Khaled Hosseini

THE KITE RUNNER

The Graphic Novel

Khaled Hosseini

THE KITE RUNNER

The Graphic Novel

Illustrated by Fabio Celoni and Mirka Andolfo

B L O O M S B U R Y

LONDON · BERLIN · NEW YORK · SYDNEY

First published in Great Britain 2011

Copyright © 2011 by Khaled and Roya Hosseini Family Charitable Remainder Unitrust

Concept and artwork copyright © 2011 by Edizione Piemme S.p.A, Italy

Illustrations: Fabio Celoni (ink) and Mirka Andolfo (colour)

Script: Tommaso Valsecchi

Art direction: Roberta Bianchi

Project supervision: Linda Kleinefeld

The moral right of the author has been asserted

Bloomsbury Publishing, London, Berlin, New York and Sydney

36 Soho Square, London W1D 3QY

A CIP catalogue record for this book is available from the British Library

ISBN 978 1 4088 1525 0
10 9 8 7 6 5 4 3 2 1

Typeset by Jim Lockwood

Printed in China by C&C Offset Printing Co., Ltd.

www.bloomsbury.com/khaledhosseini

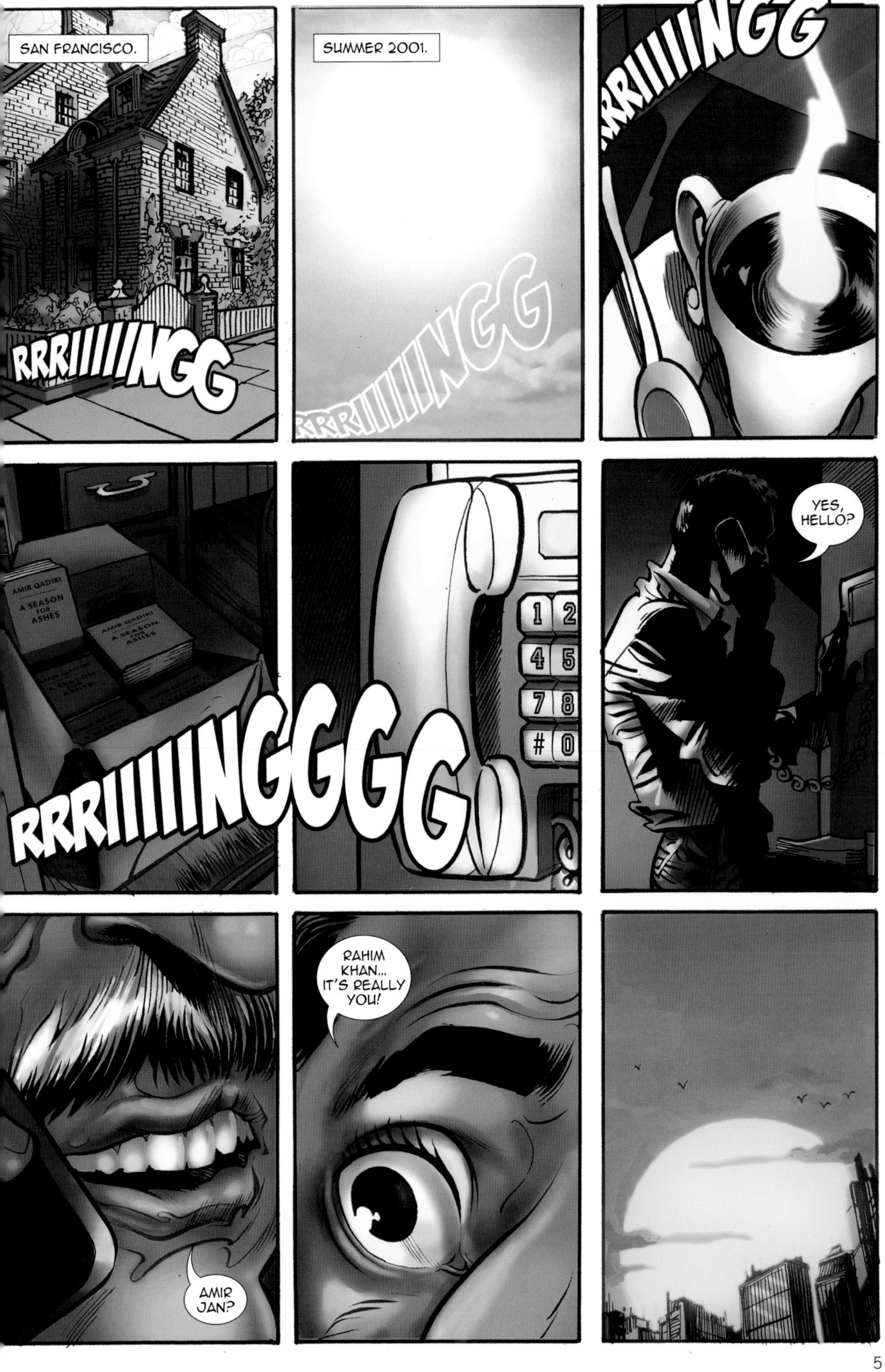
SAN FRANCISCO.
RRRIIIIIINGG
SUMMER 2001.
RRRIIIIIINGG
RRRIIIIINGG
AMIR QADIRI
A SEASON FOR ASHES
RRRIIIIIINGGGG
YES, HELLO?
AMIR JAN?
RAHIM KHAN... IT'S REALLY YOU!

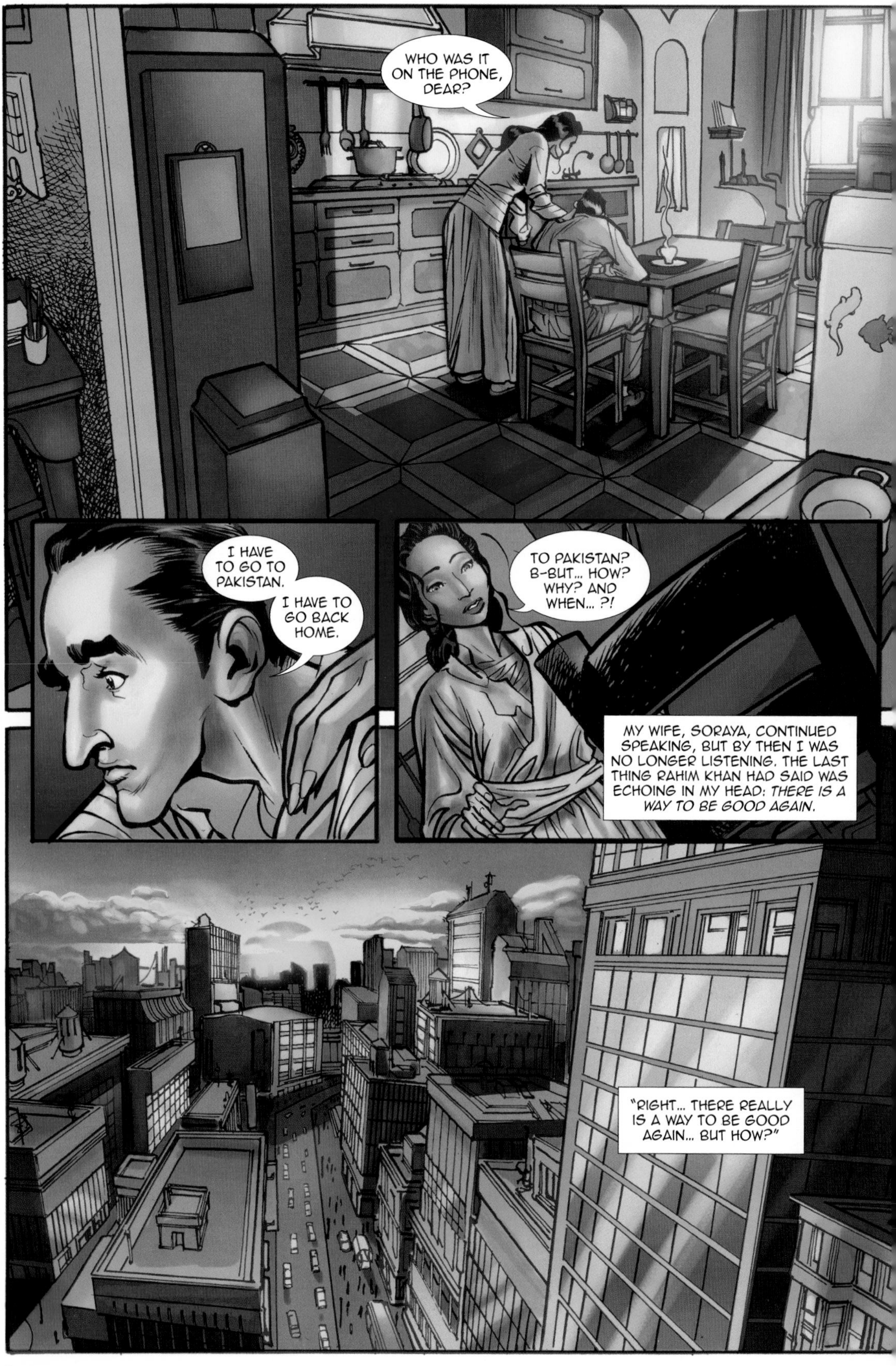
WHO WAS IT ON THE PHONE, DEAR?
I HAVE TO GO TO PAKISTAN.
I HAVE TO GO BACK HOME.
TO PAKISTAN? B-BUT... HOW? WHY? AND WHEN... ?!
MY WIFE, SORAYA, CONTINUED SPEAKING, BUT BY THEN I WAS NO LONGER LISTENING. THE LAST THING RAHIM KHAN HAD SAID WAS ECHOING IN MY HEAD: *THERE IS A WAY TO BE GOOD AGAIN.*
"RIGHT... THERE REALLY IS A WAY TO BE GOOD AGAIN... BUT HOW?"

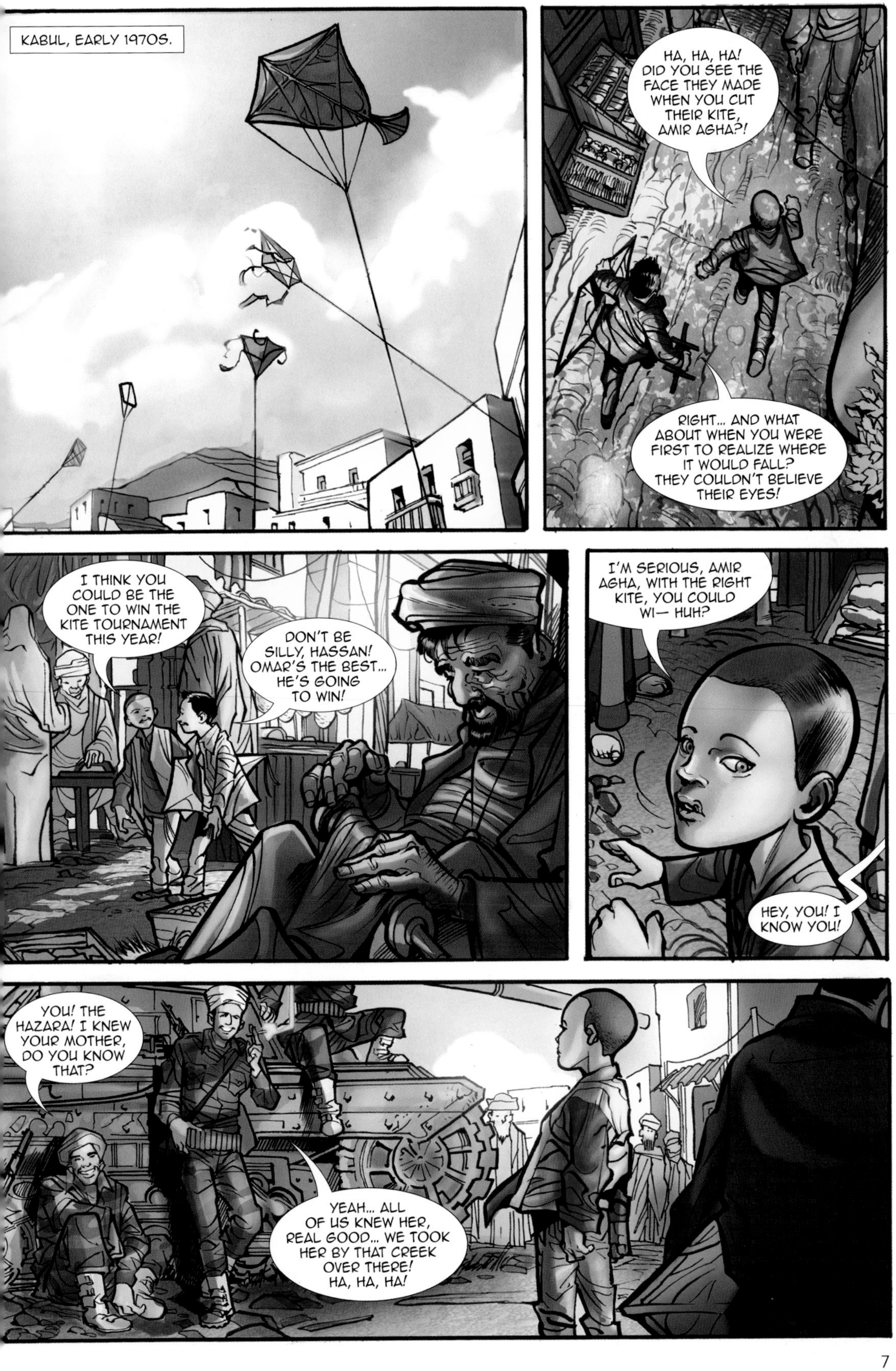
KABUL, EARLY 1970S.
HA, HA, HA! DID YOU SEE THE FACE THEY MADE WHEN YOU CUT THEIR KITE, AMIR AGHA?!
RIGHT... AND WHAT ABOUT WHEN YOU WERE FIRST TO REALIZE WHERE IT WOULD FALL? THEY COULDN'T BELIEVE THEIR EYES!
I THINK YOU COULD BE THE ONE TO WIN THE KITE TOURNAMENT THIS YEAR!
DON'T BE SILLY, HASSAN! OMAR'S THE BEST... HE'S GOING TO WIN!
I'M SERIOUS, AMIR AGHA, WITH THE RIGHT KITE, YOU COULD WI— HUH?
HEY, YOU! I KNOW YOU!
YOU! THE HAZARA! I KNEW YOUR MOTHER, DO YOU KNOW THAT?
YEAH... ALL OF US KNEW HER, REAL GOOD... WE TOOK HER BY THAT CREEK OVER THERE! HA, HA, HA!

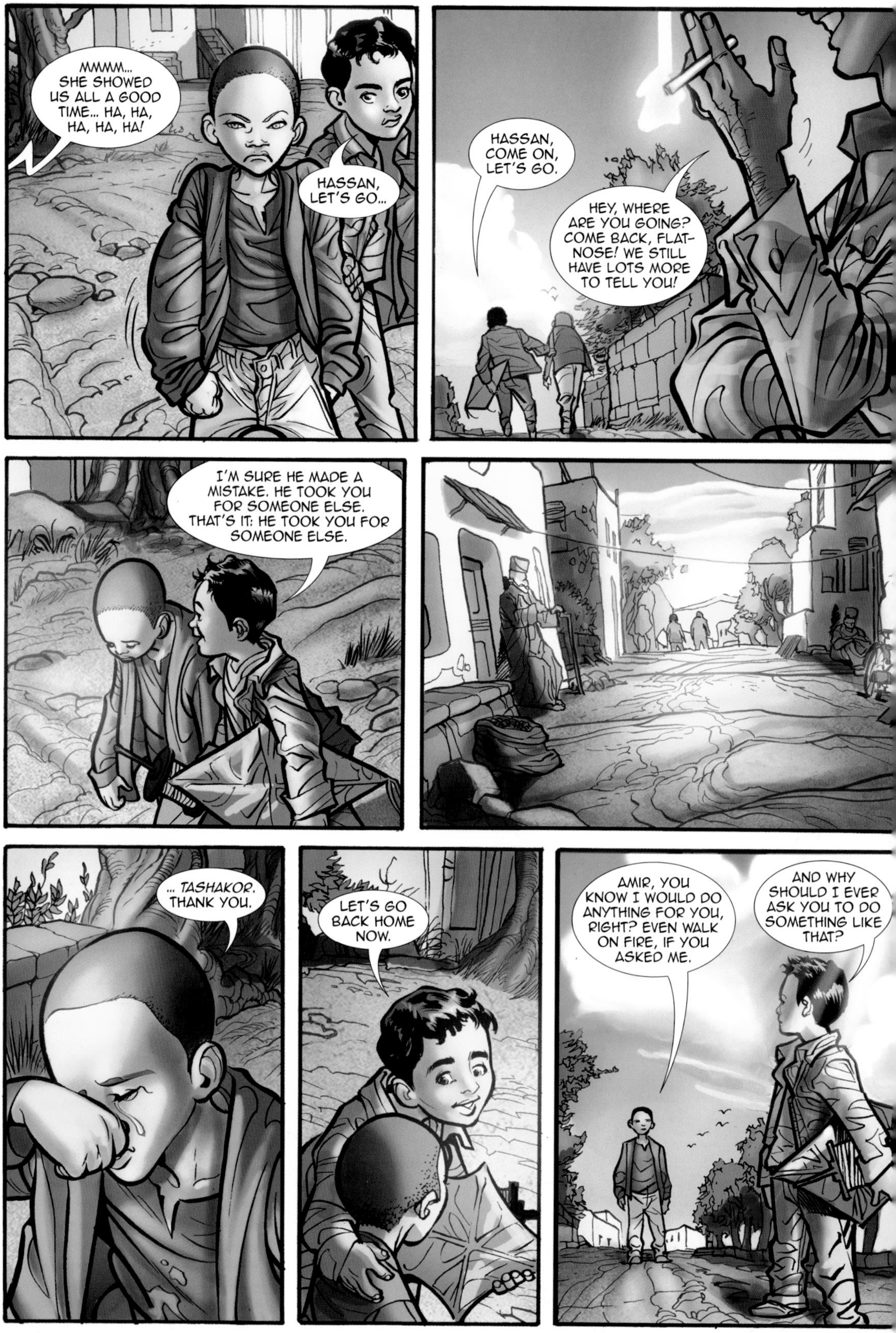
MMMM... SHE SHOWED US ALL A GOOD TIME... HA, HA, HA, HA, HA!
HASSAN, LET'S GO...
HASSAN, COME ON, LET'S GO.
HEY, WHERE ARE YOU GOING? COME BACK, FLAT-NOSE! WE STILL HAVE LOTS MORE TO TELL YOU!
I'M SURE HE MADE A MISTAKE. HE TOOK YOU FOR SOMEONE ELSE. THAT'S IT: HE TOOK YOU FOR SOMEONE ELSE.
... *TASHAKOR.* THANK YOU.
LET'S GO BACK HOME NOW.
AMIR, YOU KNOW I WOULD DO ANYTHING FOR YOU, RIGHT? EVEN WALK ON FIRE, IF YOU ASKED ME.
AND WHY SHOULD I EVER ASK YOU TO DO SOMETHING LIKE THAT?

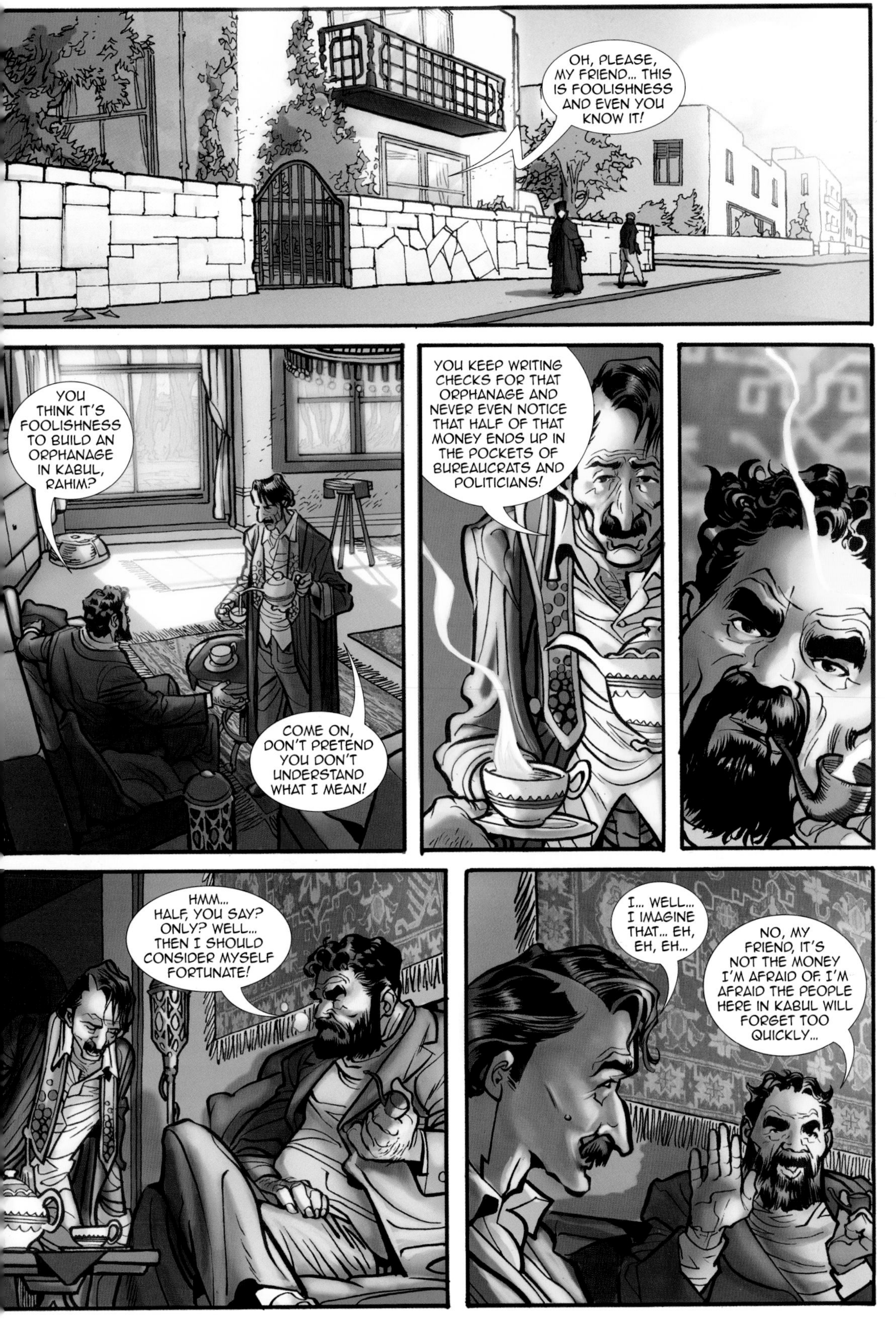
OH, PLEASE, MY FRIEND... THIS IS FOOLISHNESS AND EVEN YOU KNOW IT!
YOU THINK IT'S FOOLISHNESS TO BUILD AN ORPHANAGE IN KABUL, RAHIM?
COME ON, DON'T PRETEND YOU DON'T UNDERSTAND WHAT I MEAN!
YOU KEEP WRITING CHECKS FOR THAT ORPHANAGE AND NEVER EVEN NOTICE THAT HALF OF THAT MONEY ENDS UP IN THE POCKETS OF BUREAUCRATS AND POLITICIANS!
HMM... HALF, YOU SAY? ONLY? WELL... THEN I SHOULD CONSIDER MYSELF FORTUNATE!
I... WELL... I IMAGINE THAT... EH, EH, EH...
NO, MY FRIEND, IT'S NOT THE MONEY I'M AFRAID OF. I'M AFRAID THE PEOPLE HERE IN KABUL WILL FORGET TOO QUICKLY...

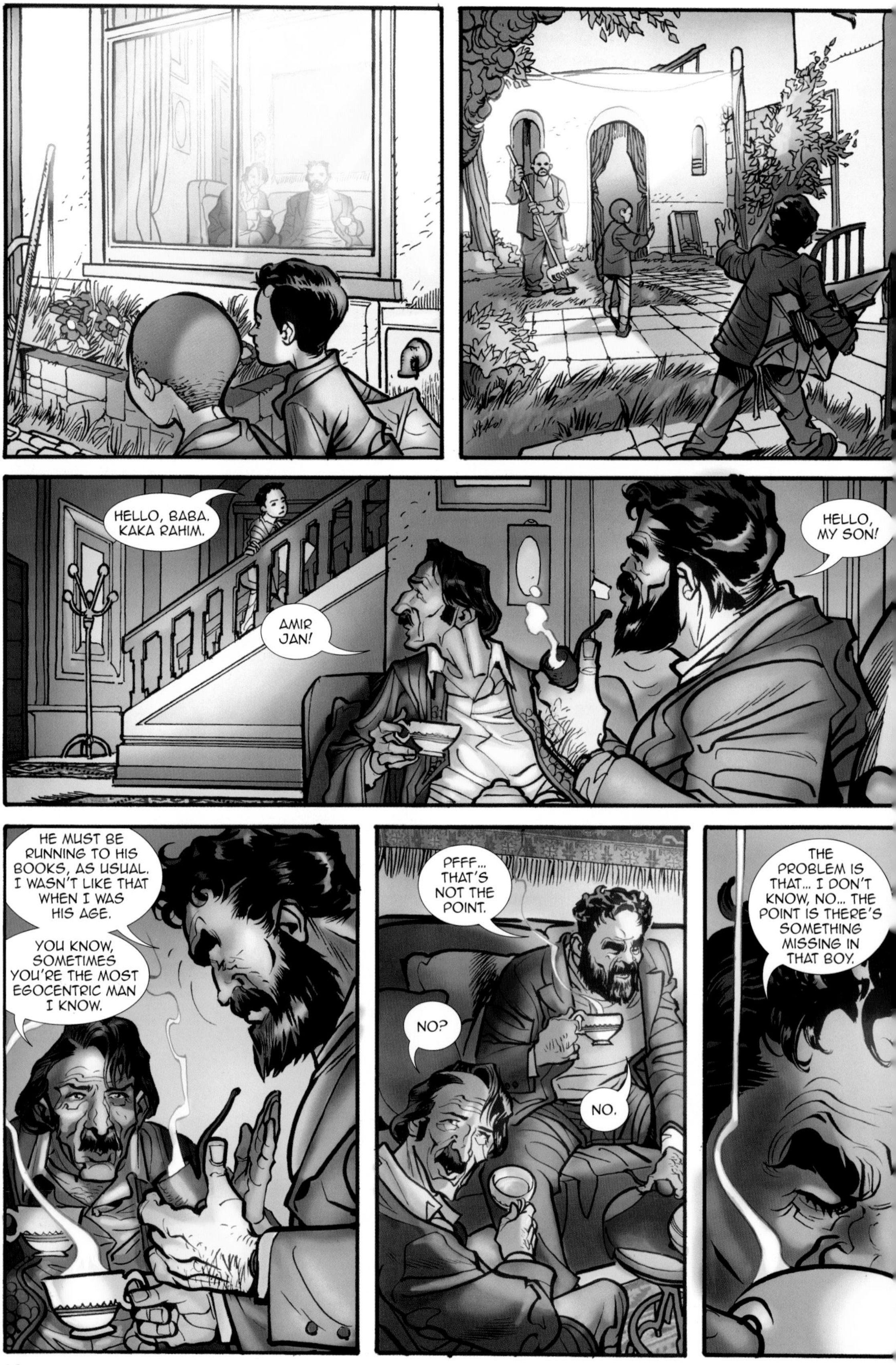

HELLO, BABA. KAKA RAHIM.
AMIR JAN!
HELLO, MY SON!
HE MUST BE RUNNING TO HIS BOOKS, AS USUAL. I WASN'T LIKE THAT WHEN I WAS HIS AGE.
YOU KNOW, SOMETIMES YOU'RE THE MOST EGOCENTRIC MAN I KNOW.
PFFF... THAT'S NOT THE POINT.
NO?
NO.
THE PROBLEM IS THAT... I DON'T KNOW, NO... THE POINT IS THERE'S SOMETHING MISSING IN THAT BOY.

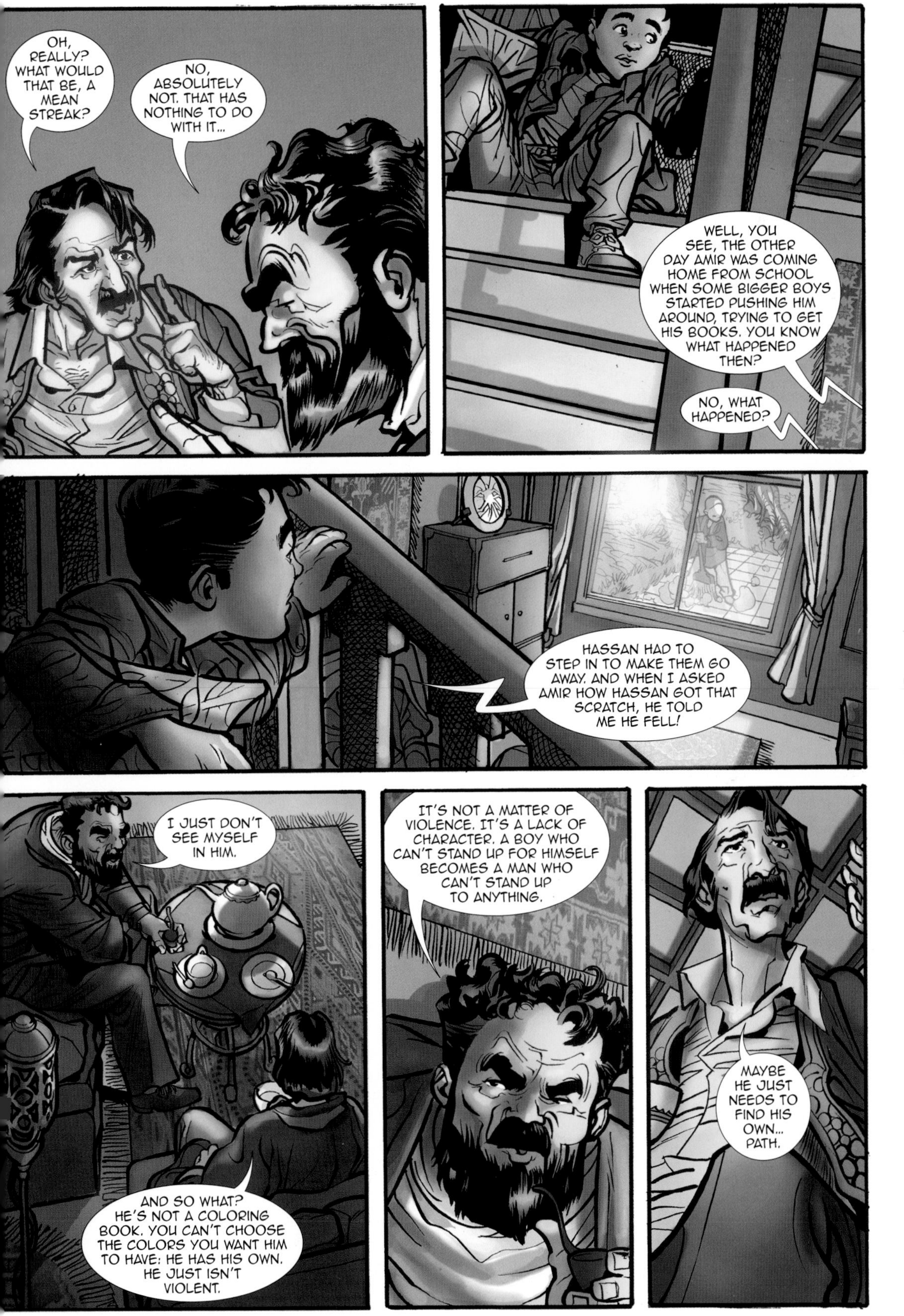
OH, REALLY? WHAT WOULD THAT BE, A MEAN STREAK?
NO, ABSOLUTELY NOT. THAT HAS NOTHING TO DO WITH IT...
WELL, YOU SEE, THE OTHER DAY AMIR WAS COMING HOME FROM SCHOOL WHEN SOME BIGGER BOYS STARTED PUSHING HIM AROUND, TRYING TO GET HIS BOOKS. YOU KNOW WHAT HAPPENED THEN?
NO, WHAT HAPPENED?
HASSAN HAD TO STEP IN TO MAKE THEM GO AWAY. AND WHEN I ASKED AMIR HOW HASSAN GOT THAT SCRATCH, HE TOLD ME HE FELL!
I JUST DON'T SEE MYSELF IN HIM.
AND SO WHAT? HE'S NOT A COLORING BOOK. YOU CAN'T CHOOSE THE COLORS YOU WANT HIM TO HAVE: HE HAS HIS OWN. HE JUST ISN'T VIOLENT.
IT'S NOT A MATTER OF VIOLENCE. IT'S A LACK OF CHARACTER. A BOY WHO CAN'T STAND UP FOR HIMSELF BECOMES A MAN WHO CAN'T STAND UP TO ANYTHING.
MAYBE HE JUST NEEDS TO FIND HIS OWN... PATH.

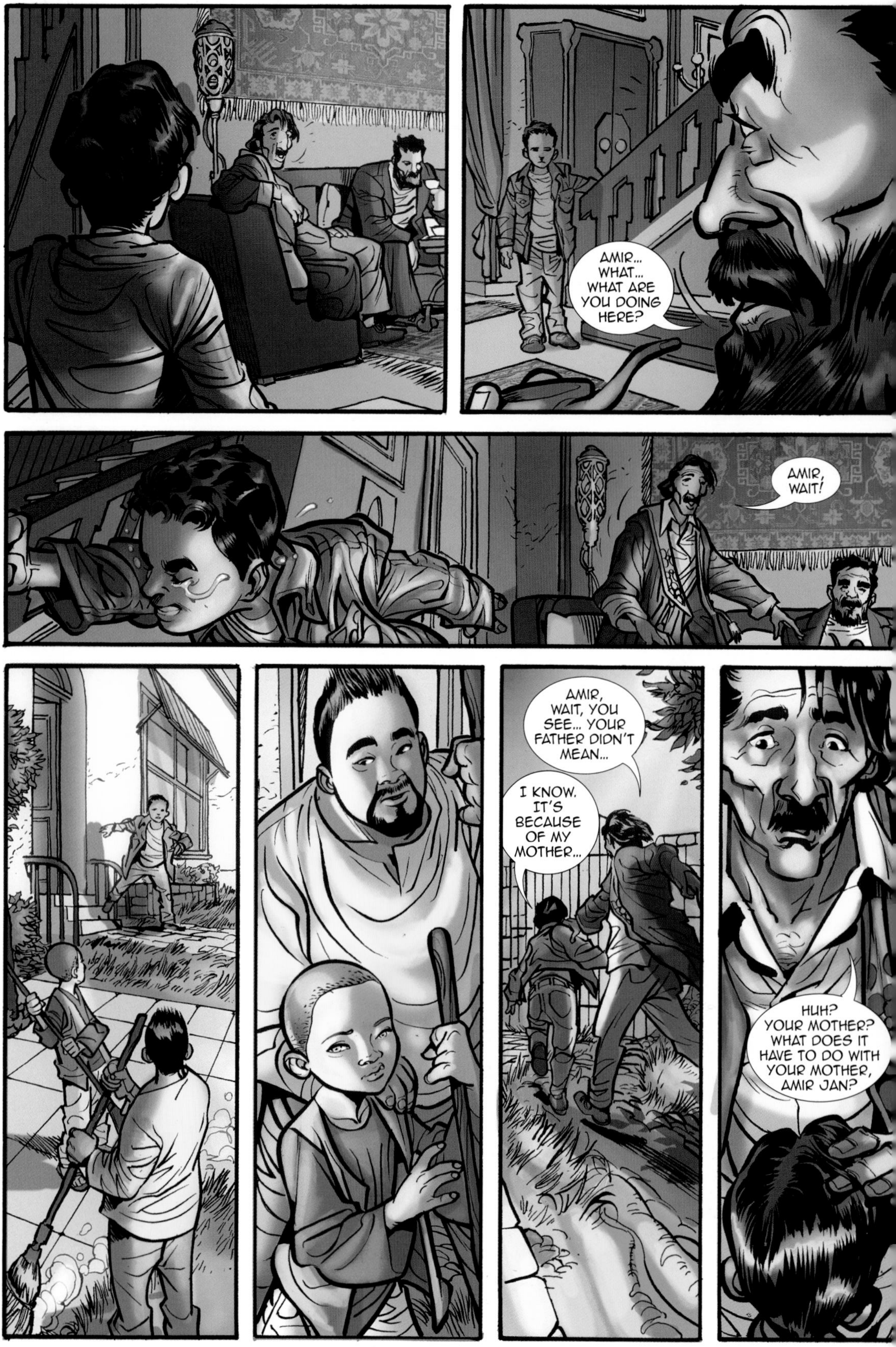
AMIR... WHAT... WHAT ARE YOU DOING HERE?
AMIR, WAIT!
AMIR, WAIT, YOU SEE... YOUR FATHER DIDN'T MEAN...
I KNOW. IT'S BECAUSE OF MY MOTHER...
HUH? YOUR MOTHER? WHAT DOES IT HAVE TO DO WITH YOUR MOTHER, AMIR JAN?

HE HATES ME BECAUSE MY MOTHER DIED GIVING BIRTH TO ME.

OH NO, AMIR JAN, DON'T SAY THAT. PLEASE DON'T SAY THAT AGAIN.

YOU SEE... BIRTH IS ALWAYS A GIFT, BUT SOMETIMES IT CAN ALSO BE A RISK. BOTH FOR MOTHER AND CHILD, AND YOU MUST BE THANKFUL YOU'RE ALIVE... THAT'S WHAT YOUR FATHER DOES: EVERY DAY HE IS THANKFUL YOU'RE HERE WITH HIM.

YOU UNDERSTAND, AMIR?

YES, KAKA RAHIM.

I KNOW. YOU'RE A SMART BOY, AMIR. BUT NOW I HAVE TO GO... I'M LEAVING FOR PAKISTAN, YOU KNOW? BUT WHEN I COME BACK, I PROMISE I'LL BRING YOU A GIFT!

REALLY. MAYBE I'LL BRING YOU A FINE NOTEBOOK TO WRITE SOME OF YOUR WONDERFUL STORIES IN. IN FACT, WHEN I GET BACK, YOU HAVE TO LET ME READ ONE!

O-OKAY...

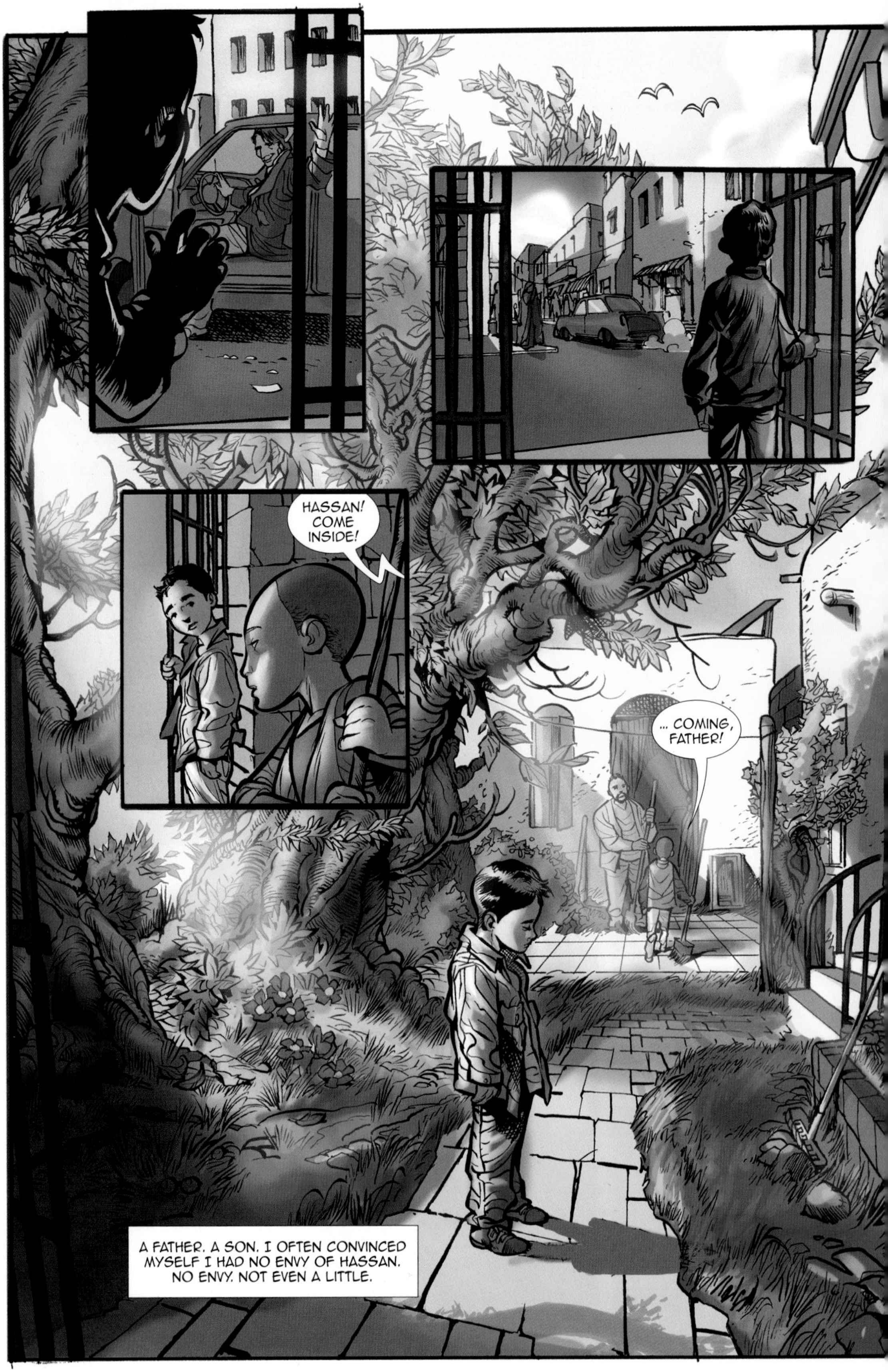
HASSAN! COME INSIDE!
... COMING, FATHER!
A FATHER. A SON. I OFTEN CONVINCED MYSELF I HAD NO ENVY OF HASSAN. NO ENVY. NOT EVEN A LITTLE.

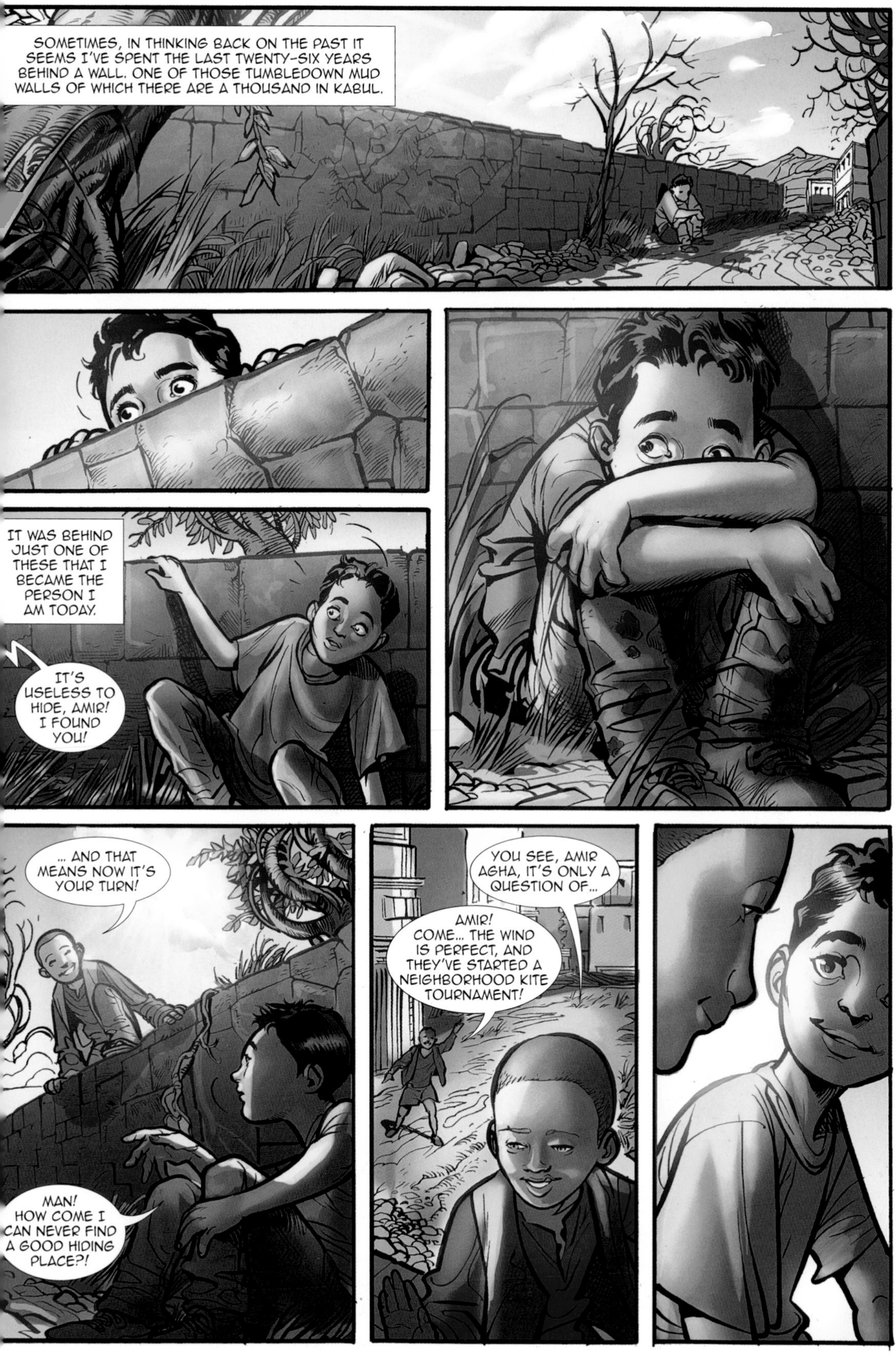
SOMETIMES, IN THINKING BACK ON THE PAST IT SEEMS I'VE SPENT THE LAST TWENTY-SIX YEARS BEHIND A WALL. ONE OF THOSE TUMBLEDOWN MUD WALLS OF WHICH THERE ARE A THOUSAND IN KABUL.
IT WAS BEHIND JUST ONE OF THESE THAT I BECAME THE PERSON I AM TODAY.
IT'S USELESS TO HIDE, AMIR! I FOUND YOU!
... AND THAT MEANS NOW IT'S YOUR TURN!
MAN! HOW COME I CAN NEVER FIND A GOOD HIDING PLACE?!
YOU SEE, AMIR AGHA, IT'S ONLY A QUESTION OF...
AMIR! COME... THE WIND IS PERFECT, AND THEY'VE STARTED A NEIGHBORHOOD KITE TOURNAMENT!

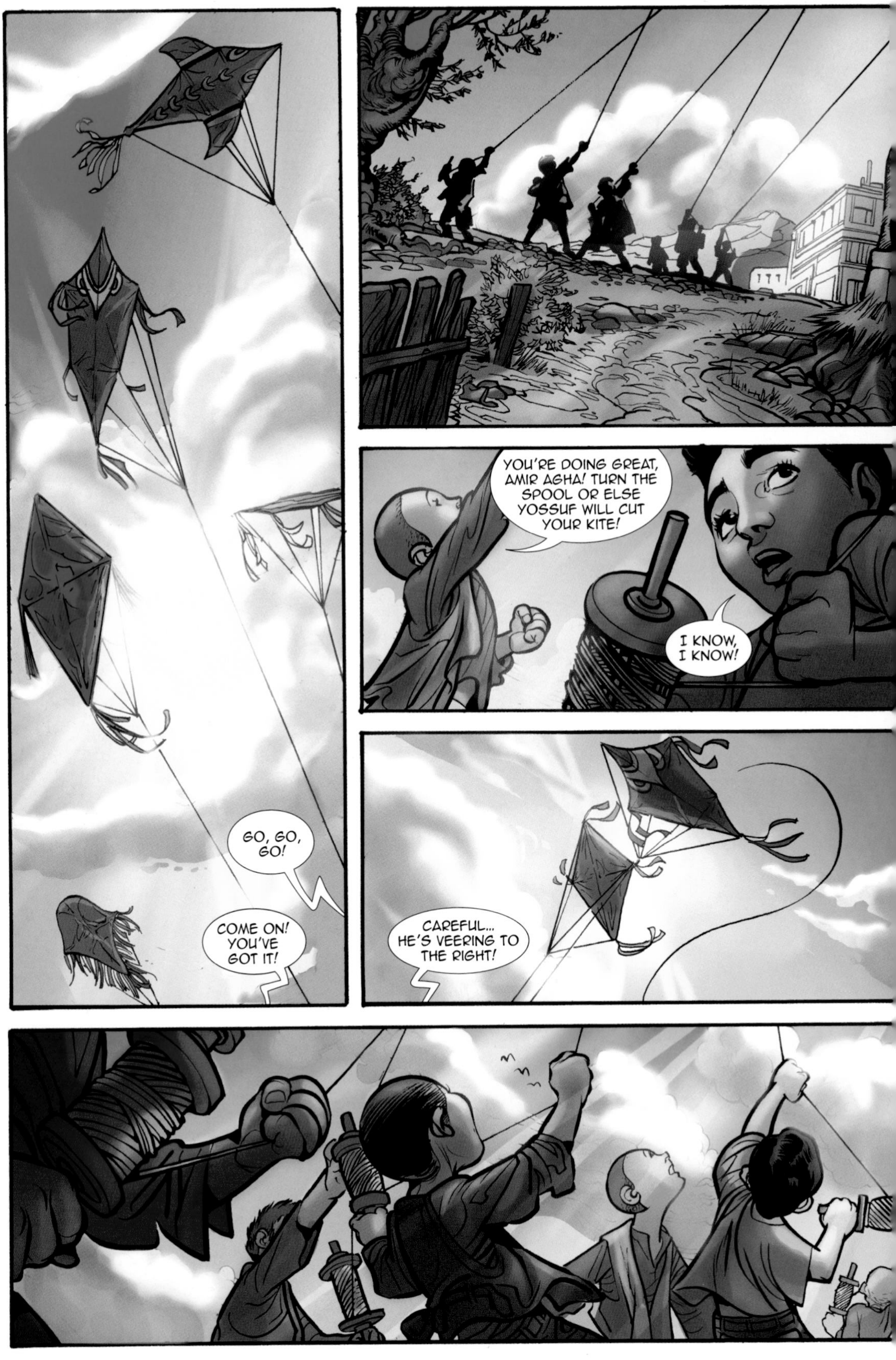

GO, GO, GO!
COME ON! YOU'VE GOT IT!
YOU'RE DOING GREAT, AMIR AGHA! TURN THE SPOOL OR ELSE YOSSUF WILL CUT YOUR KITE!
I KNOW, I KNOW!
CAREFUL... HE'S VEERING TO THE RIGHT!

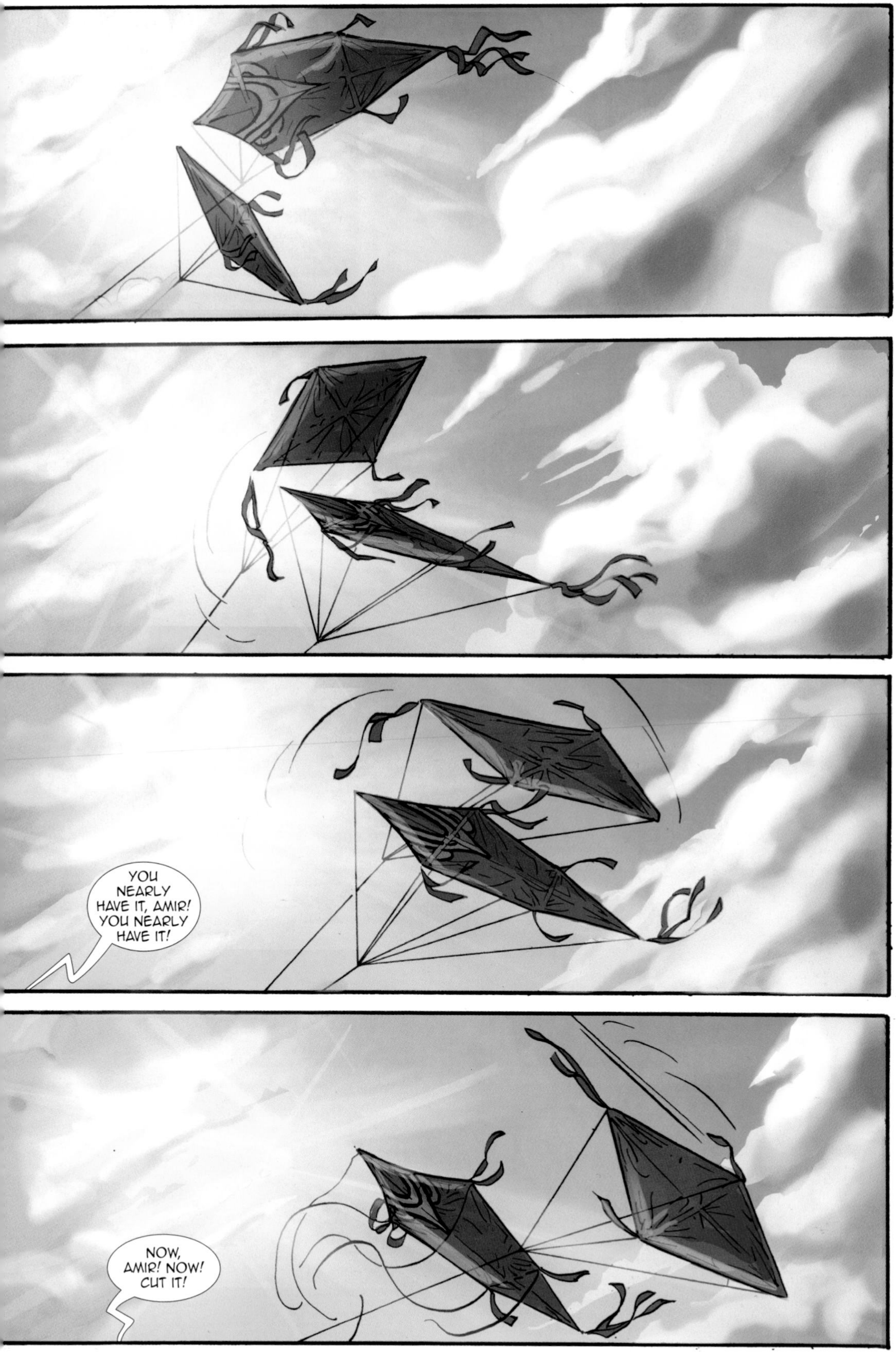
YOU NEARLY HAVE IT, AMIR! YOU NEARLY HAVE IT!
NOW, AMIR! NOW! CUT IT!

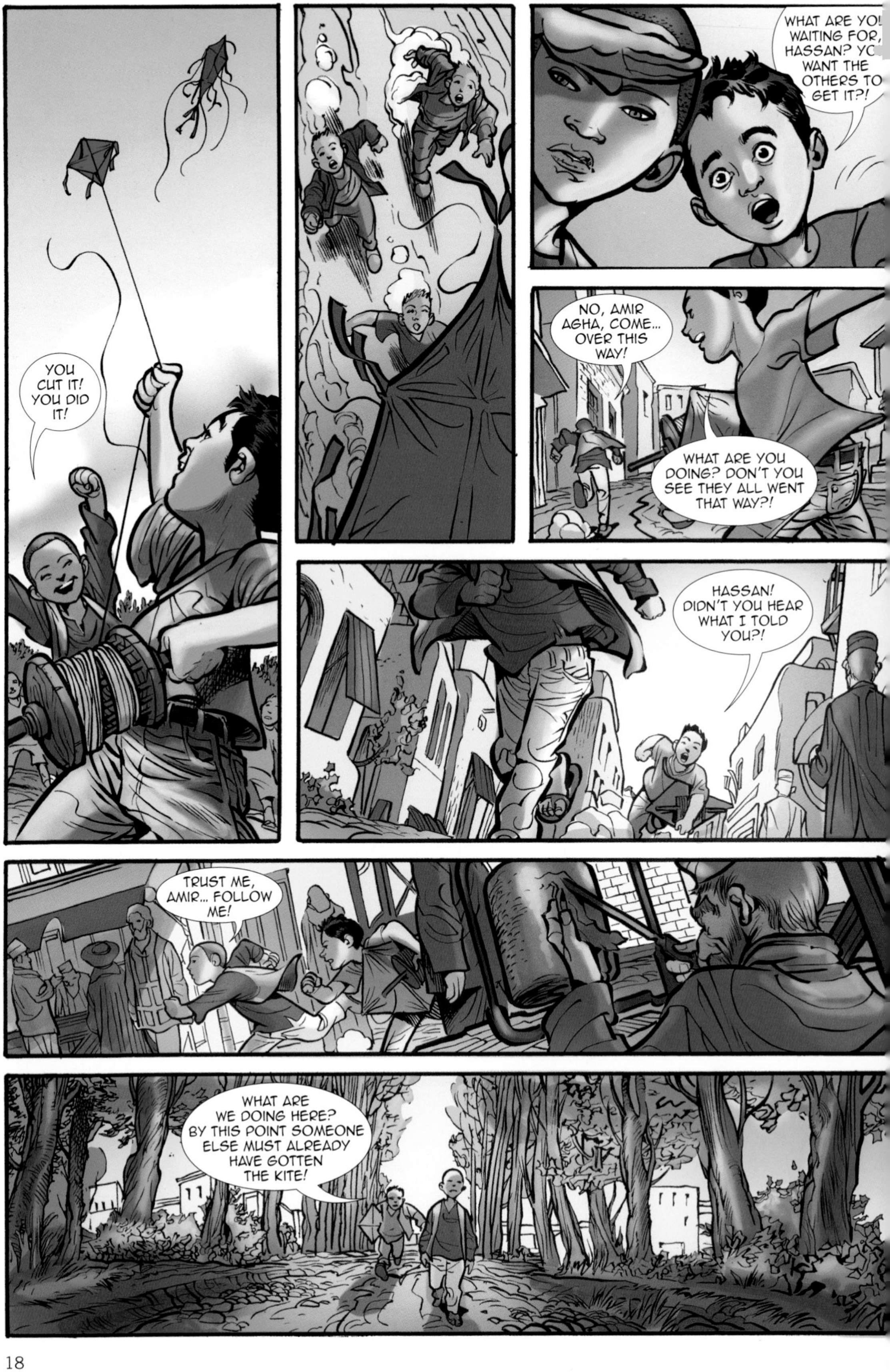
YOU CUT IT! YOU DID IT!
WHAT ARE YO WAITING FOR, HASSAN? YO WANT THE OTHERS TO GET IT?!
NO, AMIR AGHA, COME... OVER THIS WAY!
WHAT ARE YOU DOING? DON'T YOU SEE THEY ALL WENT THAT WAY?!
HASSAN! DIDN'T YOU HEAR WHAT I TOLD YOU?!
TRUST ME, AMIR... FOLLOW ME!
WHAT ARE WE DOING HERE? BY THIS POINT SOMEONE ELSE MUST ALREADY HAVE GOTTEN THE KITE!

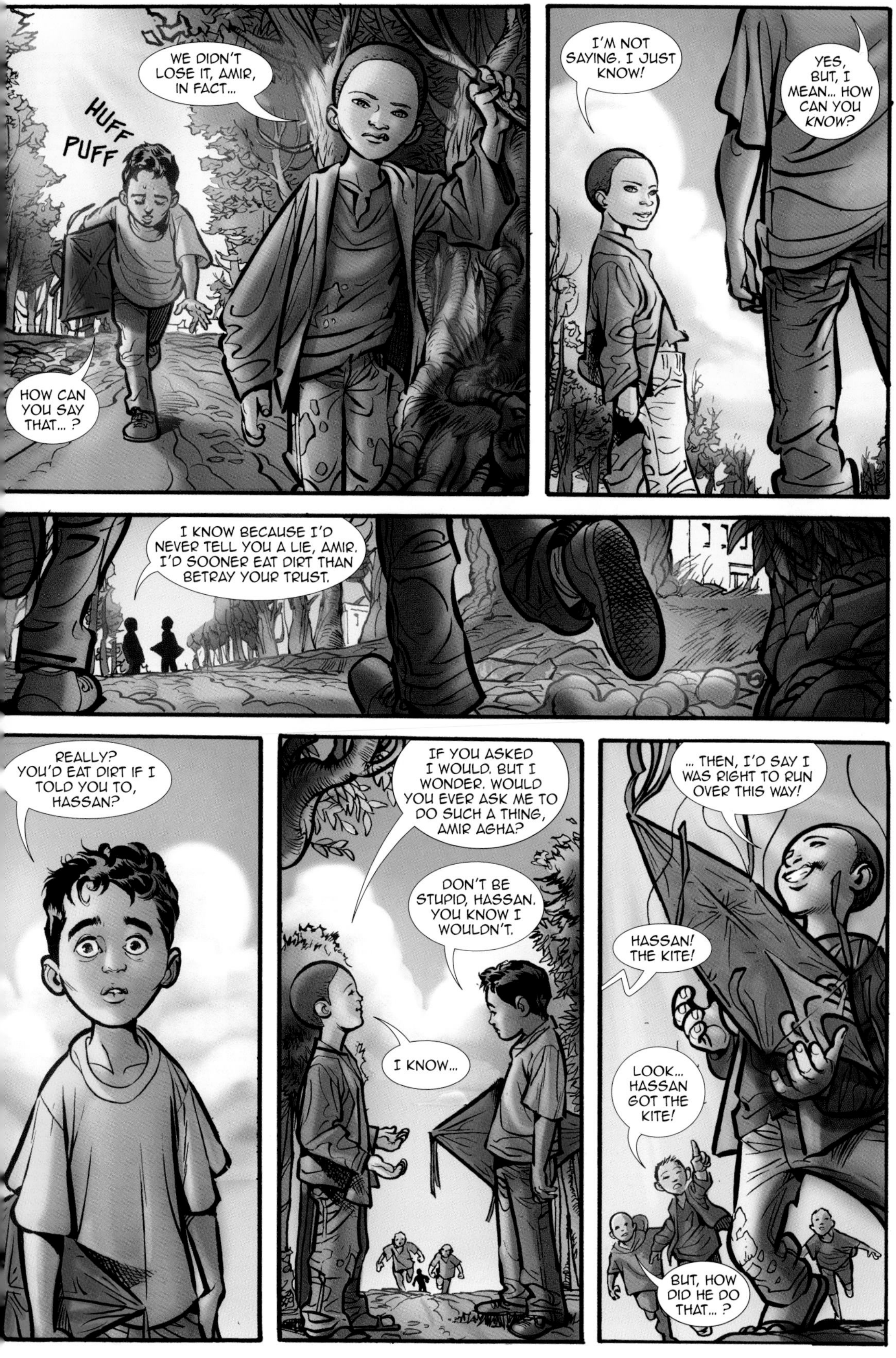
WE DIDN'T LOSE IT, AMIR, IN FACT...
HUFF PUFF
HOW CAN YOU SAY THAT... ?
I'M NOT SAYING. I JUST KNOW!
YES, BUT, I MEAN... HOW CAN YOU KNOW?
I KNOW BECAUSE I'D NEVER TELL YOU A LIE, AMIR. I'D SOONER EAT DIRT THAN BETRAY YOUR TRUST.
REALLY? YOU'D EAT DIRT IF I TOLD YOU TO, HASSAN?
IF YOU ASKED I WOULD. BUT I WONDER. WOULD YOU EVER ASK ME TO DO SUCH A THING, AMIR AGHA?
DON'T BE STUPID, HASSAN. YOU KNOW I WOULDN'T.
I KNOW...
... THEN, I'D SAY I WAS RIGHT TO RUN OVER THIS WAY!
HASSAN! THE KITE!
LOOK... HASSAN GOT THE KITE!
BUT, HOW DID HE DO THAT... ?

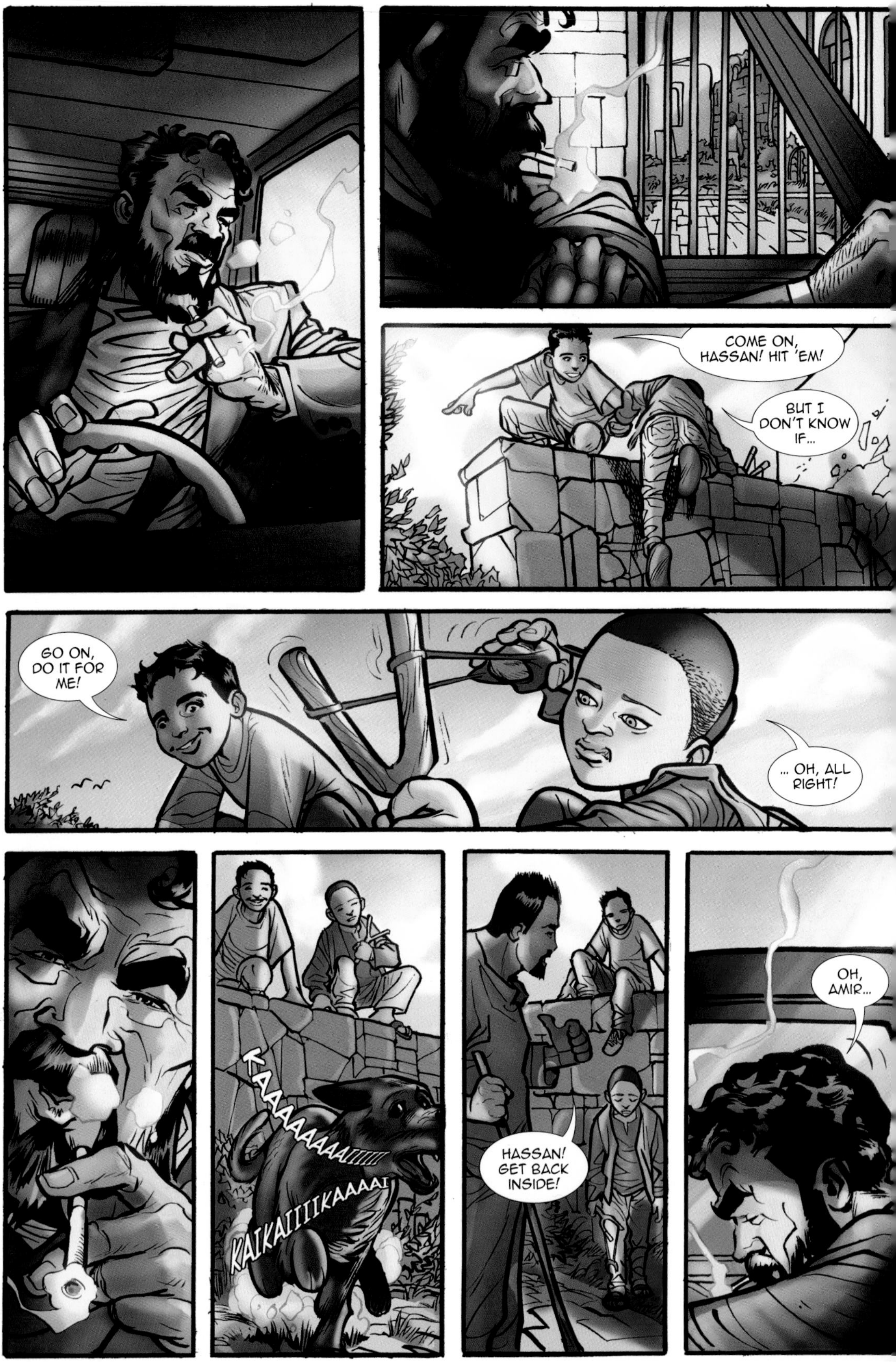
COME ON, HASSAN! HIT 'EM!
BUT I DON'T KNOW IF...
GO ON, DO IT FOR ME!
... OH, ALL RIGHT!
KAAAAAAAAIIIII
KAIKAIIIIKAAAAI
HASSAN! GET BACK INSIDE!
OH, AMIR...

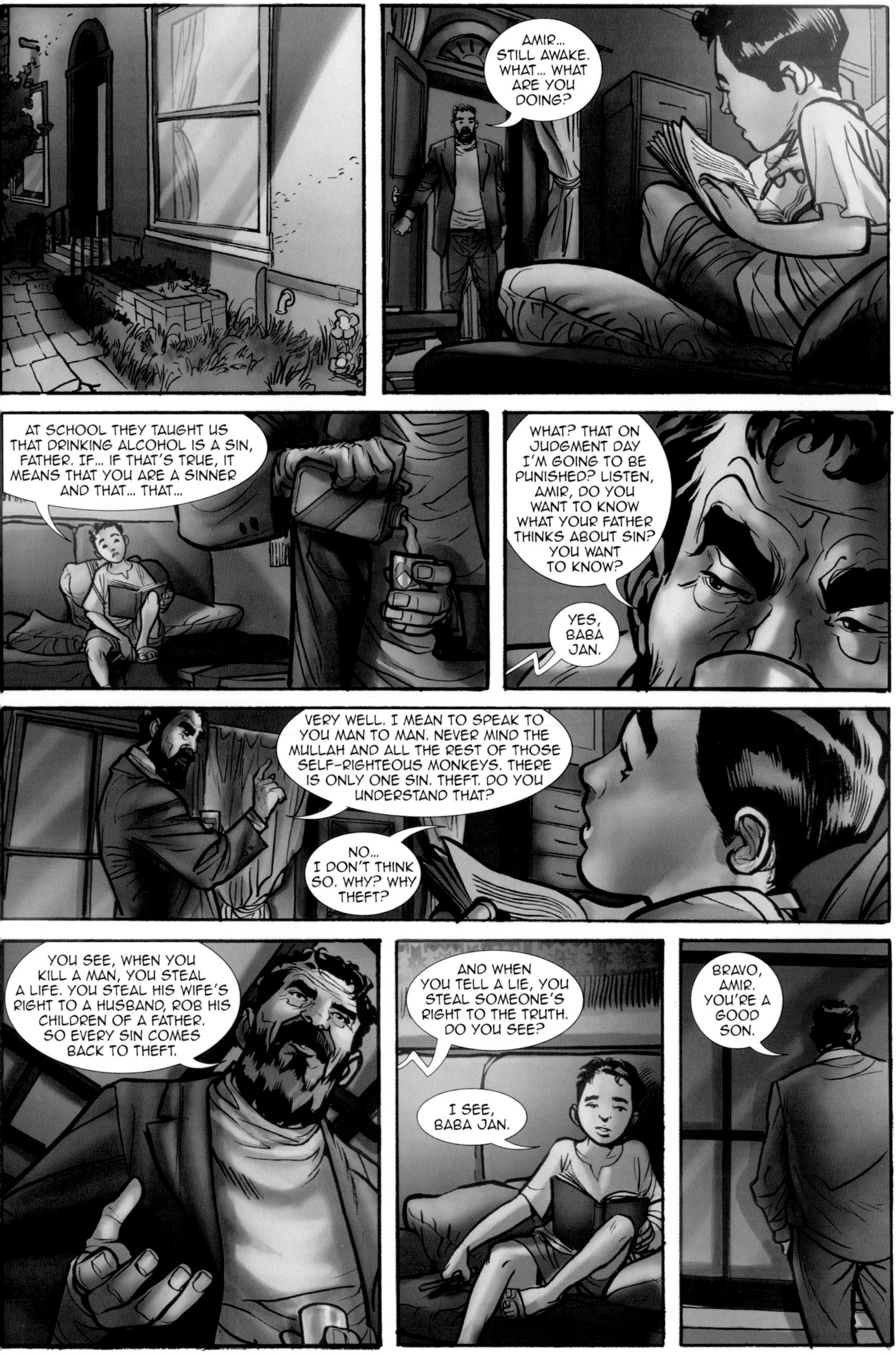
AMIR... STILL AWAKE. WHAT... WHAT ARE YOU DOING?
AT SCHOOL THEY TAUGHT US THAT DRINKING ALCOHOL IS A SIN, FATHER. IF... IF THAT'S TRUE, IT MEANS THAT YOU ARE A SINNER AND THAT... THAT...
WHAT? THAT ON JUDGMENT DAY I'M GOING TO BE PUNISHED? LISTEN, AMIR, DO YOU WANT TO KNOW WHAT YOUR FATHER THINKS ABOUT SIN? YOU WANT TO KNOW?
YES, BABA JAN.
VERY WELL. I MEAN TO SPEAK TO YOU MAN TO MAN. NEVER MIND THE MULLAH AND ALL THE REST OF THOSE SELF-RIGHTEOUS MONKEYS. THERE IS ONLY ONE SIN. THEFT. DO YOU UNDERSTAND THAT?
NO... I DON'T THINK SO. WHY? WHY THEFT?
YOU SEE, WHEN YOU KILL A MAN, YOU STEAL A LIFE. YOU STEAL HIS WIFE'S RIGHT TO A HUSBAND, ROB HIS CHILDREN OF A FATHER. SO EVERY SIN COMES BACK TO THEFT.
AND WHEN YOU TELL A LIE, YOU STEAL SOMEONE'S RIGHT TO THE TRUTH. DO YOU SEE?
I SEE, BABA JAN.
BRAVO, AMIR. YOU'RE A GOOD SON.

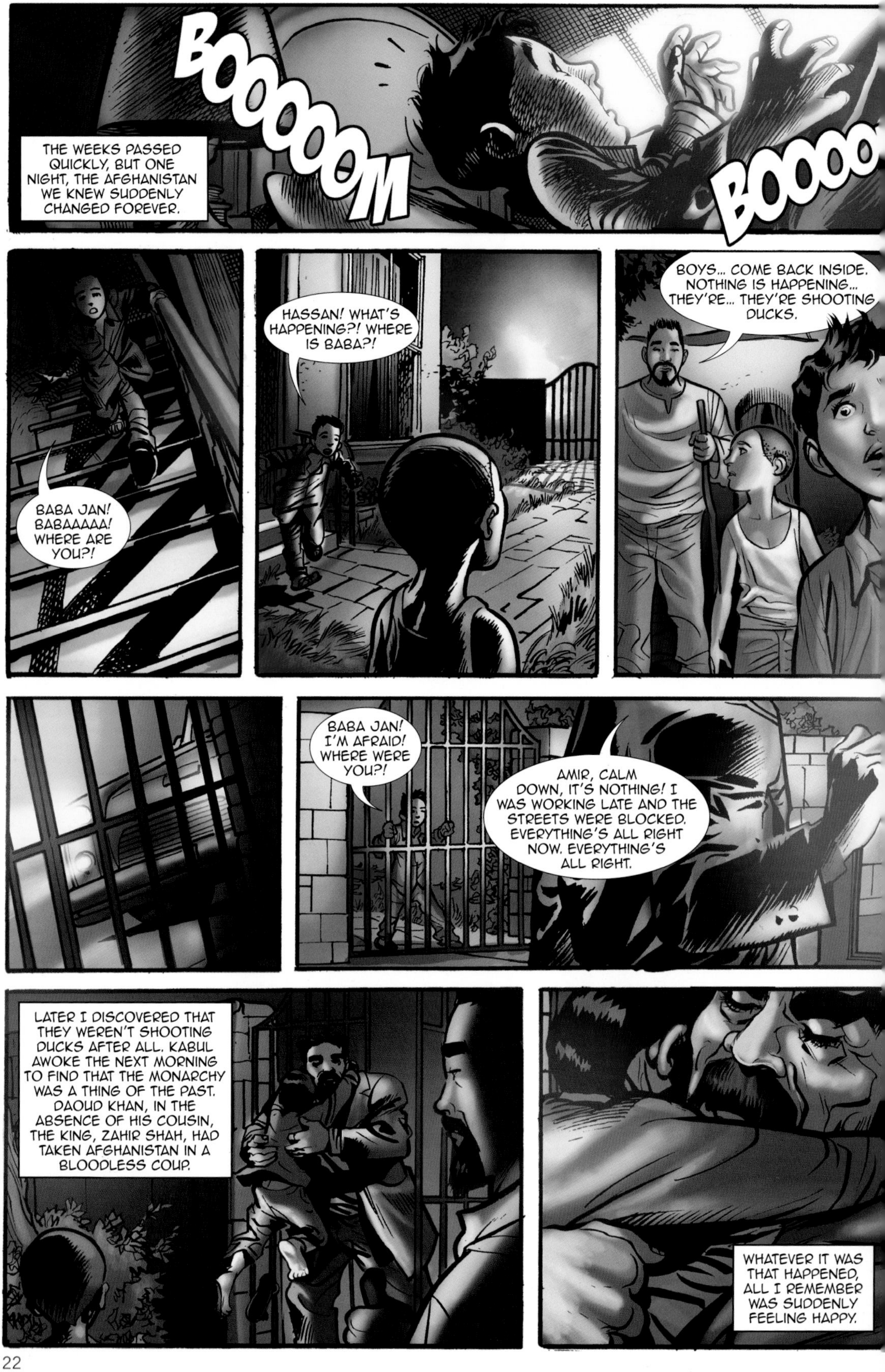
BOOOOOOM
THE WEEKS PASSED QUICKLY, BUT ONE NIGHT, THE AFGHANISTAN WE KNEW SUDDENLY CHANGED FOREVER.
BOOOO
BABA JAN! BABAAAAA! WHERE ARE YOU?!
HASSAN! WHAT'S HAPPENING?! WHERE IS BABA?!
BOYS... COME BACK INSIDE. NOTHING IS HAPPENING... THEY'RE... THEY'RE SHOOTING DUCKS.
BABA JAN! I'M AFRAID! WHERE WERE YOU?!
AMIR, CALM DOWN, IT'S NOTHING! I WAS WORKING LATE AND THE STREETS WERE BLOCKED. EVERYTHING'S ALL RIGHT NOW. EVERYTHING'S ALL RIGHT.
LATER I DISCOVERED THAT THEY WEREN'T SHOOTING DUCKS AFTER ALL. KABUL AWOKE THE NEXT MORNING TO FIND THAT THE MONARCHY WAS A THING OF THE PAST. DAOUD KHAN, IN THE ABSENCE OF HIS COUSIN, THE KING, ZAHIR SHAH, HAD TAKEN AFGHANISTAN IN A BLOODLESS COUP.
WHATEVER IT WAS THAT HAPPENED, ALL I REMEMBER WAS SUDDENLY FEELING HAPPY.

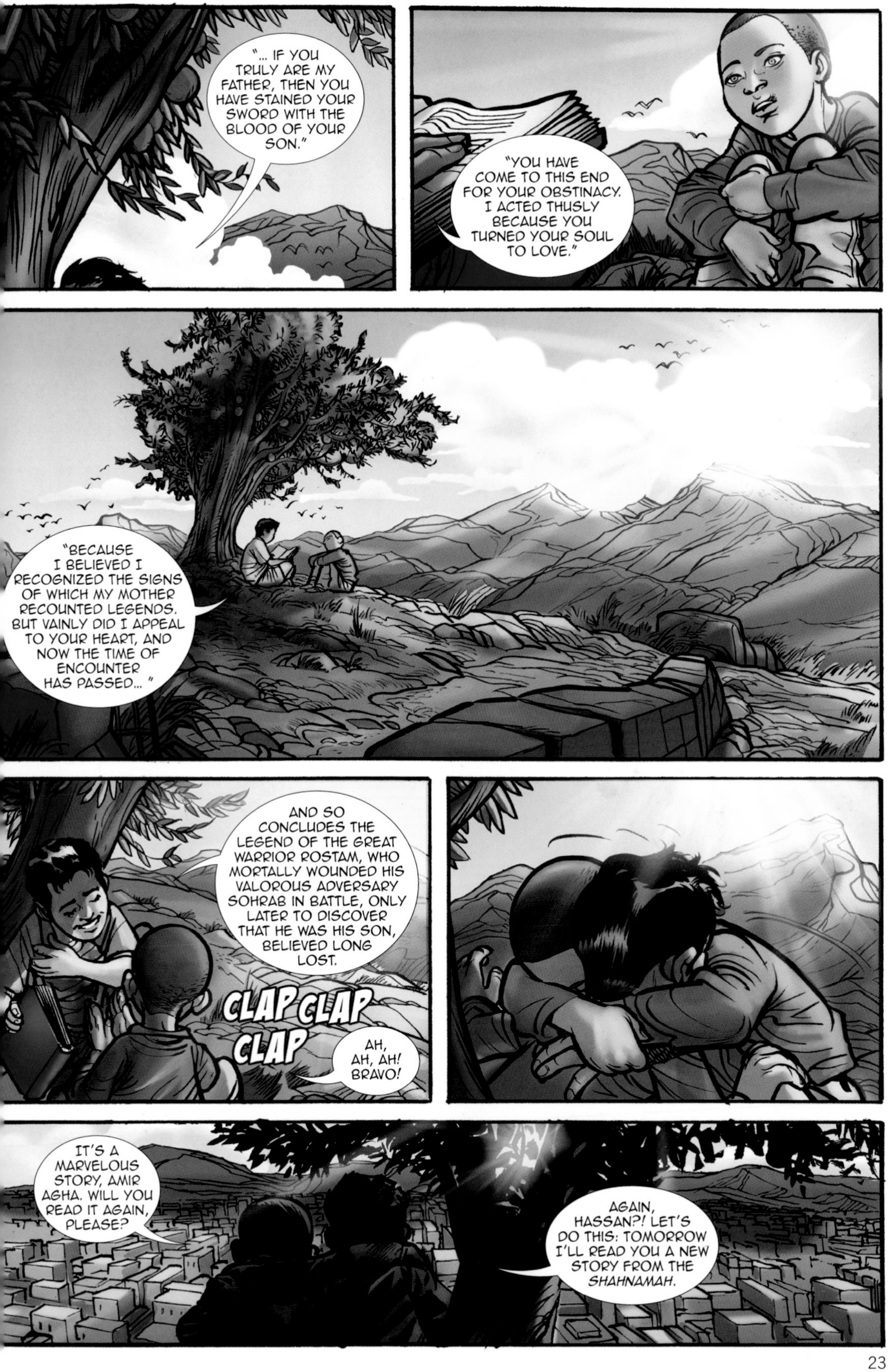
"... IF YOU TRULY ARE MY FATHER, THEN YOU HAVE STAINED YOUR SWORD WITH THE BLOOD OF YOUR SON."
"YOU HAVE COME TO THIS END FOR YOUR OBSTINACY. I ACTED THUSLY BECAUSE YOU TURNED YOUR SOUL TO LOVE."
"BECAUSE I BELIEVED I RECOGNIZED THE SIGNS OF WHICH MY MOTHER RECOUNTED LEGENDS. BUT VAINLY DID I APPEAL TO YOUR HEART, AND NOW THE TIME OF ENCOUNTER HAS PASSED..."
AND SO CONCLUDES THE LEGEND OF THE GREAT WARRIOR ROSTAM, WHO MORTALLY WOUNDED HIS VALOROUS ADVERSARY SOHRAB IN BATTLE, ONLY LATER TO DISCOVER THAT HE WAS HIS SON, BELIEVED LONG LOST.
CLAP CLAP CLAP
AH, AH, AH! BRAVO!
IT'S A MARVELOUS STORY, AMIR AGHA. WILL YOU READ IT AGAIN, PLEASE?
AGAIN, HASSAN?! LET'S DO THIS: TOMORROW I'LL READ YOU A NEW STORY FROM THE SHAHNAMAH.

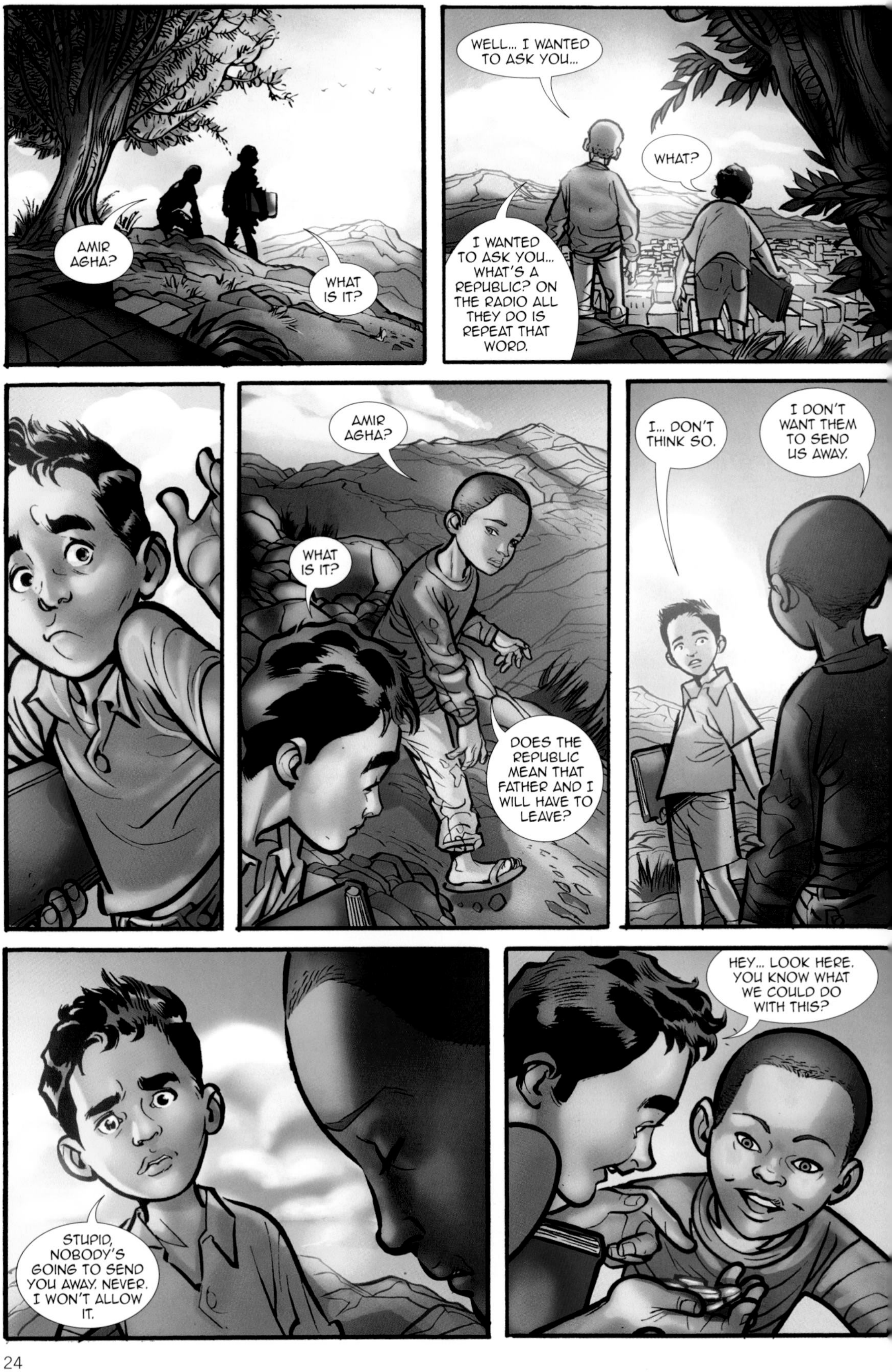
AMIR AGHA?
WHAT IS IT?
WELL... I WANTED TO ASK YOU...
WHAT?
I WANTED TO ASK YOU... WHAT'S A REPUBLIC? ON THE RADIO ALL THEY DO IS REPEAT THAT WORD.
AMIR AGHA?
WHAT IS IT?
DOES THE REPUBLIC MEAN THAT FATHER AND I WILL HAVE TO LEAVE?
I... DON'T THINK SO.
I DON'T WANT THEM TO SEND US AWAY.
STUPID, NOBODY'S GOING TO SEND YOU AWAY. NEVER. I WON'T ALLOW IT.
HEY... LOOK HERE. YOU KNOW WHAT WE COULD DO WITH THIS?

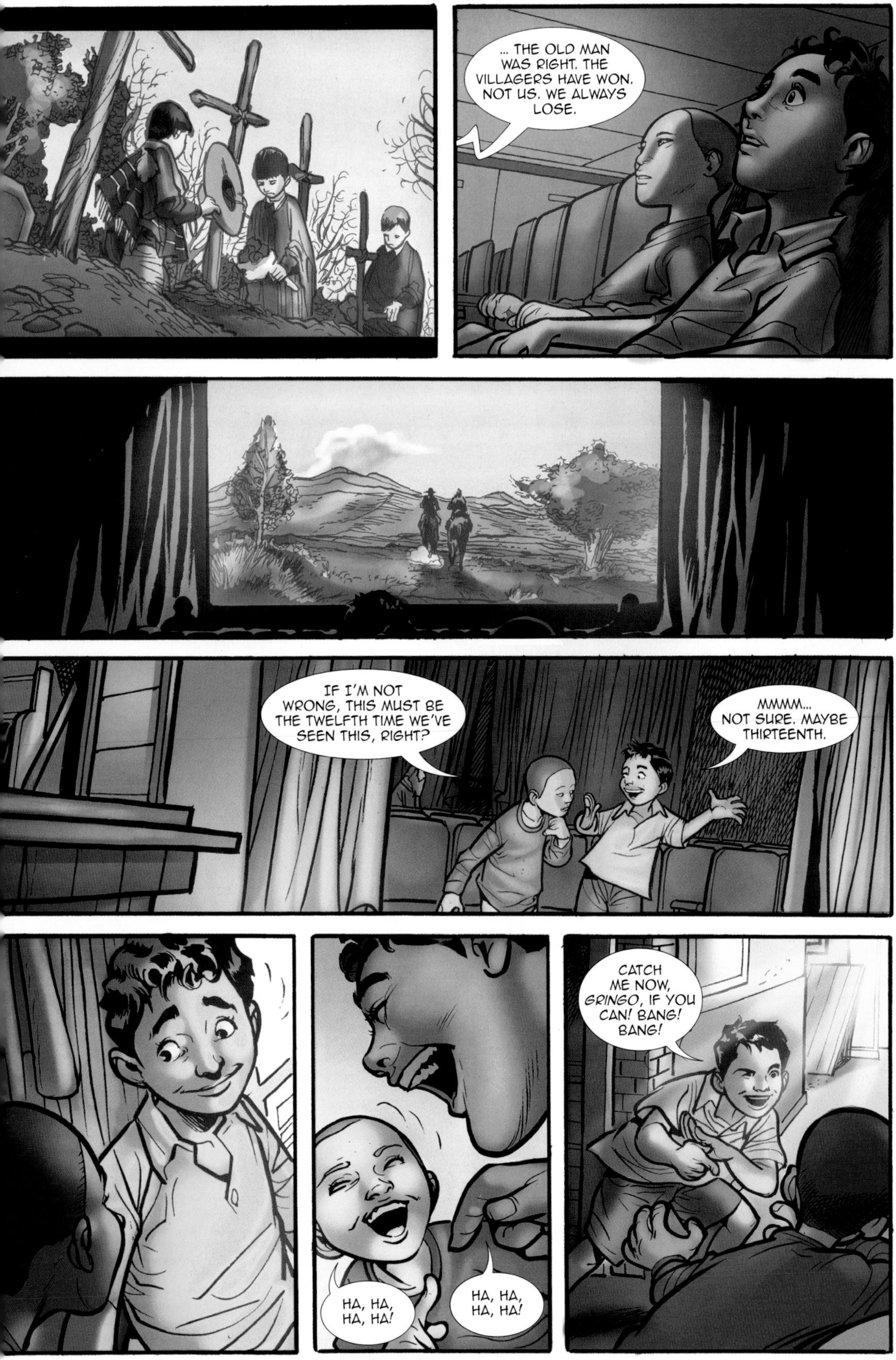
... THE OLD MAN WAS RIGHT. THE VILLAGERS HAVE WON. NOT US. WE ALWAYS LOSE.
IF I'M NOT WRONG, THIS MUST BE THE TWELFTH TIME WE'VE SEEN THIS, RIGHT?
MMMM... NOT SURE. MAYBE THIRTEENTH.
HA, HA, HA, HA!
HA, HA, HA, HA!
CATCH ME NOW, GRINGO, IF YOU CAN! BANG! BANG!

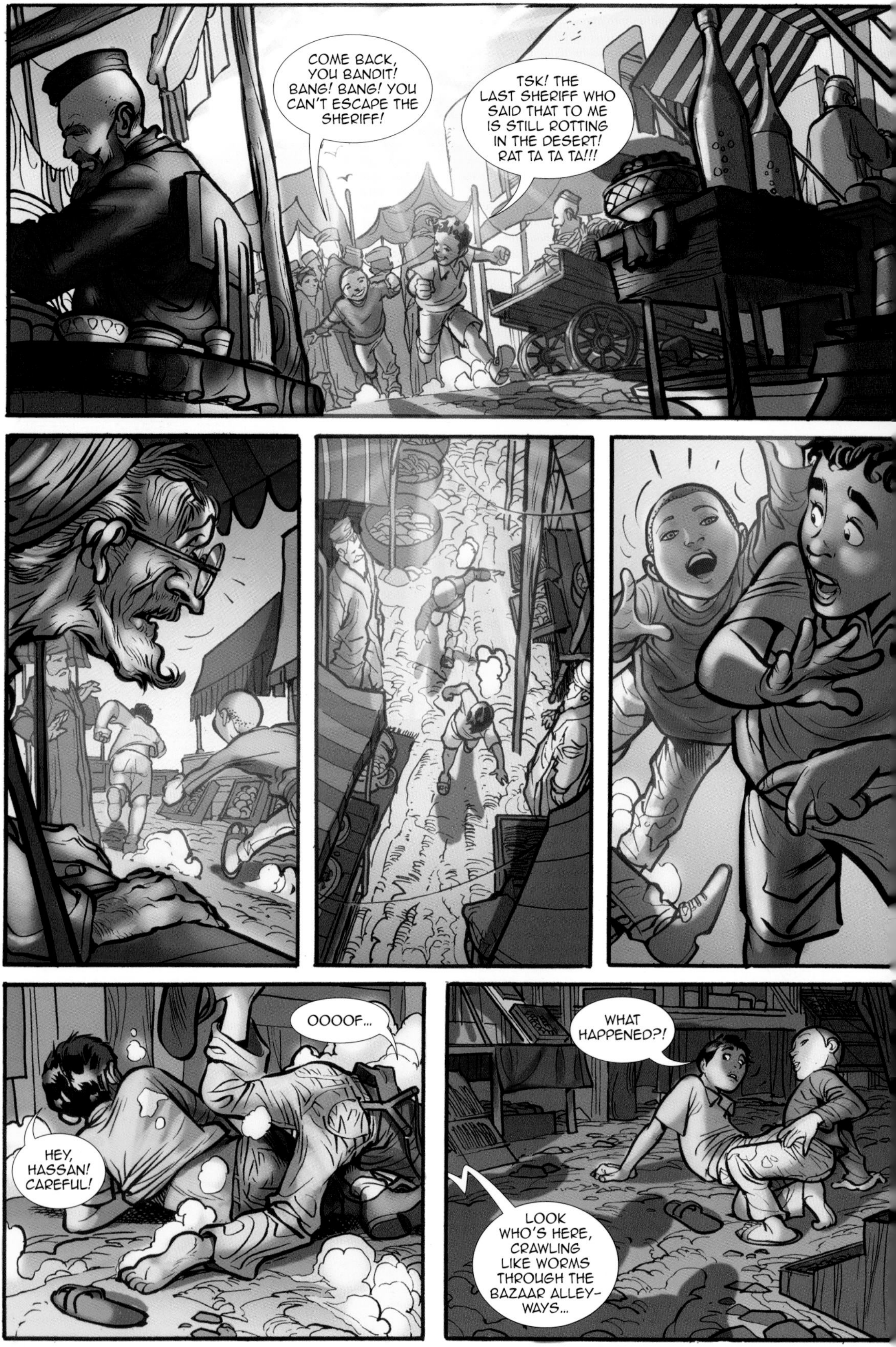
COME BACK, YOU BANDIT! BANG! BANG! YOU CAN'T ESCAPE THE SHERIFF!
TSK! THE LAST SHERIFF WHO SAID THAT TO ME IS STILL ROTTING IN THE DESERT! RAT TA TA TA!!!
OOOOF...
HEY, HASSAN! CAREFUL!
WHAT HAPPENED?!
LOOK WHO'S HERE, CRAWLING LIKE WORMS THROUGH THE BAZAAR ALLEY-WAYS...

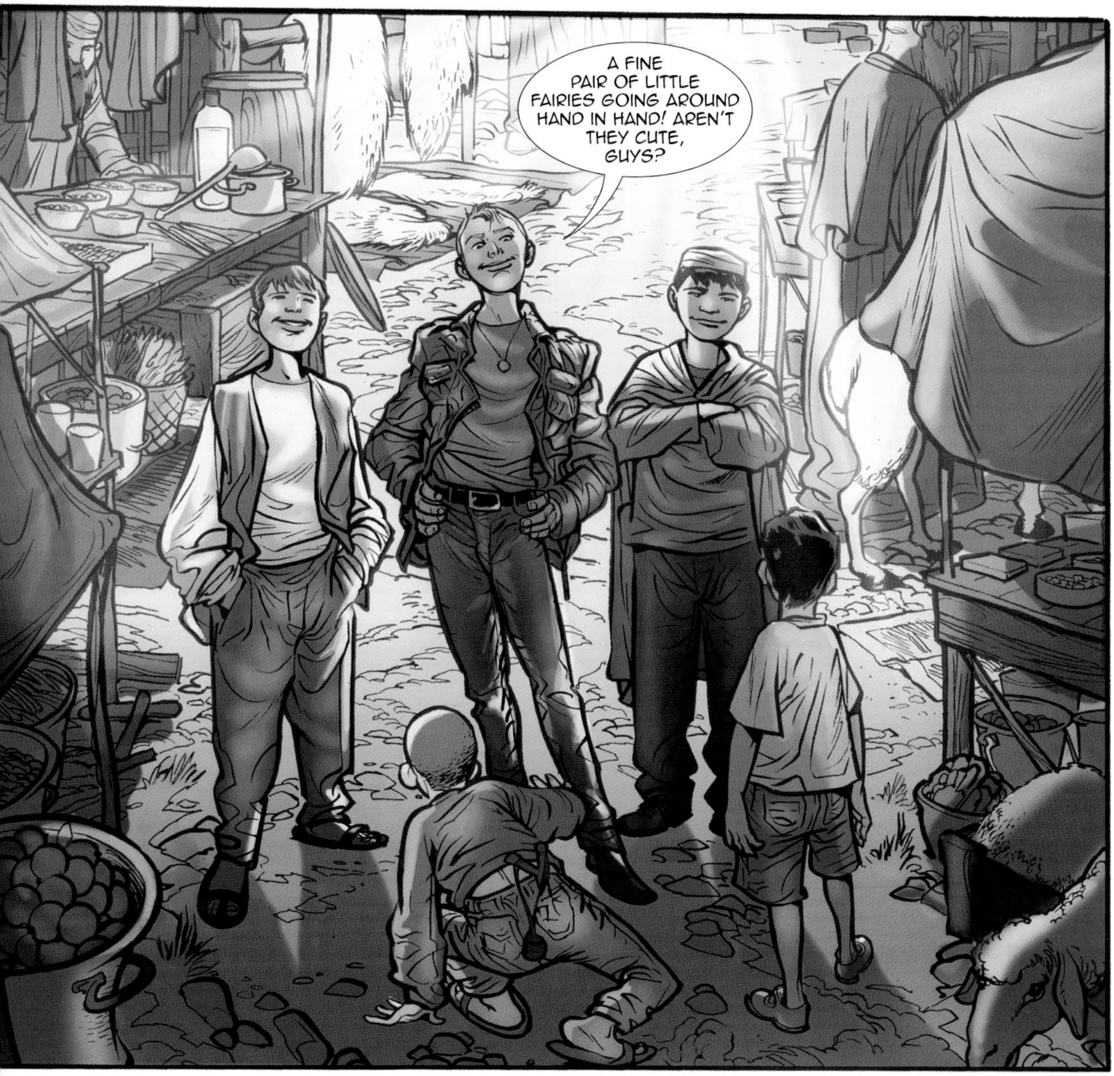
A FINE PAIR OF LITTLE FAIRIES GOING AROUND HAND IN HAND! AREN'T THEY CUTE, GUYS?

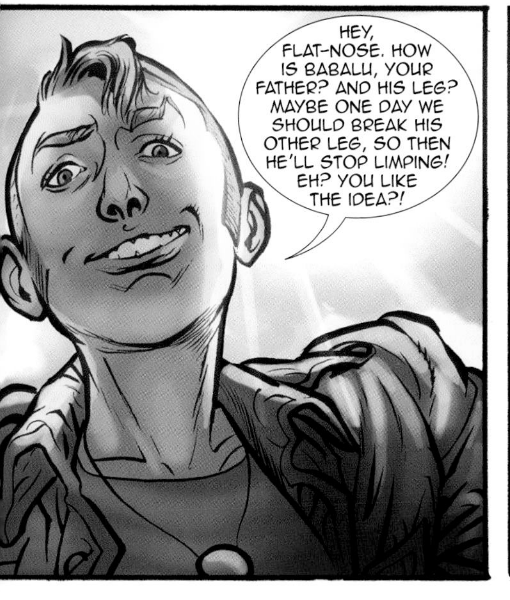
HEY, FLAT-NOSE. HOW IS BABALU, YOUR FATHER? AND HIS LEG? MAYBE ONE DAY WE SHOULD BREAK HIS OTHER LEG, SO THEN HE'LL STOP LIMPING! EH? YOU LIKE THE IDEA?!

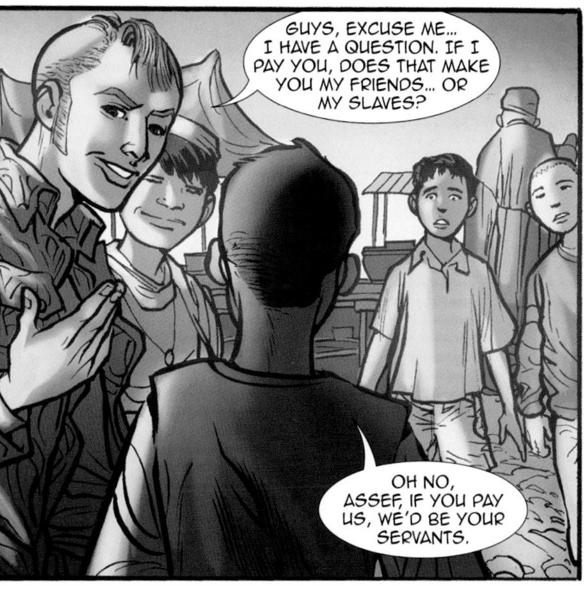
GUYS, EXCUSE ME... I HAVE A QUESTION. IF I PAY YOU, DOES THAT MAKE YOU MY FRIENDS... OR MY SLAVES?
OH NO, ASSEF, IF YOU PAY US, WE'D BE YOUR SERVANTS.

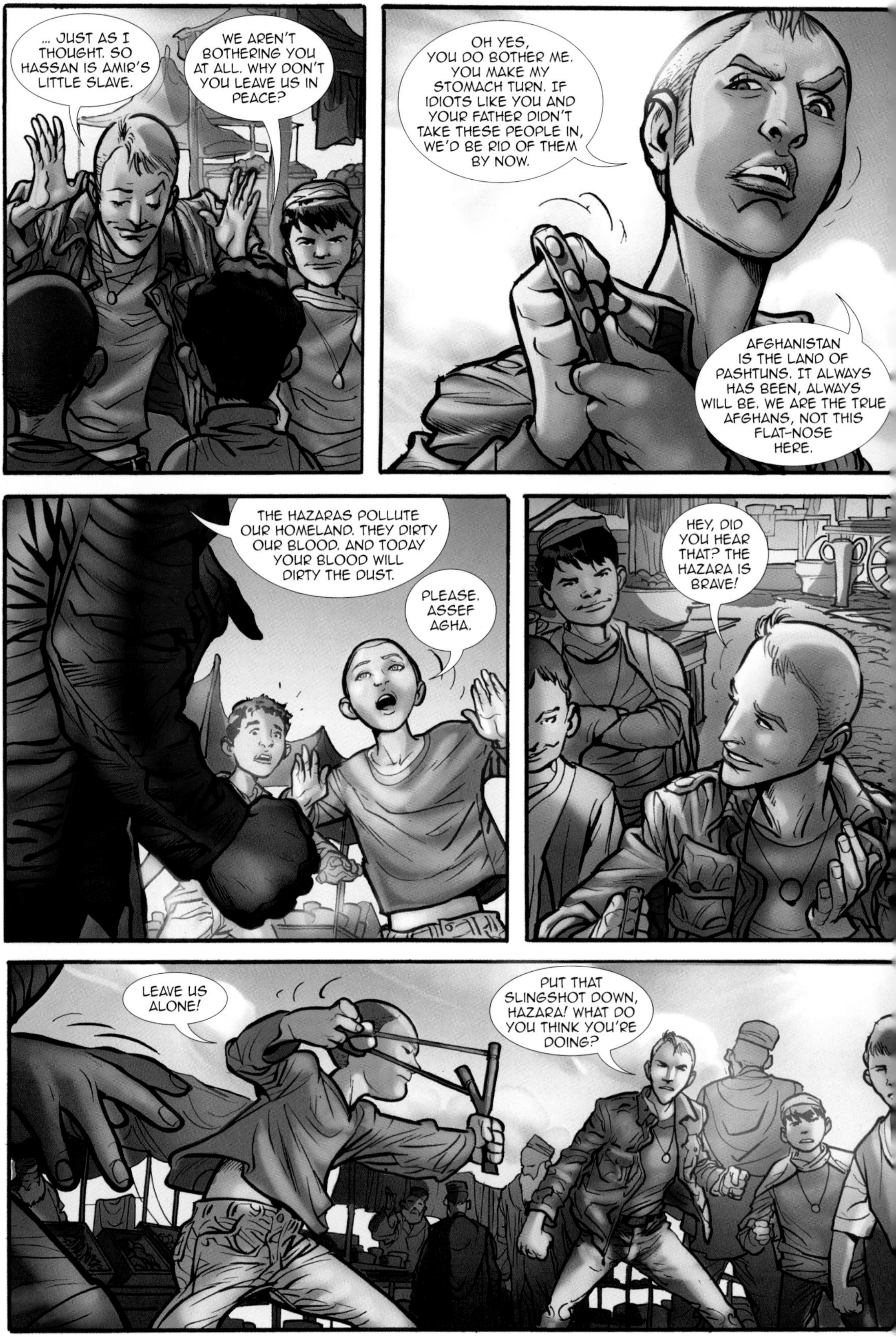
... JUST AS I THOUGHT. SO HASSAN IS AMIR'S LITTLE SLAVE.
WE AREN'T BOTHERING YOU AT ALL. WHY DON'T YOU LEAVE US IN PEACE?
OH YES, YOU DO BOTHER ME. YOU MAKE MY STOMACH TURN. IF IDIOTS LIKE YOU AND YOUR FATHER DIDN'T TAKE THESE PEOPLE IN, WE'D BE RID OF THEM BY NOW.
AFGHANISTAN IS THE LAND OF PASHTUNS. IT ALWAYS HAS BEEN, ALWAYS WILL BE. WE ARE THE TRUE AFGHANS, NOT THIS FLAT-NOSE HERE.
THE HAZARAS POLLUTE OUR HOMELAND. THEY DIRTY OUR BLOOD. AND TODAY YOUR BLOOD WILL DIRTY THE DUST.
PLEASE. ASSEF AGHA.
HEY, DID YOU HEAR THAT? THE HAZARA IS BRAVE!
LEAVE US ALONE!
PUT THAT SLINGSHOT DOWN, HAZARA! WHAT DO YOU THINK YOU'RE DOING?

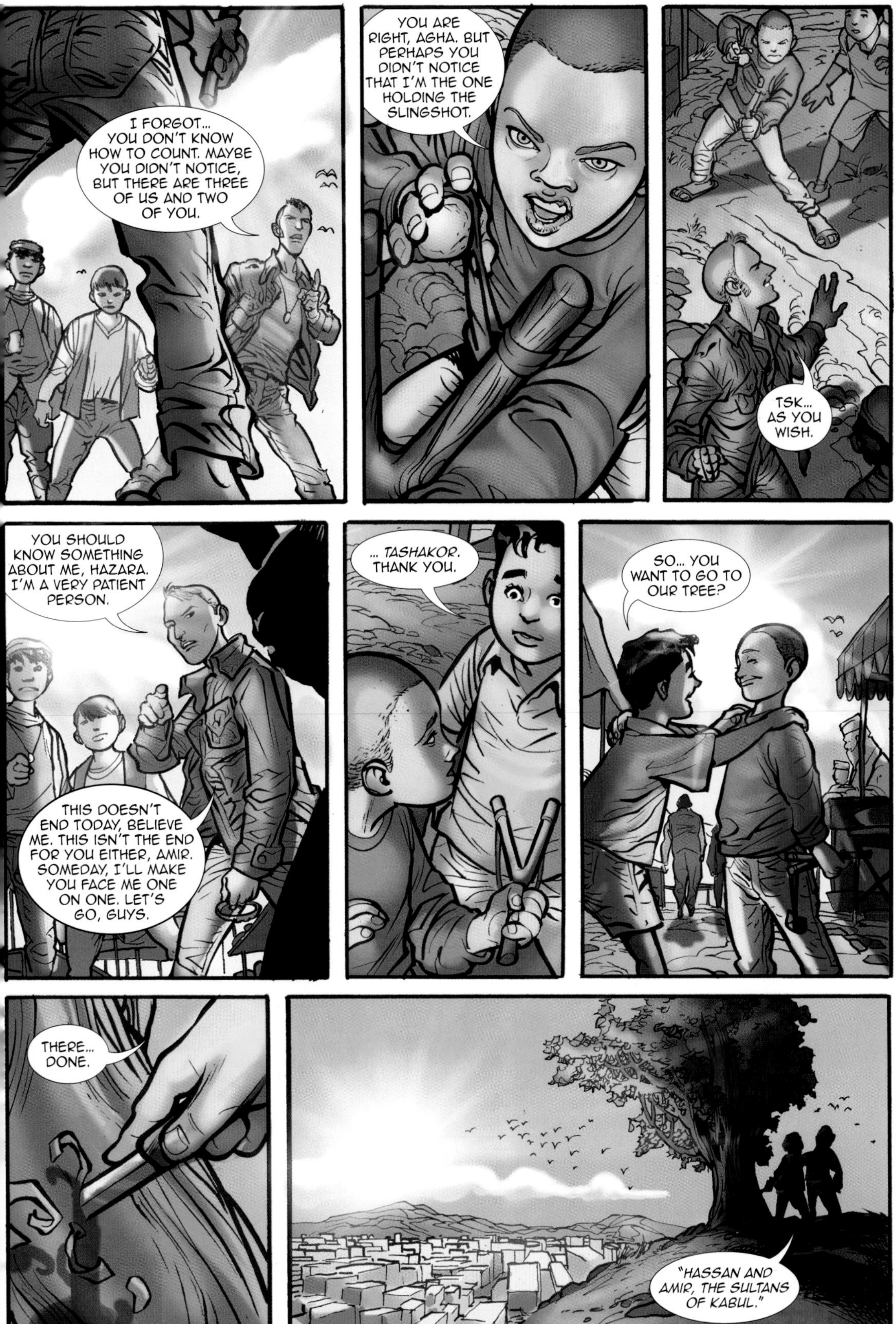
I FORGOT... YOU DON'T KNOW HOW TO COUNT. MAYBE YOU DIDN'T NOTICE, BUT THERE ARE THREE OF US AND TWO OF YOU.
YOU ARE RIGHT, AGHA. BUT PERHAPS YOU DIDN'T NOTICE THAT I'M THE ONE HOLDING THE SLINGSHOT.
TSK... AS YOU WISH.
YOU SHOULD KNOW SOMETHING ABOUT ME, HAZARA. I'M A VERY PATIENT PERSON.
THIS DOESN'T END TODAY, BELIEVE ME. THIS ISN'T THE END FOR YOU EITHER, AMIR. SOMEDAY, I'LL MAKE YOU FACE ME ONE ON ONE. LET'S GO, GUYS.
... *TASHAKOR*. THANK YOU.
SO... YOU WANT TO GO TO OUR TREE?
THERE... DONE.
"HASSAN AND AMIR, THE SULTANS OF KABUL."

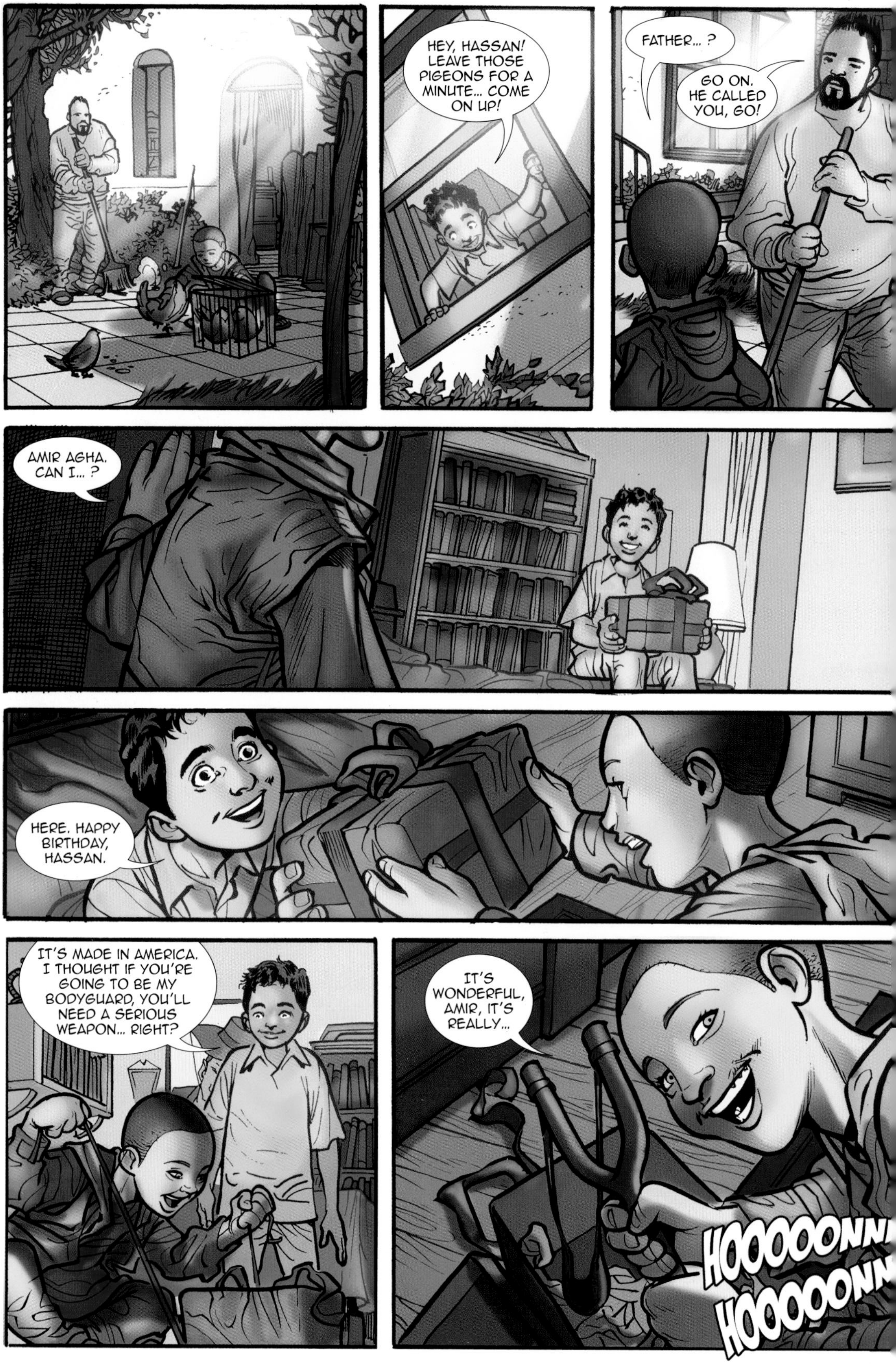

HEY, HASSAN! LEAVE THOSE PIGEONS FOR A MINUTE... COME ON UP!
FATHER... ?
GO ON. HE CALLED YOU, GO!
AMIR AGHA. CAN I... ?
HERE. HAPPY BIRTHDAY, HASSAN.
IT'S MADE IN AMERICA. I THOUGHT IF YOU'RE GOING TO BE MY BODYGUARD, YOU'LL NEED A SERIOUS WEAPON... RIGHT?
IT'S WONDERFUL, AMIR, IT'S REALLY...
HOOOOONN
HOOOOONN

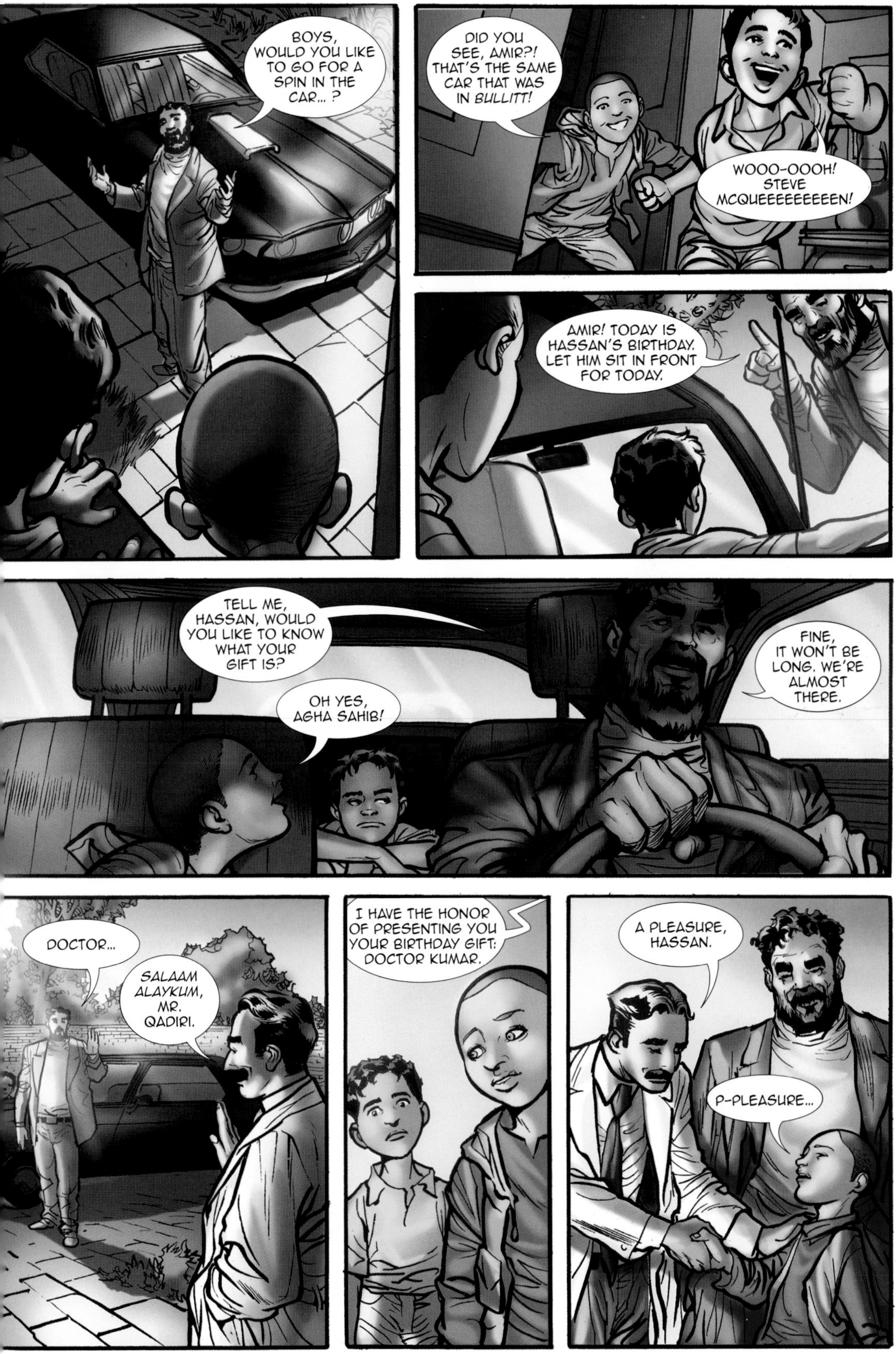
BOYS, WOULD YOU LIKE TO GO FOR A SPIN IN THE CAR... ?
DID YOU SEE, AMIR?! THAT'S THE SAME CAR THAT WAS IN BULLITT!
WOOO-OOOH! STEVE MCQUEEEEEEEEEN!
AMIR! TODAY IS HASSAN'S BIRTHDAY. LET HIM SIT IN FRONT FOR TODAY.
TELL ME, HASSAN, WOULD YOU LIKE TO KNOW WHAT YOUR GIFT IS?
OH YES, AGHA SAHIB!
FINE, IT WON'T BE LONG. WE'RE ALMOST THERE.
DOCTOR...
SALAAM ALAYKUM, MR. QADIRI.
I HAVE THE HONOR OF PRESENTING YOU YOUR BIRTHDAY GIFT: DOCTOR KUMAR.
A PLEASURE, HASSAN.
P-PLEASURE...

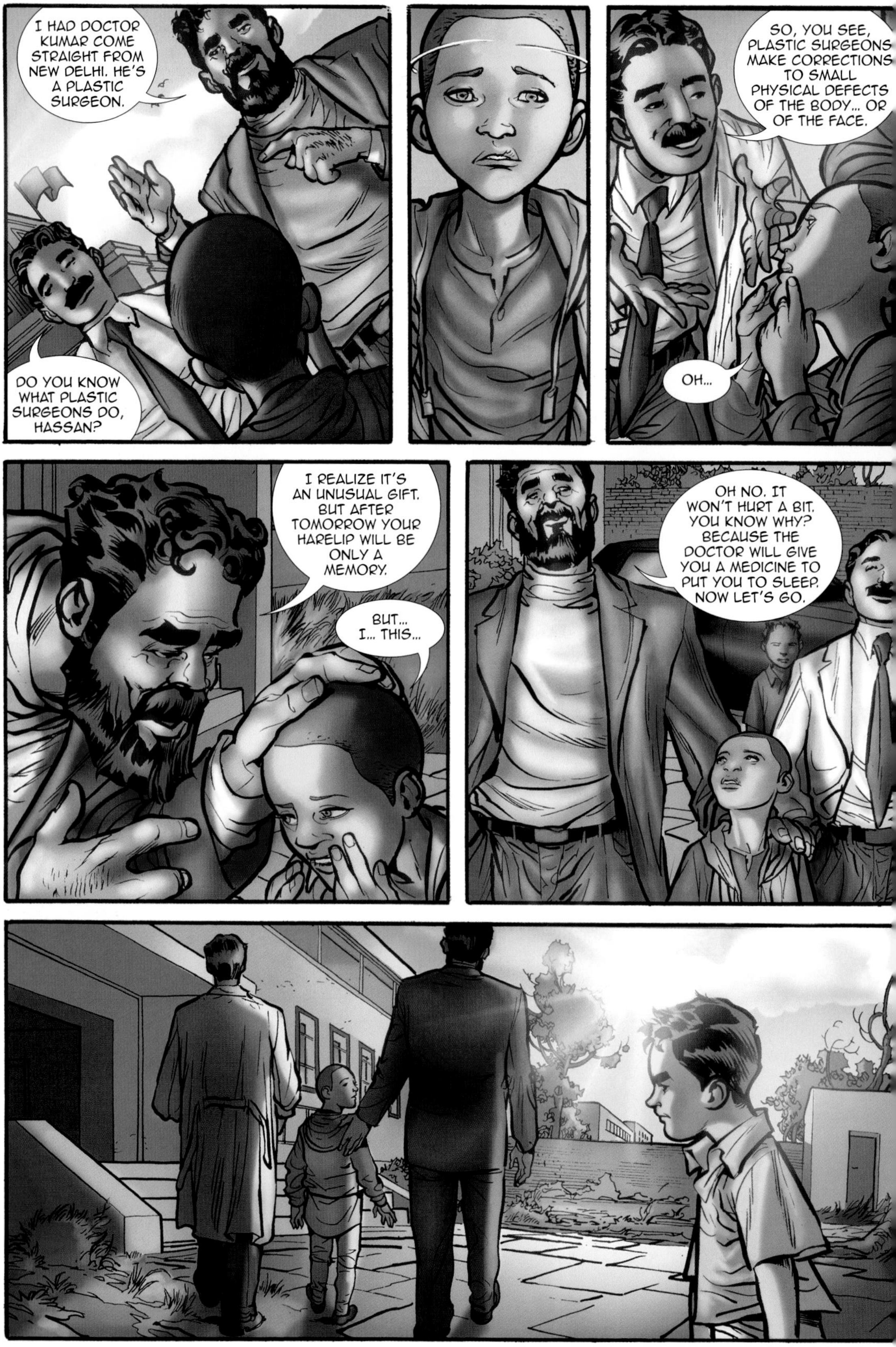
I HAD DOCTOR KUMAR COME STRAIGHT FROM NEW DELHI. HE'S A PLASTIC SURGEON.
DO YOU KNOW WHAT PLASTIC SURGEONS DO, HASSAN?
SO, YOU SEE, PLASTIC SURGEONS MAKE CORRECTIONS TO SMALL PHYSICAL DEFECTS OF THE BODY... OR OF THE FACE.
OH...
I REALIZE IT'S AN UNUSUAL GIFT. BUT AFTER TOMORROW YOUR HARELIP WILL BE ONLY A MEMORY.
BUT... I... THIS...
OH NO. IT WON'T HURT A BIT. YOU KNOW WHY? BECAUSE THE DOCTOR WILL GIVE YOU A MEDICINE TO PUT YOU TO SLEEP. NOW LET'S GO.

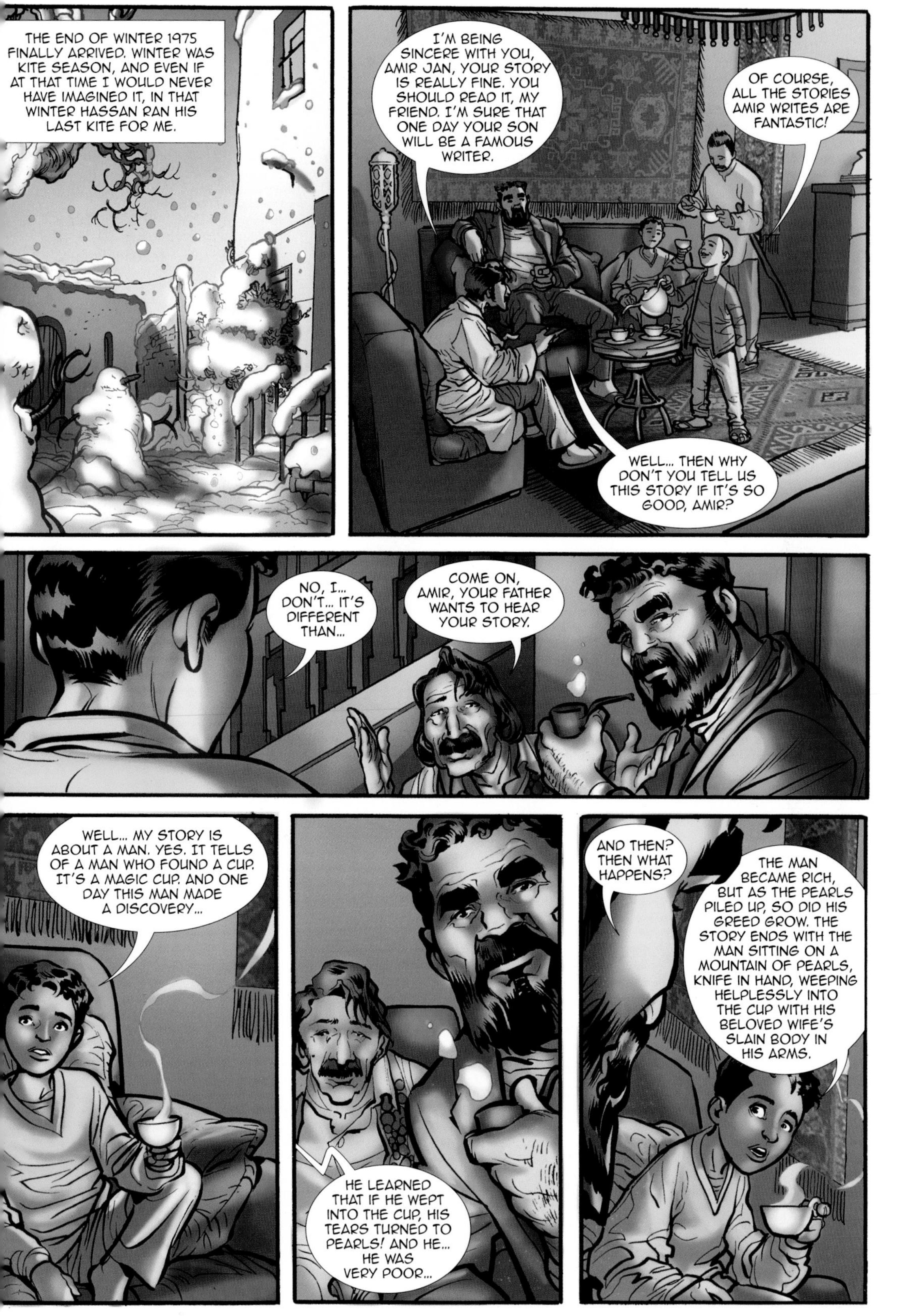
THE END OF WINTER 1975 FINALLY ARRIVED. WINTER WAS KITE SEASON, AND EVEN IF AT THAT TIME I WOULD NEVER HAVE IMAGINED IT, IN THAT WINTER HASSAN RAN HIS LAST KITE FOR ME.
I'M BEING SINCERE WITH YOU, AMIR JAN, YOUR STORY IS REALLY FINE. YOU SHOULD READ IT, MY FRIEND. I'M SURE THAT ONE DAY YOUR SON WILL BE A FAMOUS WRITER.
OF COURSE, ALL THE STORIES AMIR WRITES ARE FANTASTIC!
WELL... THEN WHY DON'T YOU TELL US THIS STORY IF IT'S SO GOOD, AMIR?
NO, I... DON'T... IT'S DIFFERENT THAN...
COME ON, AMIR, YOUR FATHER WANTS TO HEAR YOUR STORY.
WELL... MY STORY IS ABOUT A MAN. YES. IT TELLS OF A MAN WHO FOUND A CUP. IT'S A MAGIC CUP. AND ONE DAY THIS MAN MADE A DISCOVERY...
HE LEARNED THAT IF HE WEPT INTO THE CUP, HIS TEARS TURNED TO PEARLS! AND HE... HE WAS VERY POOR...
AND THEN? THEN WHAT HAPPENS?
THE MAN BECAME RICH, BUT AS THE PEARLS PILED UP, SO DID HIS GREED GROW. THE STORY ENDS WITH THE MAN SITTING ON A MOUNTAIN OF PEARLS, KNIFE IN HAND, WEEPING HELPLESSLY INTO THE CUP WITH HIS BELOVED WIFE'S SLAIN BODY IN HIS ARMS.

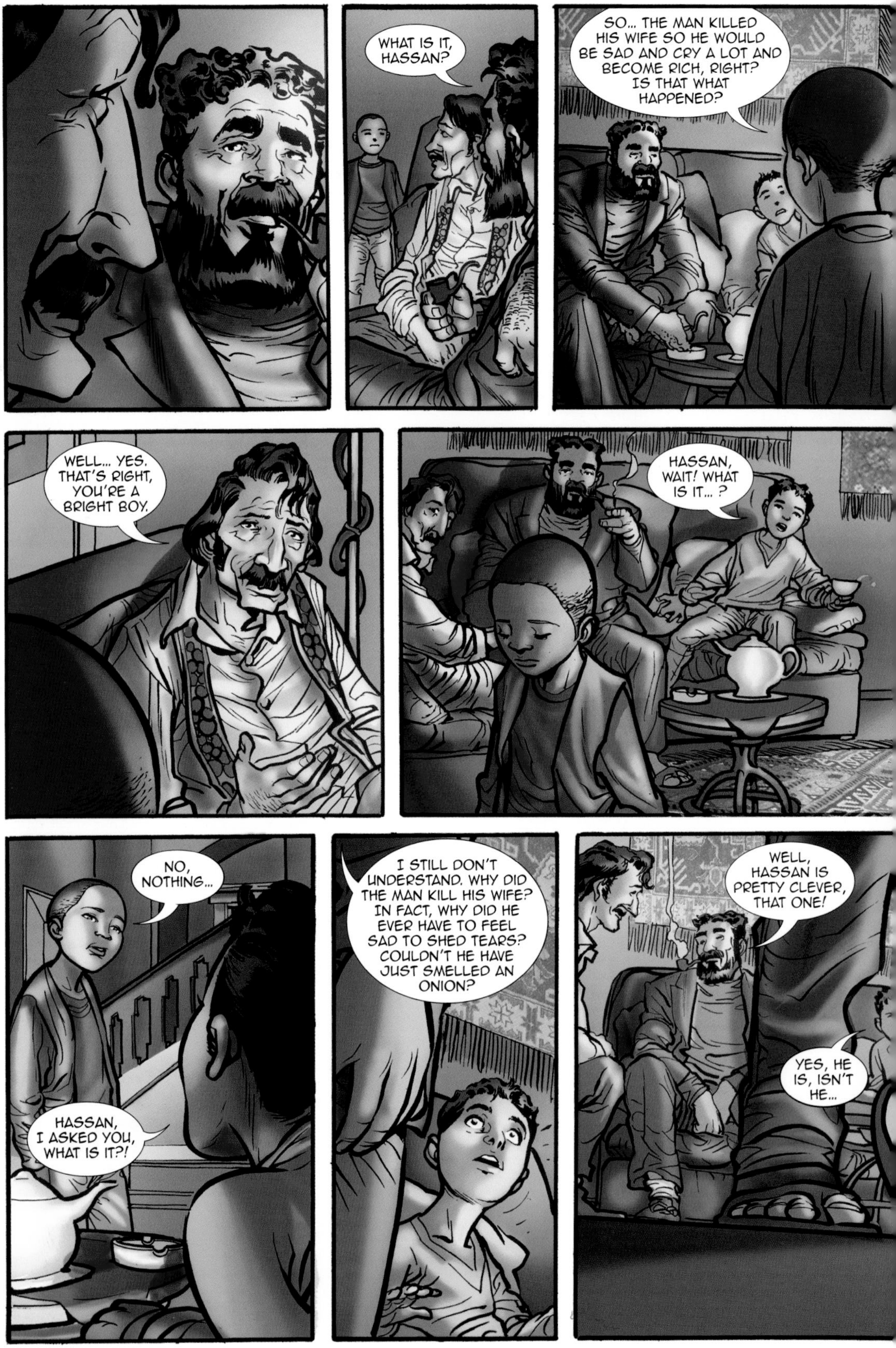
WHAT IS IT, HASSAN?
SO... THE MAN KILLED HIS WIFE SO HE WOULD BE SAD AND CRY A LOT AND BECOME RICH, RIGHT? IS THAT WHAT HAPPENED?
WELL... YES. THAT'S RIGHT, YOU'RE A BRIGHT BOY.
HASSAN, WAIT! WHAT IS IT... ?
NO, NOTHING...
HASSAN, I ASKED YOU, WHAT IS IT?!
I STILL DON'T UNDERSTAND. WHY DID THE MAN KILL HIS WIFE? IN FACT, WHY DID HE EVER HAVE TO FEEL SAD TO SHED TEARS? COULDN'T HE HAVE JUST SMELLED AN ONION?
WELL, HASSAN IS PRETTY CLEVER, THAT ONE!
YES, HE IS, ISN'T HE...

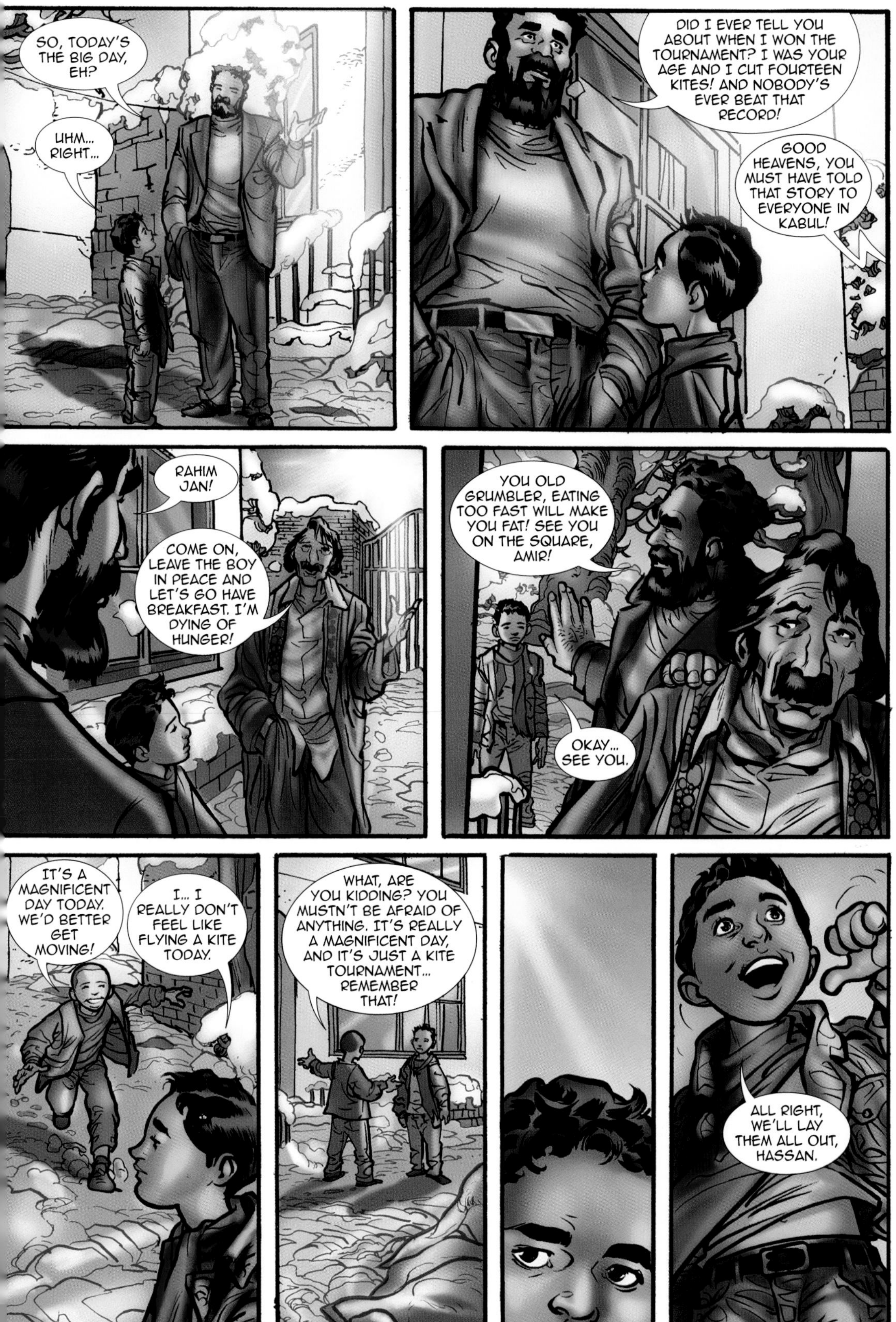
SO, TODAY'S THE BIG DAY, EH?
UHM... RIGHT...
DID I EVER TELL YOU ABOUT WHEN I WON THE TOURNAMENT? I WAS YOUR AGE AND I CUT FOURTEEN KITES! AND NOBODY'S EVER BEAT THAT RECORD!
GOOD HEAVENS, YOU MUST HAVE TOLD THAT STORY TO EVERYONE IN KABUL!
RAHIM JAN!
COME ON, LEAVE THE BOY IN PEACE AND LET'S GO HAVE BREAKFAST. I'M DYING OF HUNGER!
YOU OLD GRUMBLER, EATING TOO FAST WILL MAKE YOU FAT! SEE YOU ON THE SQUARE, AMIR!
OKAY... SEE YOU.
IT'S A MAGNIFICENT DAY TODAY. WE'D BETTER GET MOVING!
I... I REALLY DON'T FEEL LIKE FLYING A KITE TODAY.
WHAT, ARE YOU KIDDING? YOU MUSTN'T BE AFRAID OF ANYTHING. IT'S REALLY A MAGNIFICENT DAY, AND IT'S JUST A KITE TOURNAMENT... REMEMBER THAT!
ALL RIGHT, WE'LL LAY THEM ALL OUT, HASSAN.

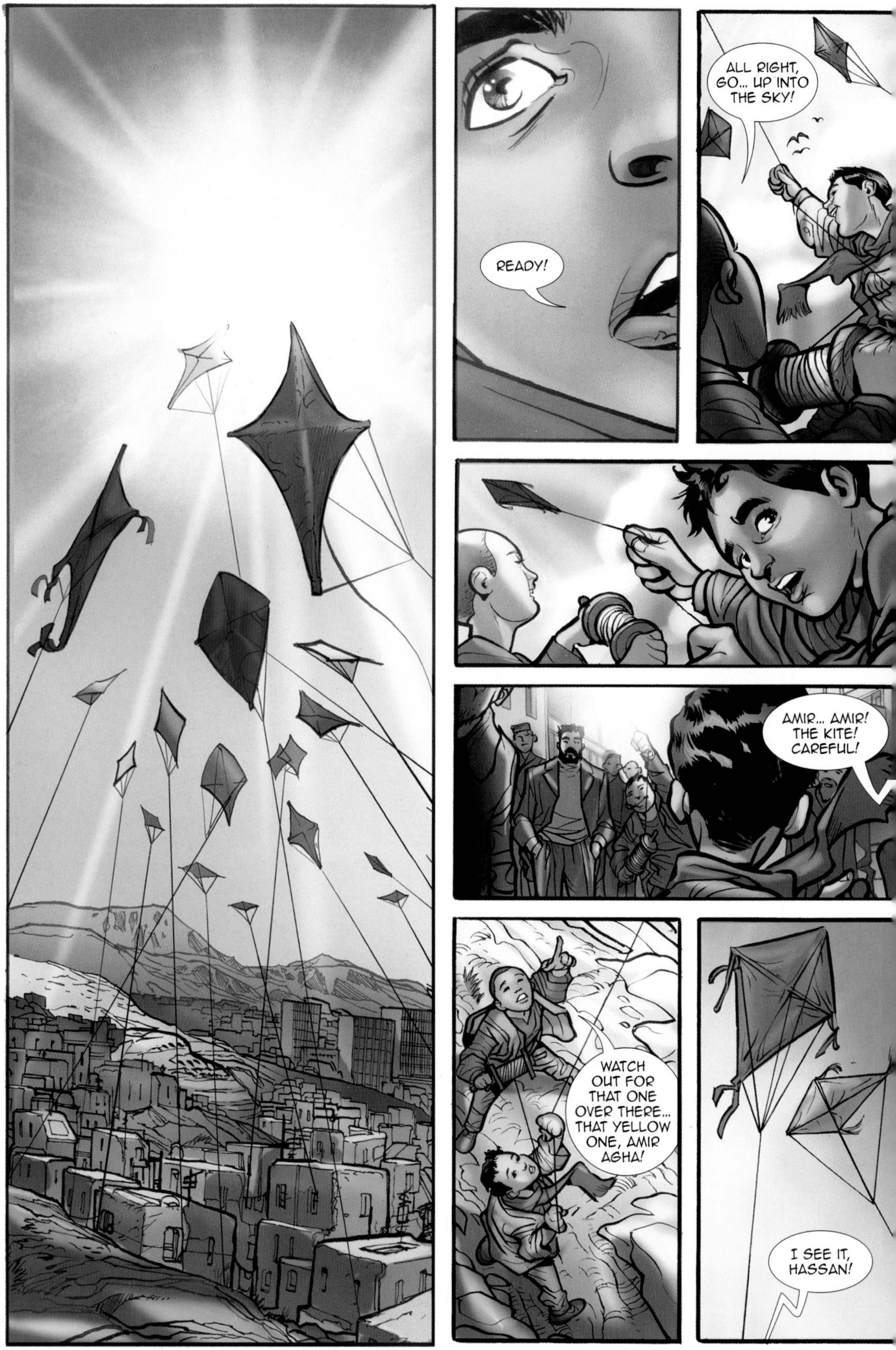
READY!
ALL RIGHT, GO... UP INTO THE SKY!
AMIR... AMIR! THE KITE! CAREFUL!
WATCH OUT FOR THAT ONE OVER THERE... THAT YELLOW ONE, AMIR AGHA!
I SEE IT, HASSAN!

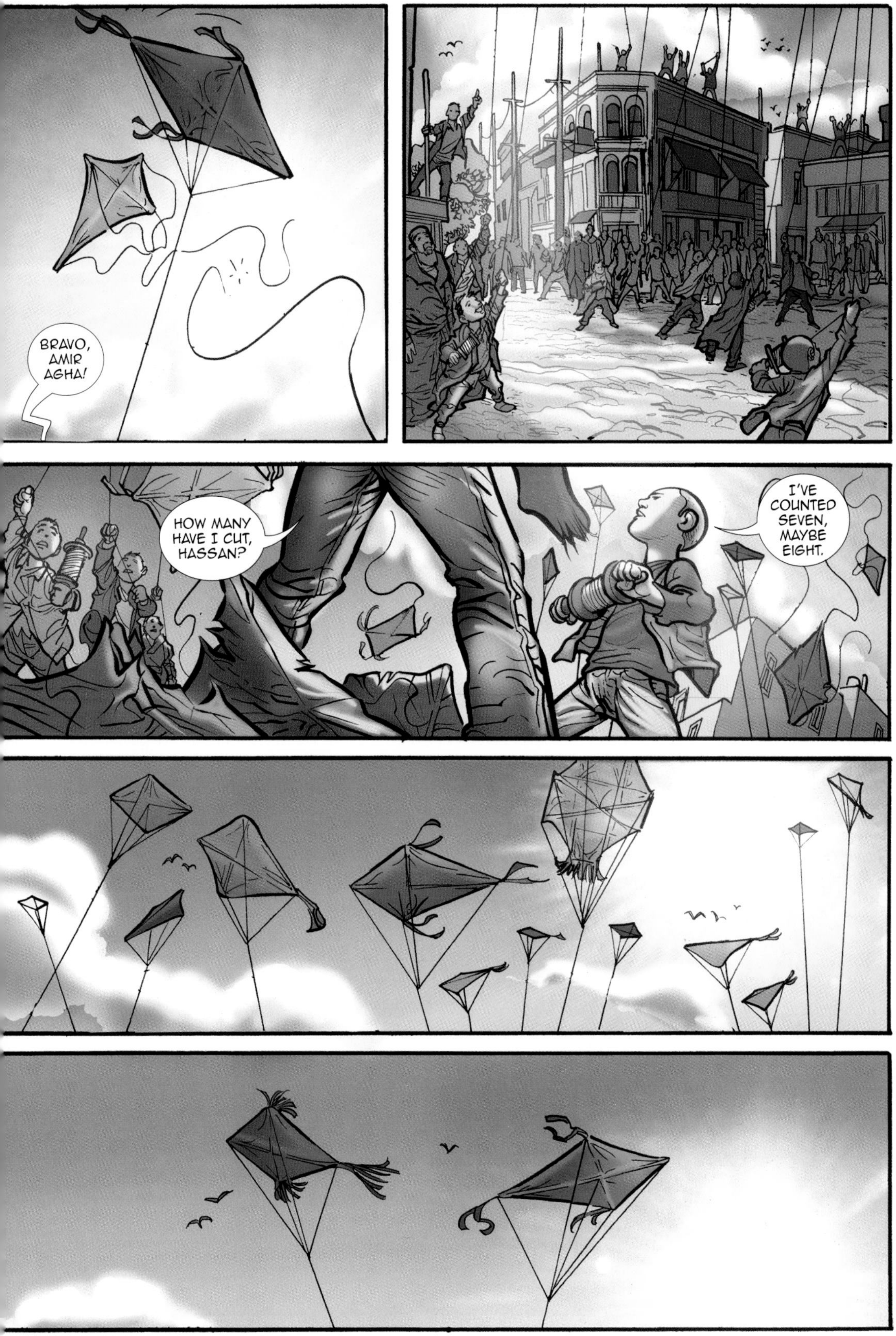
BRAVO, AMIR AGHA!
HOW MANY HAVE I CUT, HASSAN?
I'VE COUNTED SEVEN, MAYBE EIGHT.

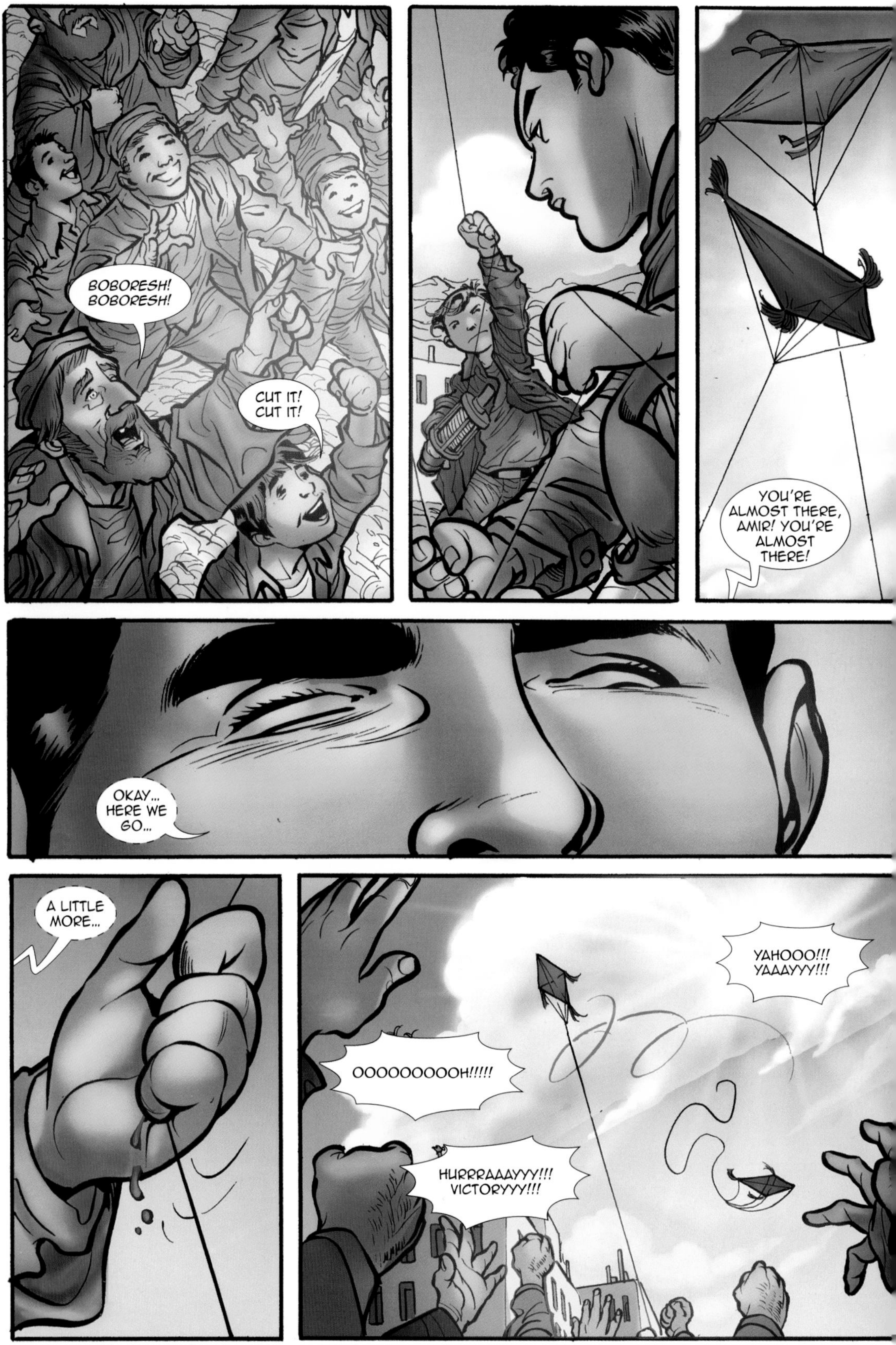
BOBORESH! BOBORESH!
CUT IT! CUT IT!
YOU'RE ALMOST THERE, AMIR! YOU'RE ALMOST THERE!
OKAY... HERE WE GO...
A LITTLE MORE...
YAHOOO!!! YAAAYYY!!!
OOOOOOOOOH!!!!!
HURRRAAAYYY!!! VICTORYYY!!!

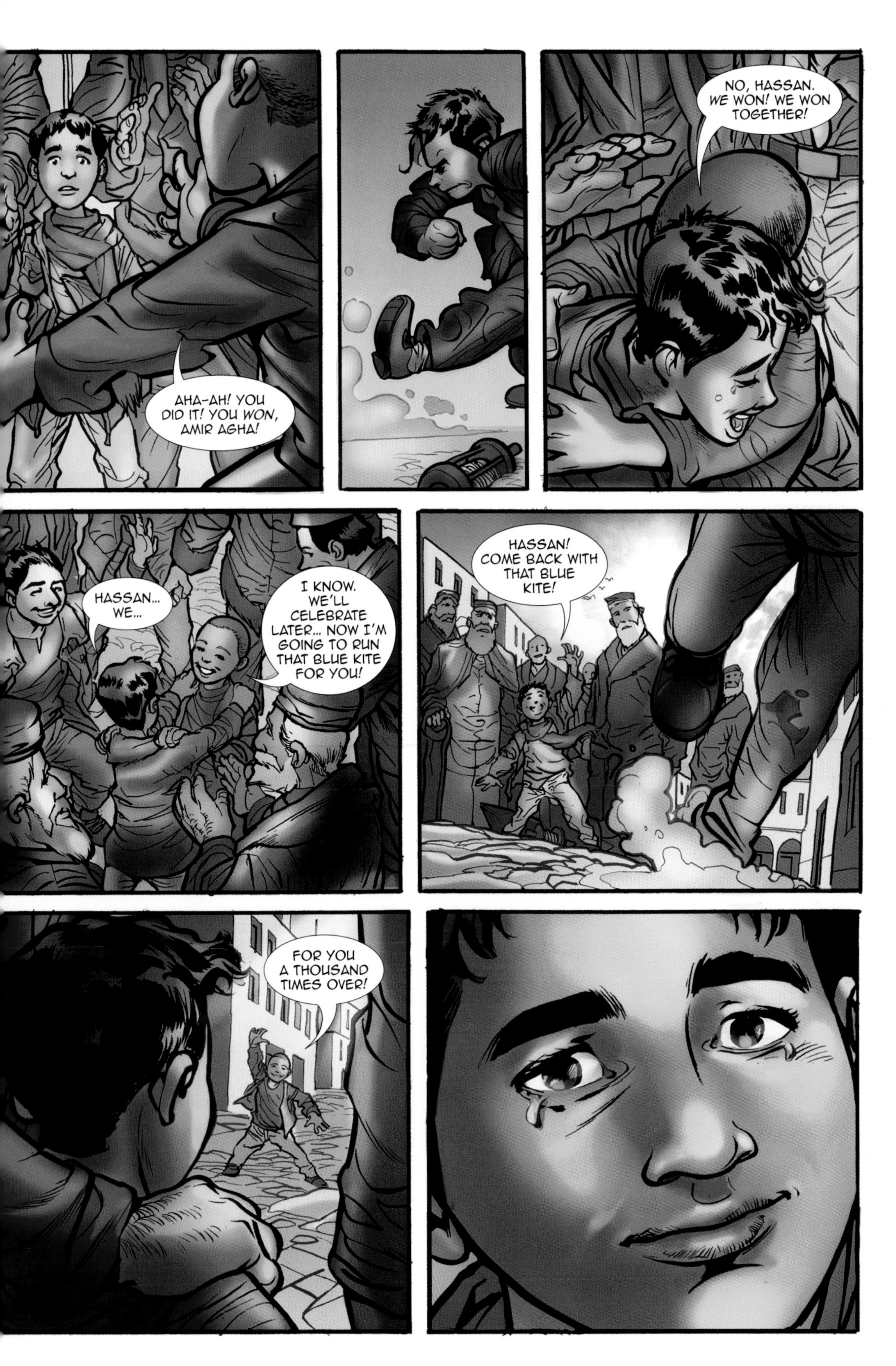
AHA-AH! YOU DID IT! YOU WON, AMIR AGHA!
NO, HASSAN. WE WON! WE WON TOGETHER!
HASSAN... WE...
I KNOW. WE'LL CELEBRATE LATER... NOW I'M GOING TO RUN THAT BLUE KITE FOR YOU!
HASSAN! COME BACK WITH THAT BLUE KITE!
FOR YOU A THOUSAND TIMES OVER!

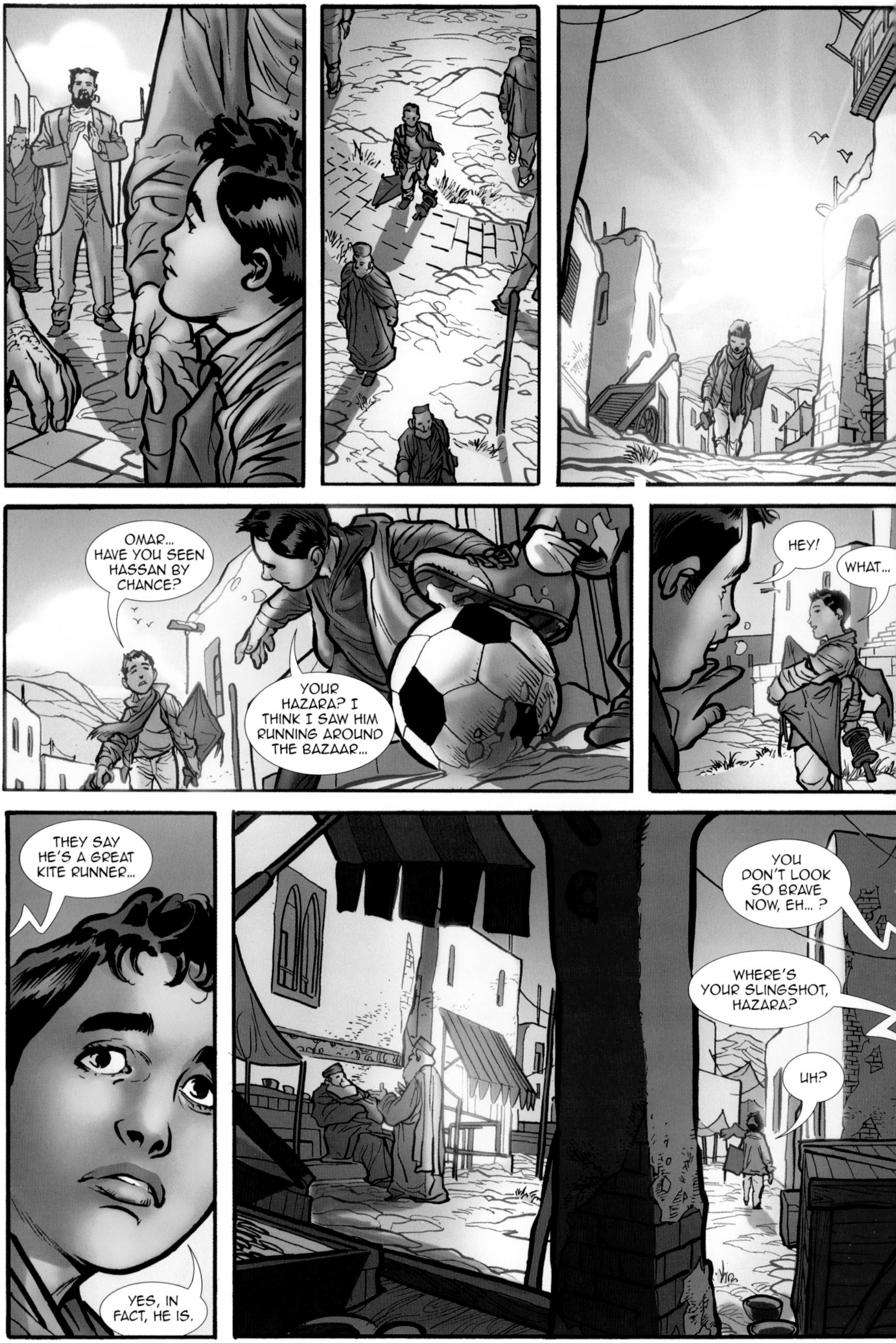

OMAR... HAVE YOU SEEN HASSAN BY CHANCE?
YOUR HAZARA? I THINK I SAW HIM RUNNING AROUND THE BAZAAR...
HEY!
WHAT...
THEY SAY HE'S A GREAT KITE RUNNER...
YES, IN FACT, HE IS.
YOU DON'T LOOK SO BRAVE NOW, EH... ?
WHERE'S YOUR SLINGSHOT, HAZARA?
UH?

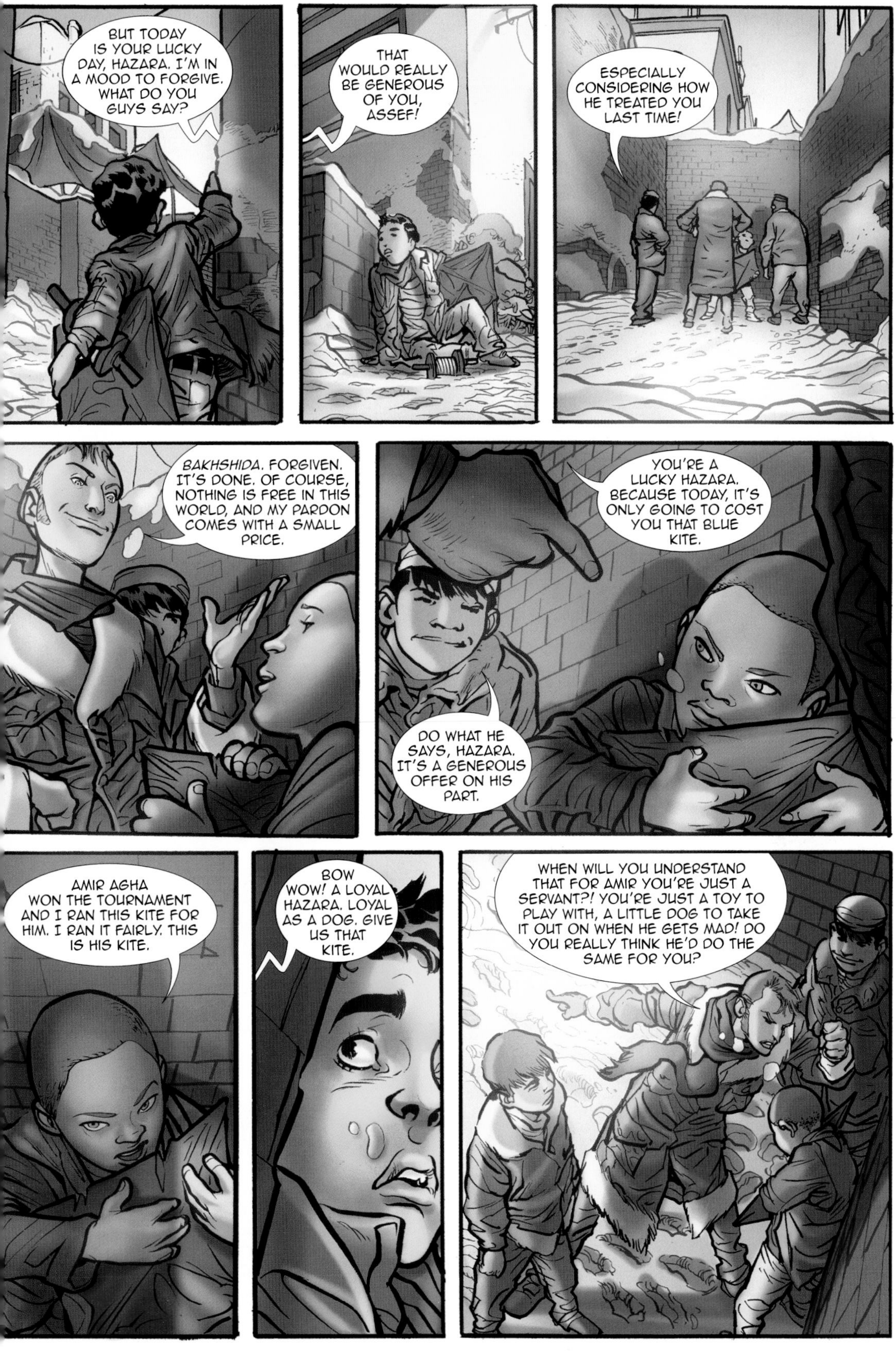
BUT TODAY IS YOUR LUCKY DAY, HAZARA. I'M IN A MOOD TO FORGIVE. WHAT DO YOU GUYS SAY?
THAT WOULD REALLY BE GENEROUS OF YOU, ASSEF!
ESPECIALLY CONSIDERING HOW HE TREATED YOU LAST TIME!
BAKHSHIDA. FORGIVEN. IT'S DONE. OF COURSE, NOTHING IS FREE IN THIS WORLD, AND MY PARDON COMES WITH A SMALL PRICE.
YOU'RE A LUCKY HAZARA. BECAUSE TODAY, IT'S ONLY GOING TO COST YOU THAT BLUE KITE.
DO WHAT HE SAYS, HAZARA. IT'S A GENEROUS OFFER ON HIS PART.
AMIR AGHA WON THE TOURNAMENT AND I RAN THIS KITE FOR HIM. I RAN IT FAIRLY. THIS IS HIS KITE.
BOW WOW! A LOYAL HAZARA. LOYAL AS A DOG. GIVE US THAT KITE.
WHEN WILL YOU UNDERSTAND THAT FOR AMIR YOU'RE JUST A SERVANT?! YOU'RE JUST A TOY TO PLAY WITH, A LITTLE DOG TO TAKE IT OUT ON WHEN HE GETS MAD! DO YOU REALLY THINK HE'D DO THE SAME FOR YOU?

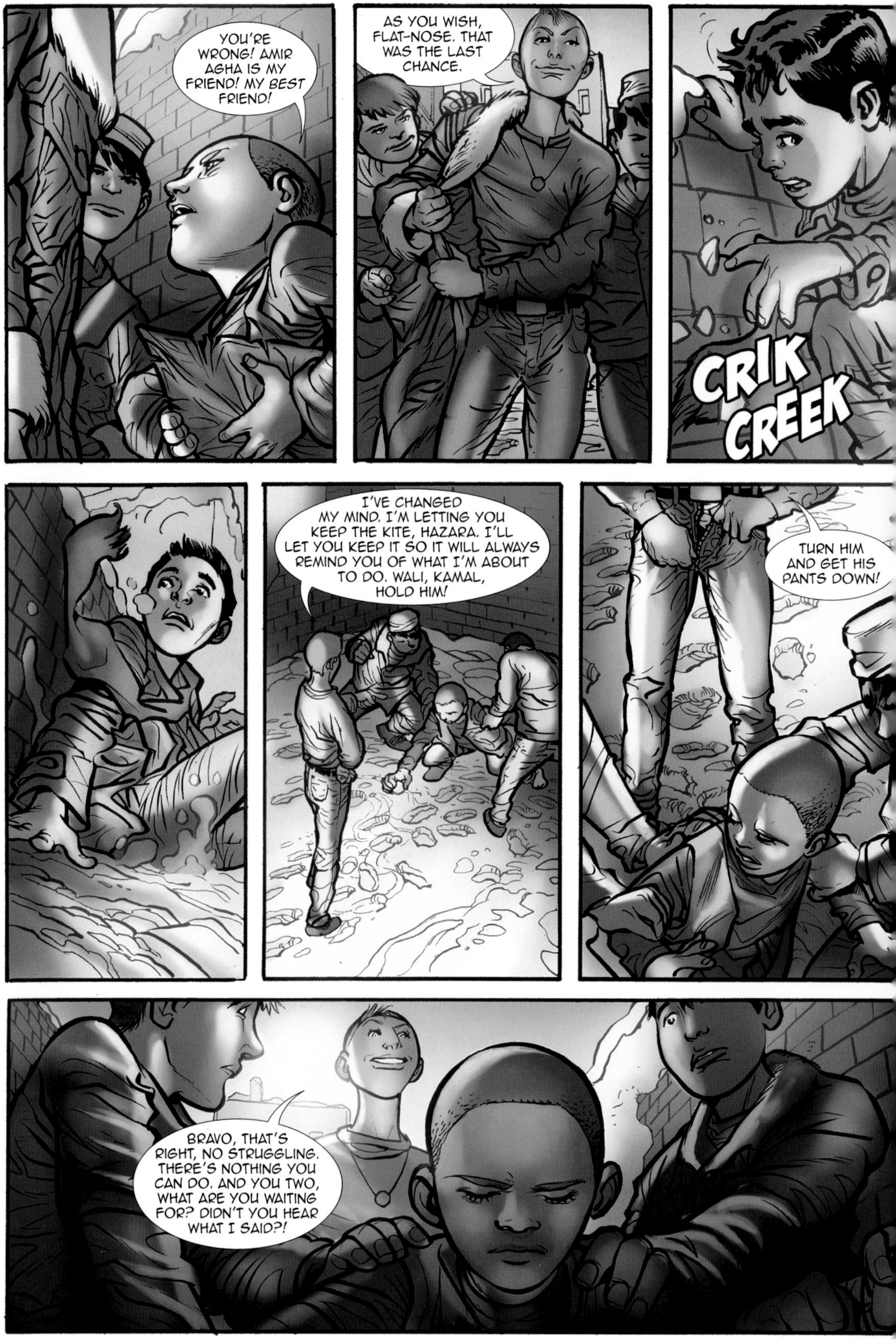
YOU'RE WRONG! AMIR AGHA IS MY FRIEND! MY BEST FRIEND!
AS YOU WISH, FLAT-NOSE. THAT WAS THE LAST CHANCE.
CRIK CREEK
I'VE CHANGED MY MIND. I'M LETTING YOU KEEP THE KITE, HAZARA. I'LL LET YOU KEEP IT SO IT WILL ALWAYS REMIND YOU OF WHAT I'M ABOUT TO DO. WALI, KAMAL, HOLD HIM!
TURN HIM AND GET HIS PANTS DOWN!
BRAVO, THAT'S RIGHT, NO STRUGGLING. THERE'S NOTHING YOU CAN DO. AND YOU TWO, WHAT ARE YOU WAITING FOR? DIDN'T YOU HEAR WHAT I SAID?!

READY, HAZARA?

I RAN AWAY. I RAN BECAUSE I WAS A COWARD.

I TOLD MYSELF I WAS AFRAID OF ASSEF AND THE HARM HE WOULD HAVE DONE ME.

BUT THE REAL REASON I WAS RUNNING WAS THAT ASSEF WAS RIGHT: NOTHING WAS FREE IN THIS WORLD.

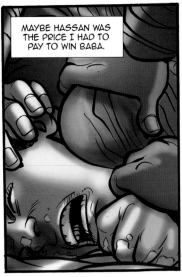

MAYBE HASSAN WAS THE PRICE I HAD TO PAY TO WIN BABA.

WAS IT A FAIR PRICE? THE ANSWER FLOATED TO MY CONSCIOUS MIND BEFORE I COULD THWART IT.

AFTER ALL, HE WAS JUST A HAZARA, WASN'T HE?

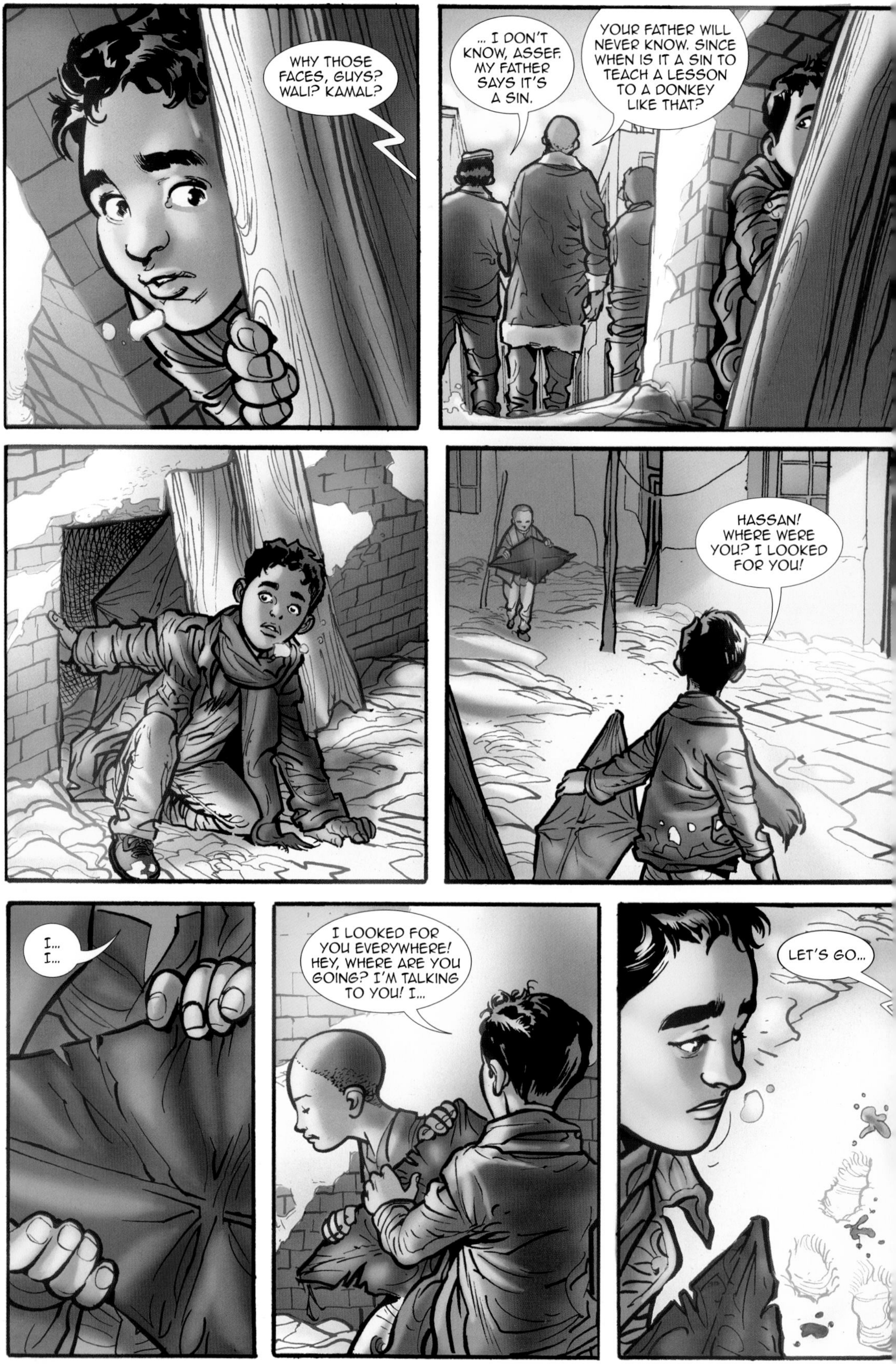
WHY THOSE FACES, GUYS? WALI? KAMAL?
... I DON'T KNOW, ASSEF. MY FATHER SAYS IT'S A SIN.
YOUR FATHER WILL NEVER KNOW. SINCE WHEN IS IT A SIN TO TEACH A LESSON TO A DONKEY LIKE THAT?
HASSAN! WHERE WERE YOU? I LOOKED FOR YOU!
I... I...
I LOOKED FOR YOU EVERYWHERE! HEY, WHERE ARE YOU GOING? I'M TALKING TO YOU! I...
LET'S GO...

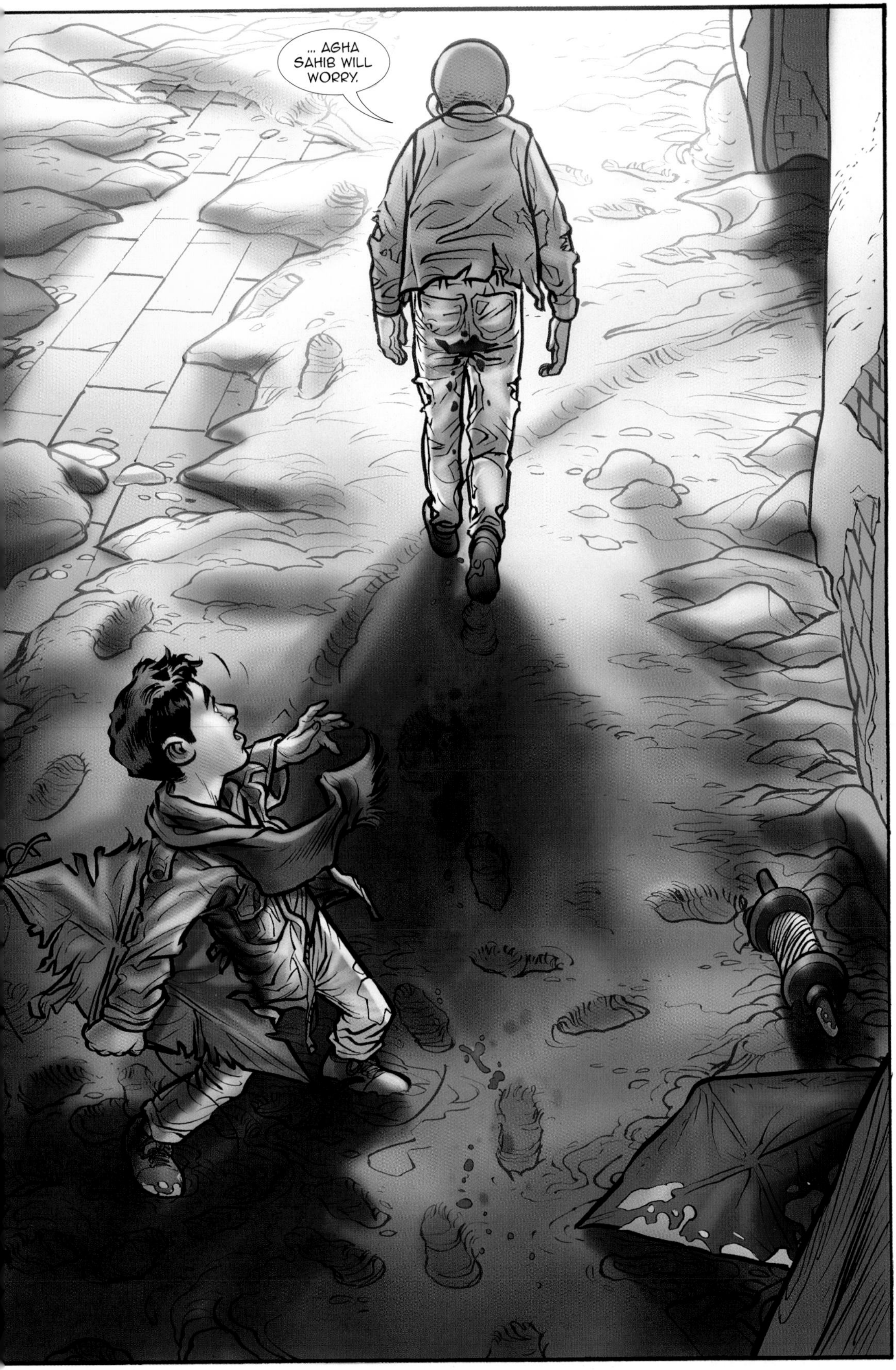
... AGHA SAHIB WILL WORRY.

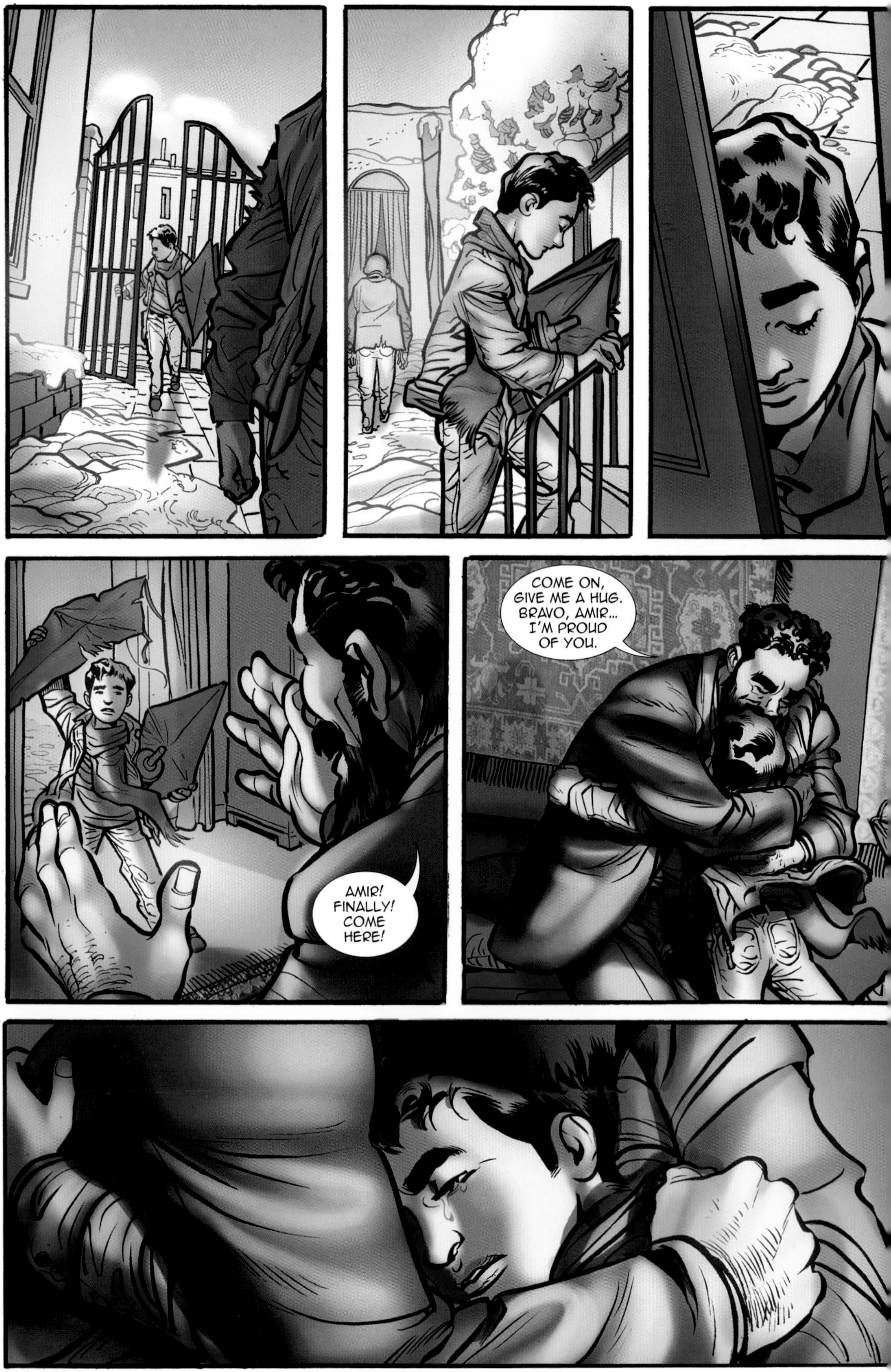
AMIR!
FINALLY!
COME
HERE!
COME ON,
GIVE ME A HUG.
BRAVO, AMIR...
I'M PROUD
OF YOU.

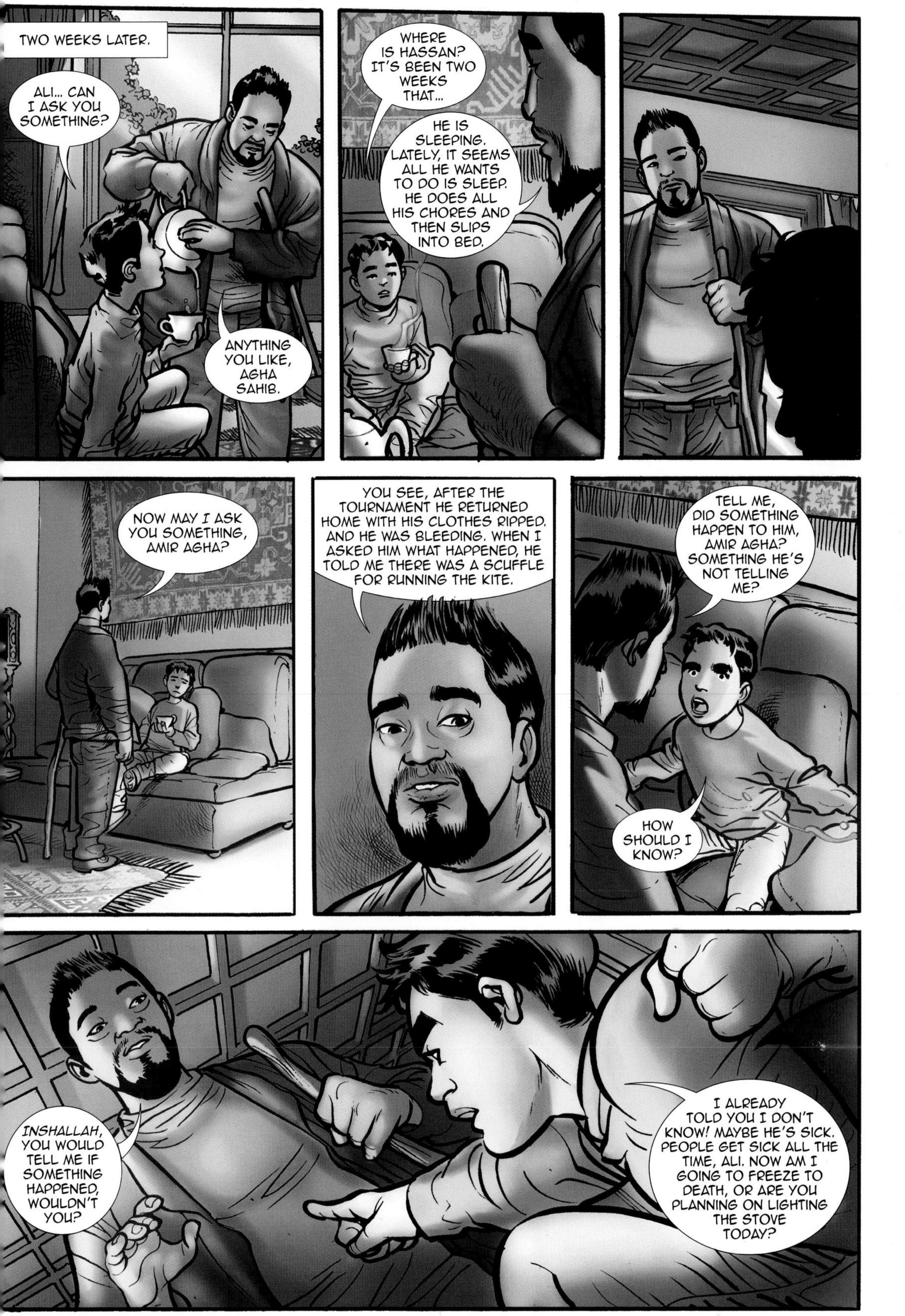
TWO WEEKS LATER.
ALI... CAN I ASK YOU SOMETHING?
ANYTHING YOU LIKE, AGHA SAHIB.
WHERE IS HASSAN? IT'S BEEN TWO WEEKS THAT...
HE IS SLEEPING. LATELY, IT SEEMS ALL HE WANTS TO DO IS SLEEP. HE DOES ALL HIS CHORES AND THEN SLIPS INTO BED.
NOW MAY *I* ASK YOU SOMETHING, AMIR AGHA?
YOU SEE, AFTER THE TOURNAMENT HE RETURNED HOME WITH HIS CLOTHES RIPPED. AND HE WAS BLEEDING. WHEN I ASKED HIM WHAT HAPPENED, HE TOLD ME THERE WAS A SCUFFLE FOR RUNNING THE KITE.
TELL ME, DID SOMETHING HAPPEN TO HIM, AMIR AGHA? SOMETHING HE'S NOT TELLING ME?
HOW SHOULD I KNOW?
INSHALLAH, YOU WOULD TELL ME IF SOMETHING HAPPENED, WOULDN'T YOU?
I ALREADY TOLD YOU I DON'T KNOW! MAYBE HE'S SICK. PEOPLE GET SICK ALL THE TIME, ALI. NOW AM I GOING TO FREEZE TO DEATH, OR ARE YOU PLANNING ON LIGHTING THE STOVE TODAY?

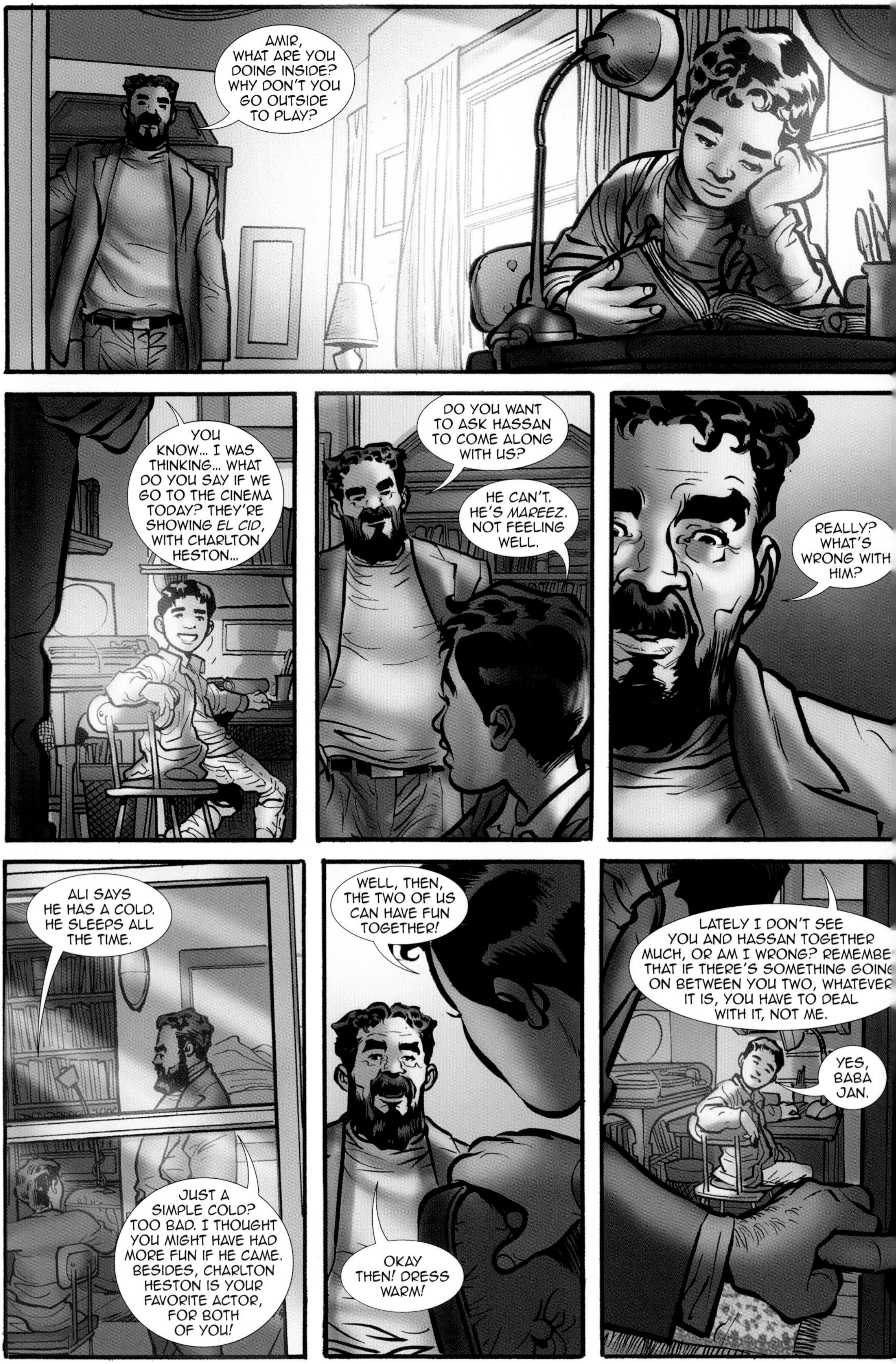
AMIR, WHAT ARE YOU DOING INSIDE? WHY DON'T YOU GO OUTSIDE TO PLAY?
YOU KNOW... I WAS THINKING... WHAT DO YOU SAY IF WE GO TO THE CINEMA TODAY? THEY'RE SHOWING *EL CID*, WITH CHARLTON HESTON...
DO YOU WANT TO ASK HASSAN TO COME ALONG WITH US?
HE CAN'T. HE'S *MAREEZ*. NOT FEELING WELL.
REALLY? WHAT'S WRONG WITH HIM?
ALI SAYS HE HAS A COLD. HE SLEEPS ALL THE TIME.
JUST A SIMPLE COLD? TOO BAD. I THOUGHT YOU MIGHT HAVE HAD MORE FUN IF HE CAME. BESIDES, CHARLTON HESTON IS YOUR FAVORITE ACTOR, FOR BOTH OF YOU!
WELL, THEN, THE TWO OF US CAN HAVE FUN TOGETHER!
OKAY THEN! DRESS WARM!
LATELY I DON'T SEE YOU AND HASSAN TOGETHER MUCH, OR AM I WRONG? REMEMBE THAT IF THERE'S SOMETHING GOIN ON BETWEEN YOU TWO, WHATEVER IT IS, YOU HAVE TO DEAL WITH IT, NOT ME.
YES, BABA JAN.

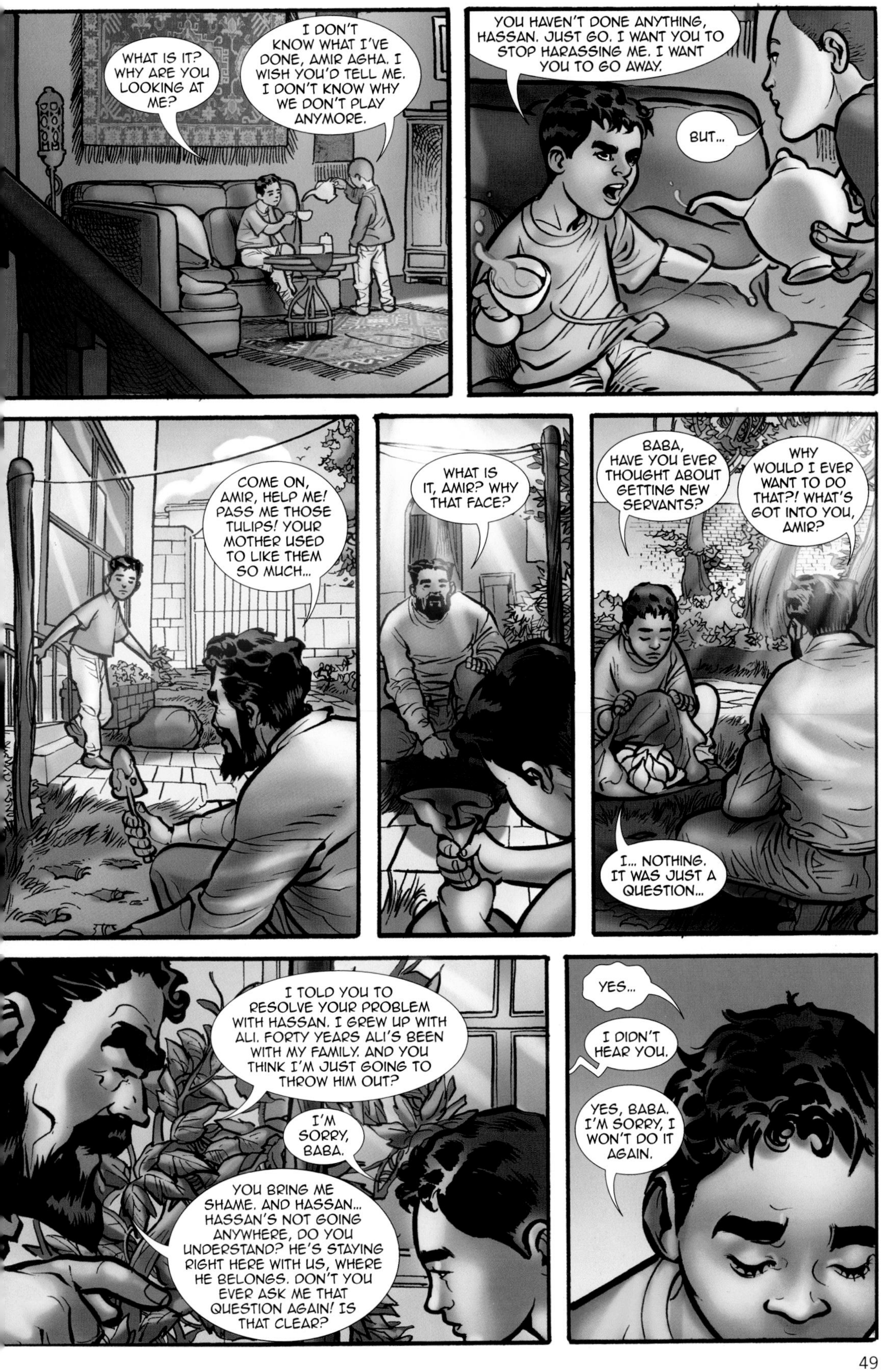
WHAT IS IT? WHY ARE YOU LOOKING AT ME?
I DON'T KNOW WHAT I'VE DONE, AMIR AGHA. I WISH YOU'D TELL ME. I DON'T KNOW WHY WE DON'T PLAY ANYMORE.
YOU HAVEN'T DONE ANYTHING, HASSAN. JUST GO. I WANT YOU TO STOP HARASSING ME. I WANT YOU TO GO AWAY.
BUT...
COME ON, AMIR, HELP ME! PASS ME THOSE TULIPS! YOUR MOTHER USED TO LIKE THEM SO MUCH...
WHAT IS IT, AMIR? WHY THAT FACE?
BABA, HAVE YOU EVER THOUGHT ABOUT GETTING NEW SERVANTS?
WHY WOULD I EVER WANT TO DO THAT?! WHAT'S GOT INTO YOU, AMIR?
I... NOTHING. IT WAS JUST A QUESTION...
I TOLD YOU TO RESOLVE YOUR PROBLEM WITH HASSAN. I GREW UP WITH ALI. FORTY YEARS ALI'S BEEN WITH MY FAMILY. AND YOU THINK I'M JUST GOING TO THROW HIM OUT?
I'M SORRY, BABA.
YOU BRING ME SHAME. AND HASSAN... HASSAN'S NOT GOING ANYWHERE, DO YOU UNDERSTAND? HE'S STAYING RIGHT HERE WITH US, WHERE HE BELONGS. DON'T YOU EVER ASK ME THAT QUESTION AGAIN! IS THAT CLEAR?
YES...
I DIDN'T HEAR YOU.
YES, BABA. I'M SORRY, I WON'T DO IT AGAIN.

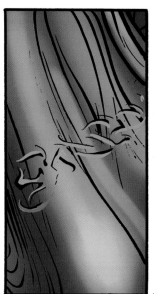

AMIR AGHA, I BROUGHT YOU YOUR STORY! THE ONE YOU PROMISED TO READ ME, REMEMBER?

HUH?

BUT WHY, INSTEAD OF ASKING ME, DON'T YOU LEARN TO READ BY YOURSELF?

I... I AM LEARNING, SLOWLY... BUT WHAT'S WRONG? IT'S YOUR STORY...

MY STORIES ARE STUPID.

DON'T SAY THAT, AMIR! I LIKE THEM A LOT!

TELL ME... WHAT WOULD YOU DO IF I HIT YOU WITH ONE OF THESE?

WHY ARE YOU DOING... ?

SLLLAAAPPP

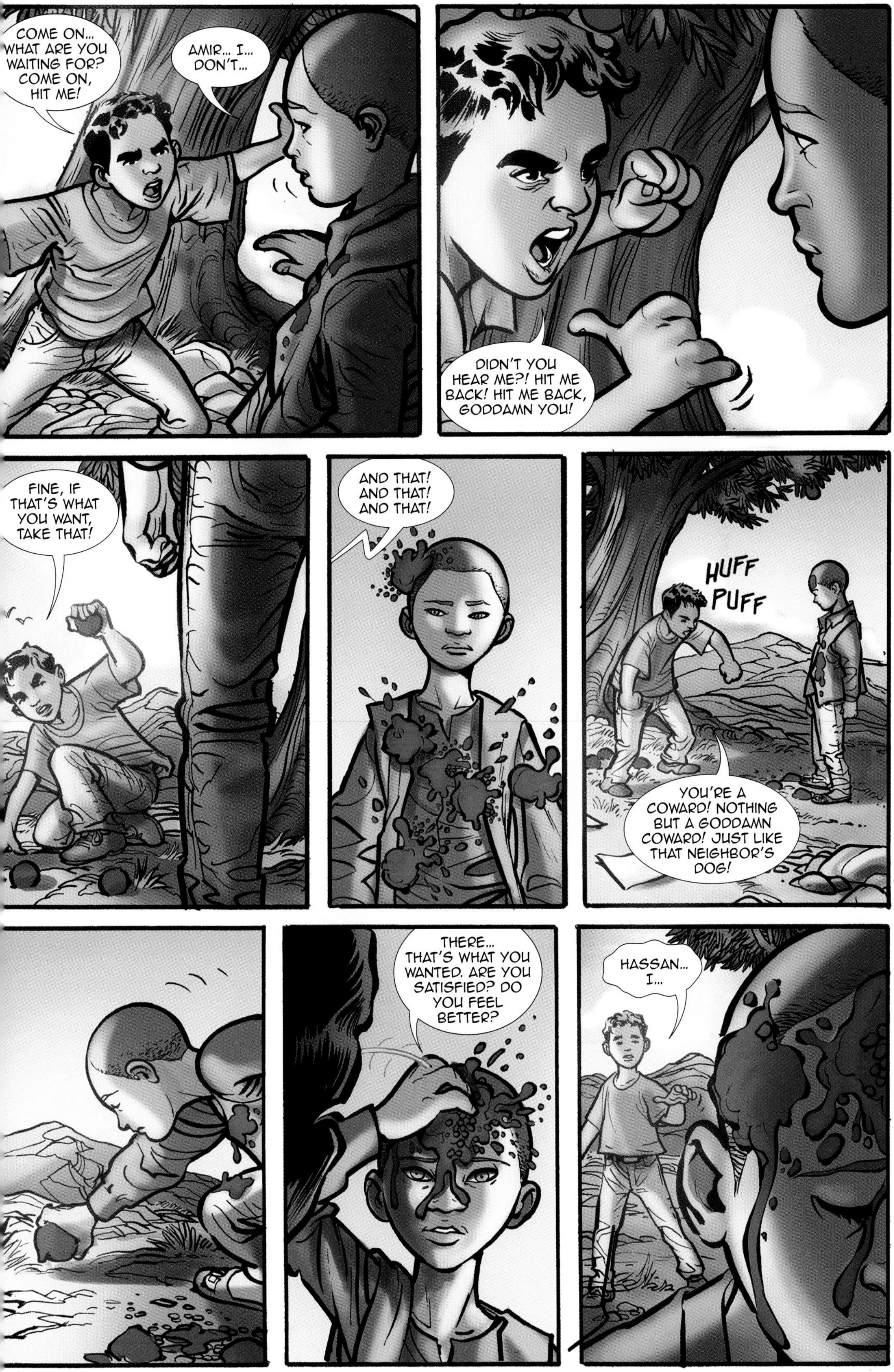
COME ON... WHAT ARE YOU WAITING FOR? COME ON, HIT ME!
AMIR... I... DON'T...
DIDN'T YOU HEAR ME?! HIT ME BACK! HIT ME BACK, GODDAMN YOU!
FINE, IF THAT'S WHAT YOU WANT, TAKE THAT!
AND THAT! AND THAT! AND THAT!
HUFF
PUFF
YOU'RE A COWARD! NOTHING BUT A GODDAMN COWARD! JUST LIKE THAT NEIGHBOR'S DOG!
THERE... THAT'S WHAT YOU WANTED. ARE YOU SATISFIED? DO YOU FEEL BETTER?
HASSAN... I...

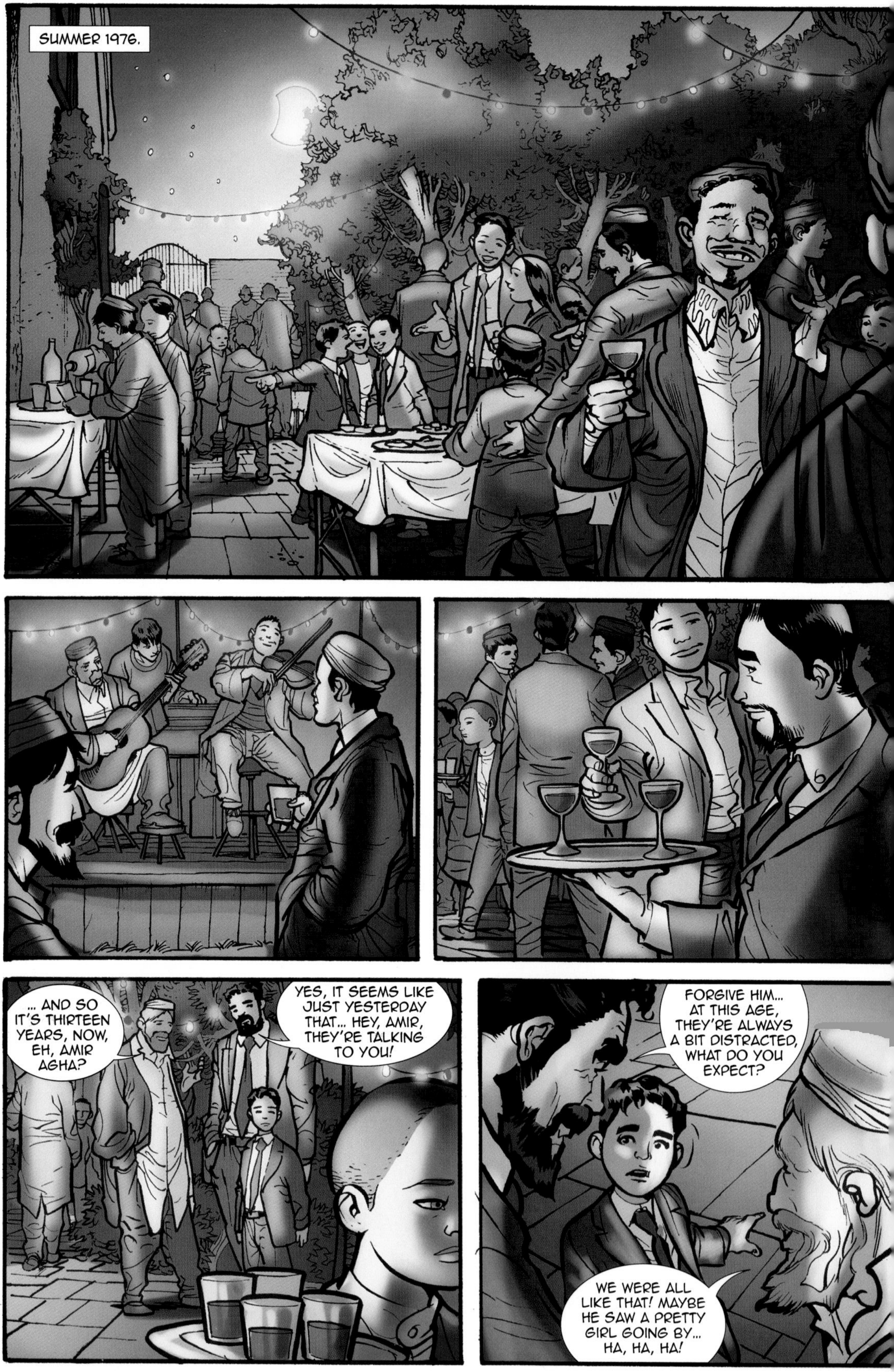
SUMMER 1976.
... AND SO IT'S THIRTEEN YEARS, NOW, EH, AMIR AGHA?
YES, IT SEEMS LIKE JUST YESTERDAY THAT... HEY, AMIR, THEY'RE TALKING TO YOU!
FORGIVE HIM... AT THIS AGE, THEY'RE ALWAYS A BIT DISTRACTED, WHAT DO YOU EXPECT?
WE WERE ALL LIKE THAT! MAYBE HE SAW A PRETTY GIRL GOING BY... HA, HA, HA!

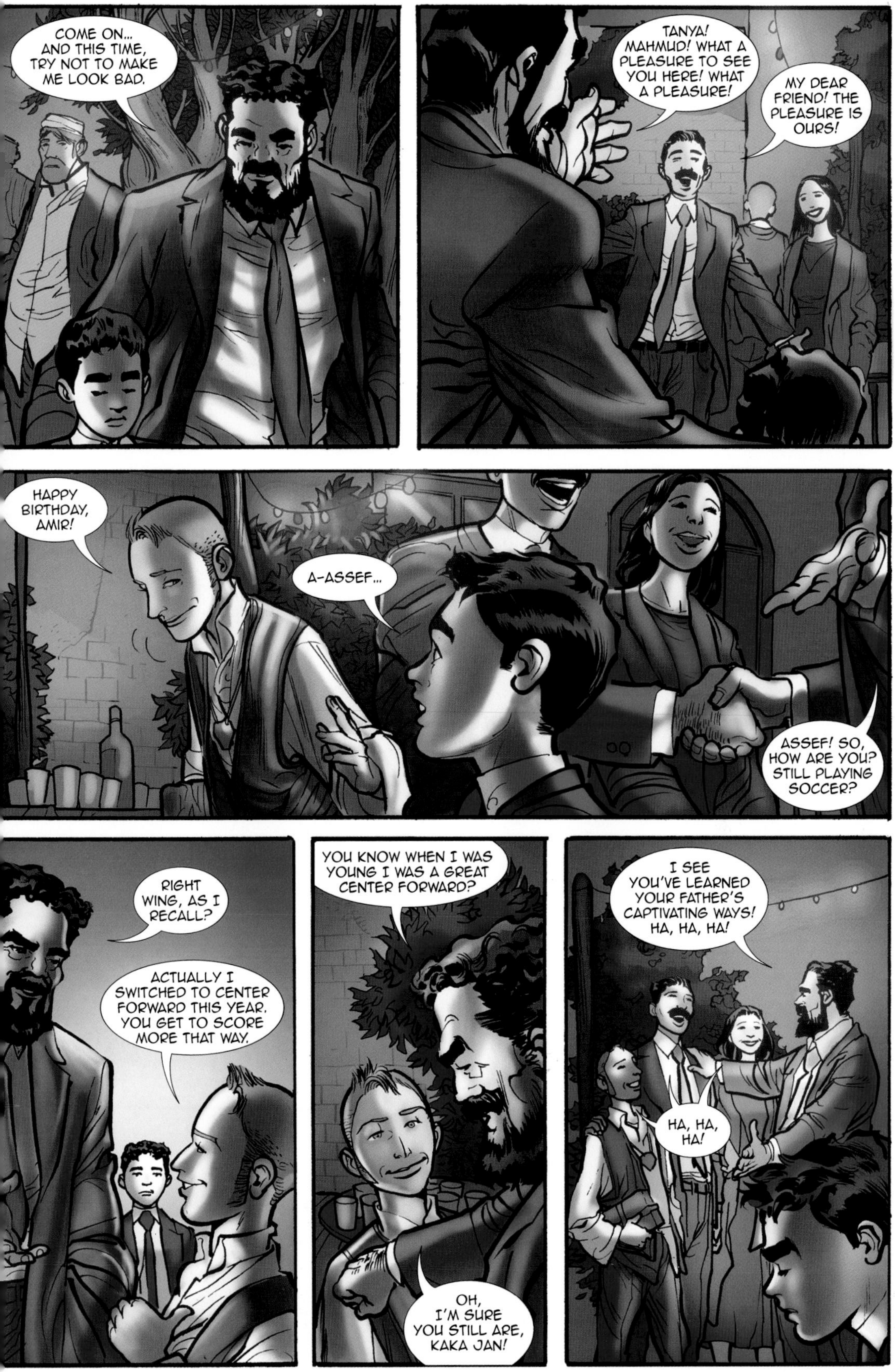
COME ON... AND THIS TIME, TRY NOT TO MAKE ME LOOK BAD.
TANYA! MAHMUD! WHAT A PLEASURE TO SEE YOU HERE! WHAT A PLEASURE!
MY DEAR FRIEND! THE PLEASURE IS OURS!
HAPPY BIRTHDAY, AMIR!
A-ASSEF...
ASSEF! SO, HOW ARE YOU? STILL PLAYING SOCCER?
RIGHT WING, AS I RECALL?
ACTUALLY I SWITCHED TO CENTER FORWARD THIS YEAR. YOU GET TO SCORE MORE THAT WAY.
YOU KNOW WHEN I WAS YOUNG I WAS A GREAT CENTER FORWARD?
OH, I'M SURE YOU STILL ARE, KAKA JAN!
I SEE YOU'VE LEARNED YOUR FATHER'S CAPTIVATING WAYS! HA, HA, HA!
HA, HA, HA!

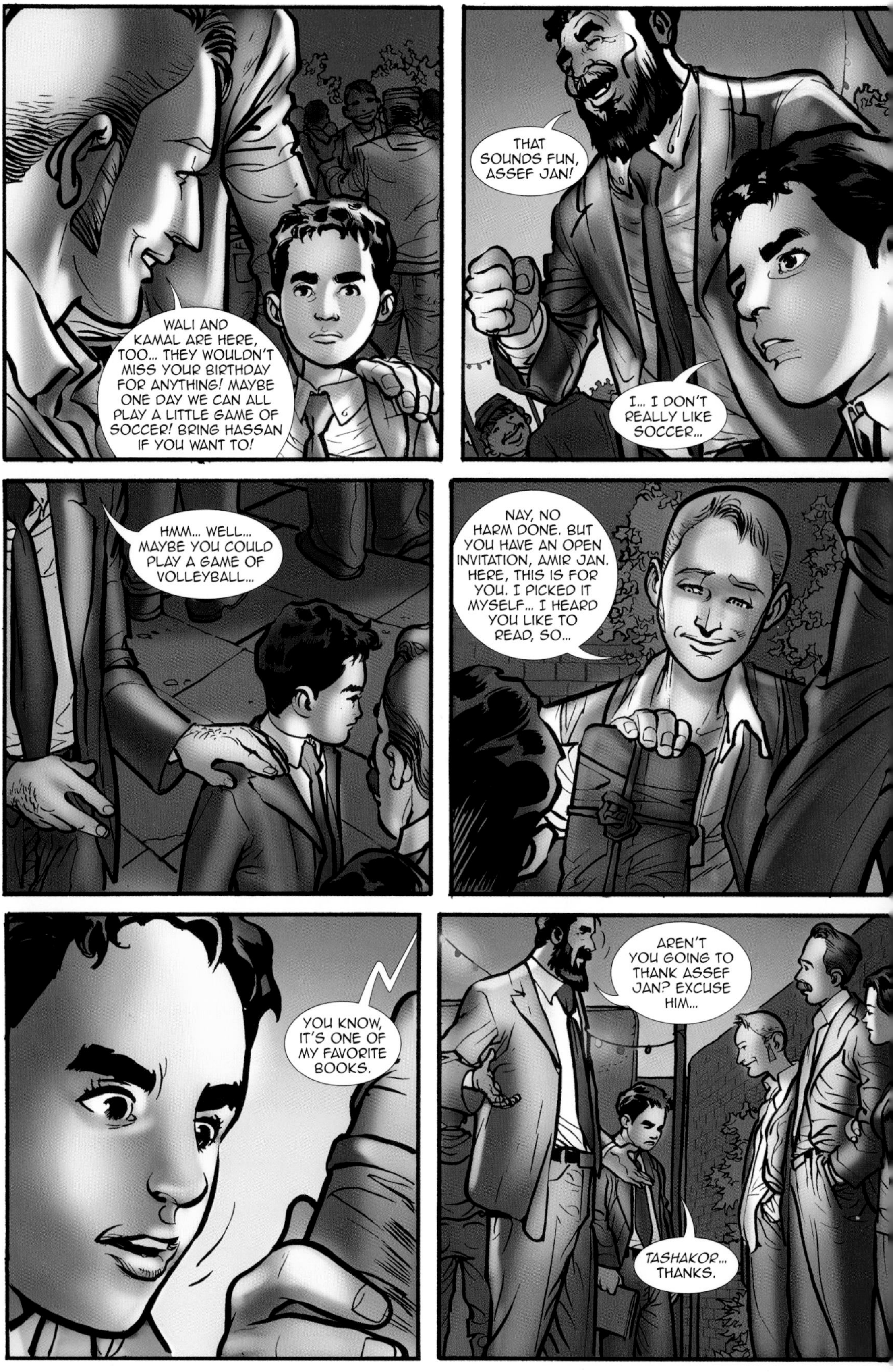
WALI AND KAMAL ARE HERE, TOO... THEY WOULDN'T MISS YOUR BIRTHDAY FOR ANYTHING! MAYBE ONE DAY WE CAN ALL PLAY A LITTLE GAME OF SOCCER! BRING HASSAN IF YOU WANT TO!
THAT SOUNDS FUN, ASSEF JAN!
I... I DON'T REALLY LIKE SOCCER...
HMM... WELL... MAYBE YOU COULD PLAY A GAME OF VOLLEYBALL...
NAY, NO HARM DONE. BUT YOU HAVE AN OPEN INVITATION, AMIR JAN. HERE, THIS IS FOR YOU. I PICKED IT MYSELF... I HEARD YOU LIKE TO READ, SO...
YOU KNOW, IT'S ONE OF MY FAVORITE BOOKS.
AREN'T YOU GOING TO THANK ASSEF JAN? EXCUSE HIM...
TASHAKOR... THANKS.

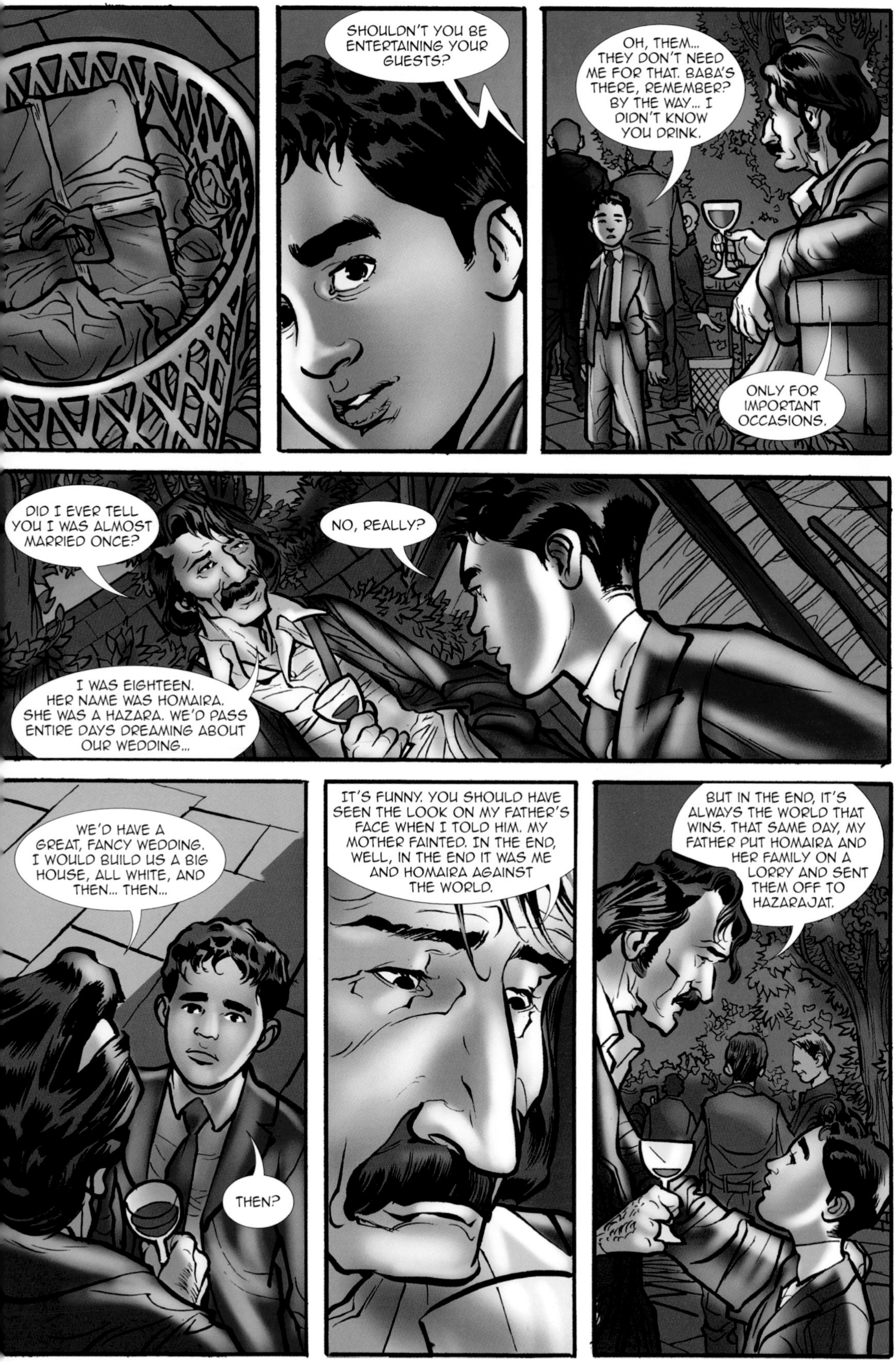
SHOULDN'T YOU BE ENTERTAINING YOUR GUESTS?
OH, THEM... THEY DON'T NEED ME FOR THAT. BABA'S THERE, REMEMBER? BY THE WAY... I DIDN'T KNOW YOU DRINK.
ONLY FOR IMPORTANT OCCASIONS.
DID I EVER TELL YOU I WAS ALMOST MARRIED ONCE?
NO, REALLY?
I WAS EIGHTEEN. HER NAME WAS HOMAIRA. SHE WAS A HAZARA. WE'D PASS ENTIRE DAYS DREAMING ABOUT OUR WEDDING...
WE'D HAVE A GREAT, FANCY WEDDING. I WOULD BUILD US A BIG HOUSE, ALL WHITE, AND THEN... THEN...
THEN?
IT'S FUNNY. YOU SHOULD HAVE SEEN THE LOOK ON MY FATHER'S FACE WHEN I TOLD HIM. MY MOTHER FAINTED. IN THE END, WELL, IN THE END IT WAS ME AND HOMAIRA AGAINST THE WORLD.
BUT IN THE END, IT'S ALWAYS THE WORLD THAT WINS. THAT SAME DAY, MY FATHER PUT HOMAIRA AND HER FAMILY ON A LORRY AND SENT THEM OFF TO HAZARAJAT.

I'M SORRY...

OH WELL, IT WAS PROBABLY FOR THE BEST, THOUGH. WHAT I WANTED TO TELL YOU IS THAT YOU CAN TELL ME ANYTHING YOU WANT, AMIR. ANYTIME.

HAPPY BIRTHDAY, AMIR! FOR YOUR STORIES.

THANK YOU, KAKA RAHIM!

THANKS, IT'S BEAUTIFUL, THANK YOU!

OOPS, I ALMOST FORGOT...

ALI ASKED ME TO GIVE YOU THIS... IT'S FROM HASSAN.

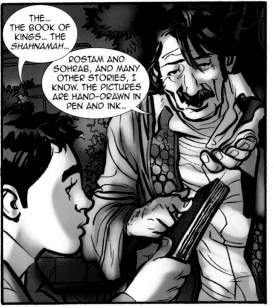

THE... THE BOOK OF KINGS... THE SHAHNAMAH...

ROSTAM AND SOHRAB, AND MANY OTHER STORIES, I KNOW. THE PICTURES ARE HAND-DRAWN IN PEN AND INK...

KAPOOOO

... FIREWORKS. JUST LIKE YOUR FATHER.

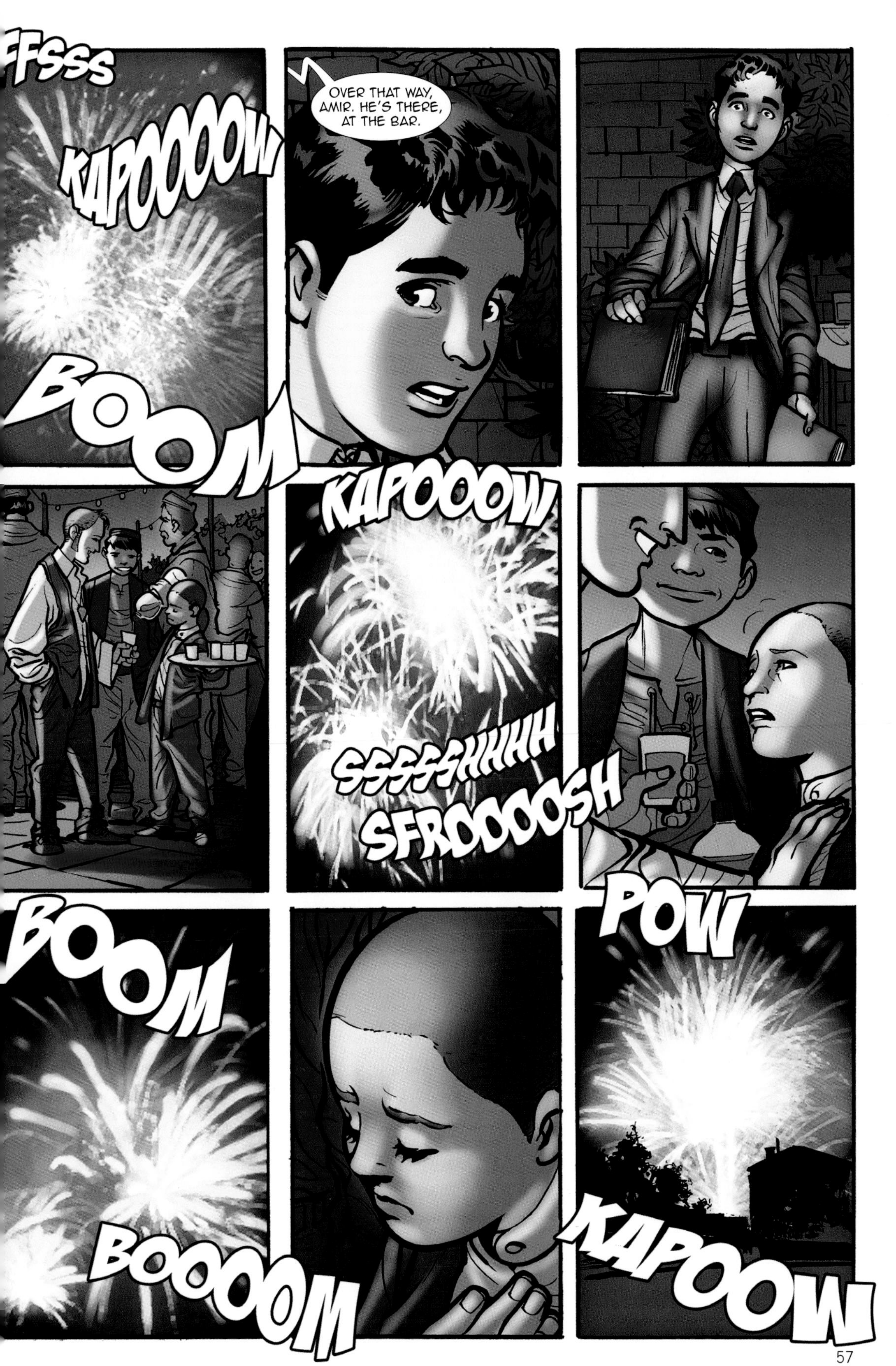
FFSSS
KAPOOOOW
BOOM
OVER THAT WAY, AMIR. HE'S THERE, AT THE BAR.
KAPOOOW
SSSSSHHHH
SFROOOOSH
BOOM
BOOOOM
POW
KAPOOW

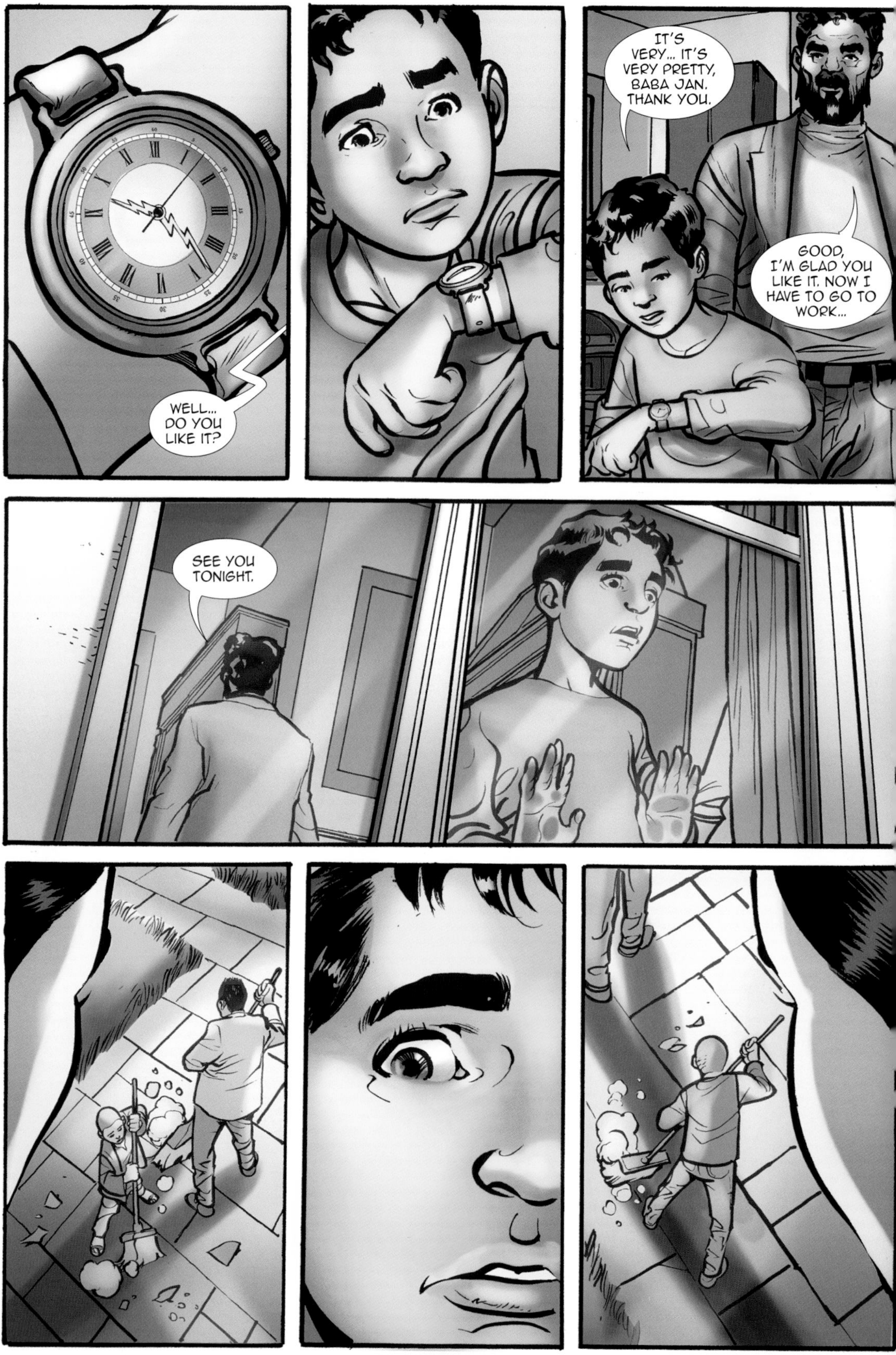
WELL... DO YOU LIKE IT?
IT'S VERY... IT'S VERY PRETTY, BABA JAN. THANK YOU.
GOOD, I'M GLAD YOU LIKE IT. NOW I HAVE TO GO TO WORK...
SEE YOU TONIGHT.

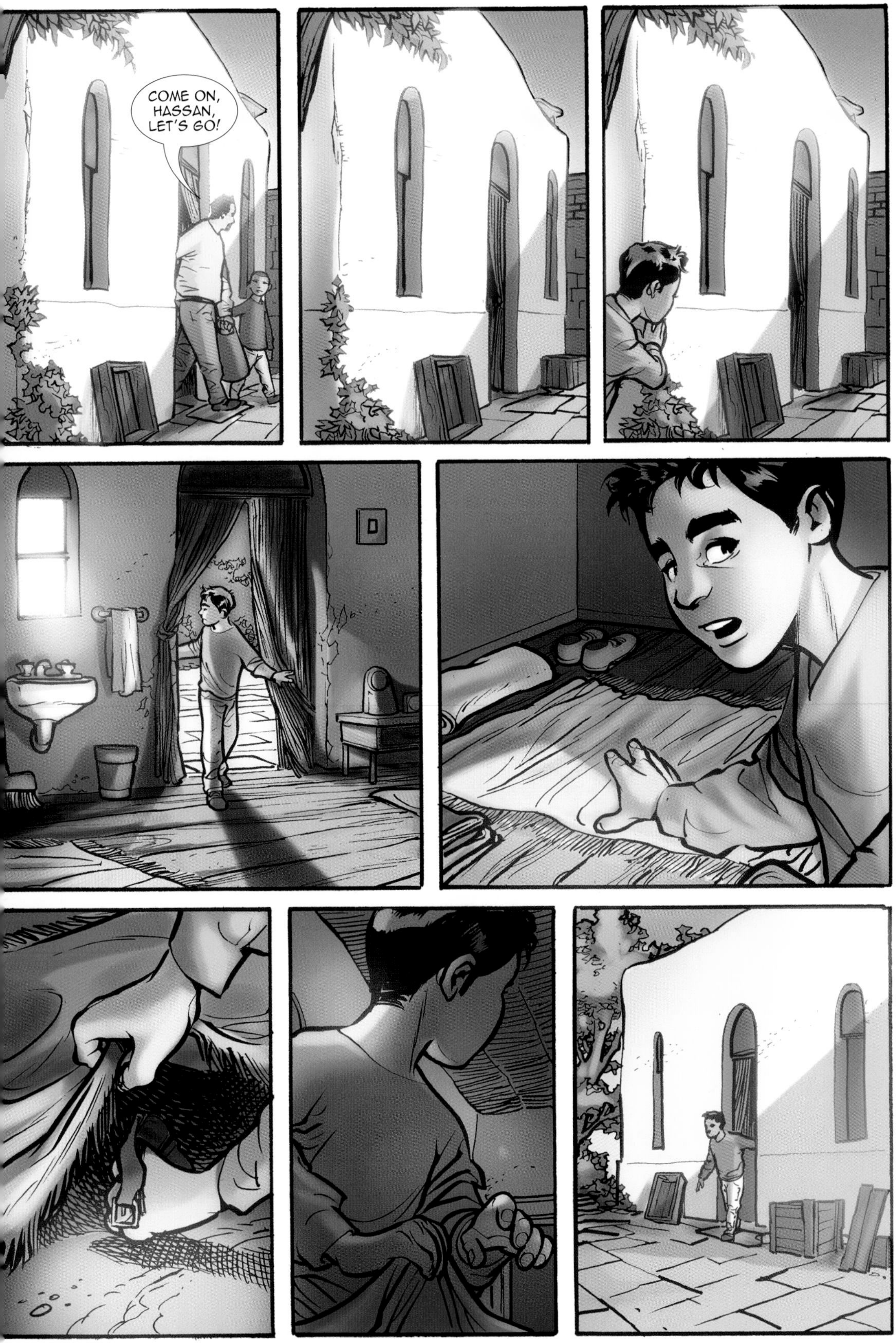
COME ON, HASSAN, LET'S GO!

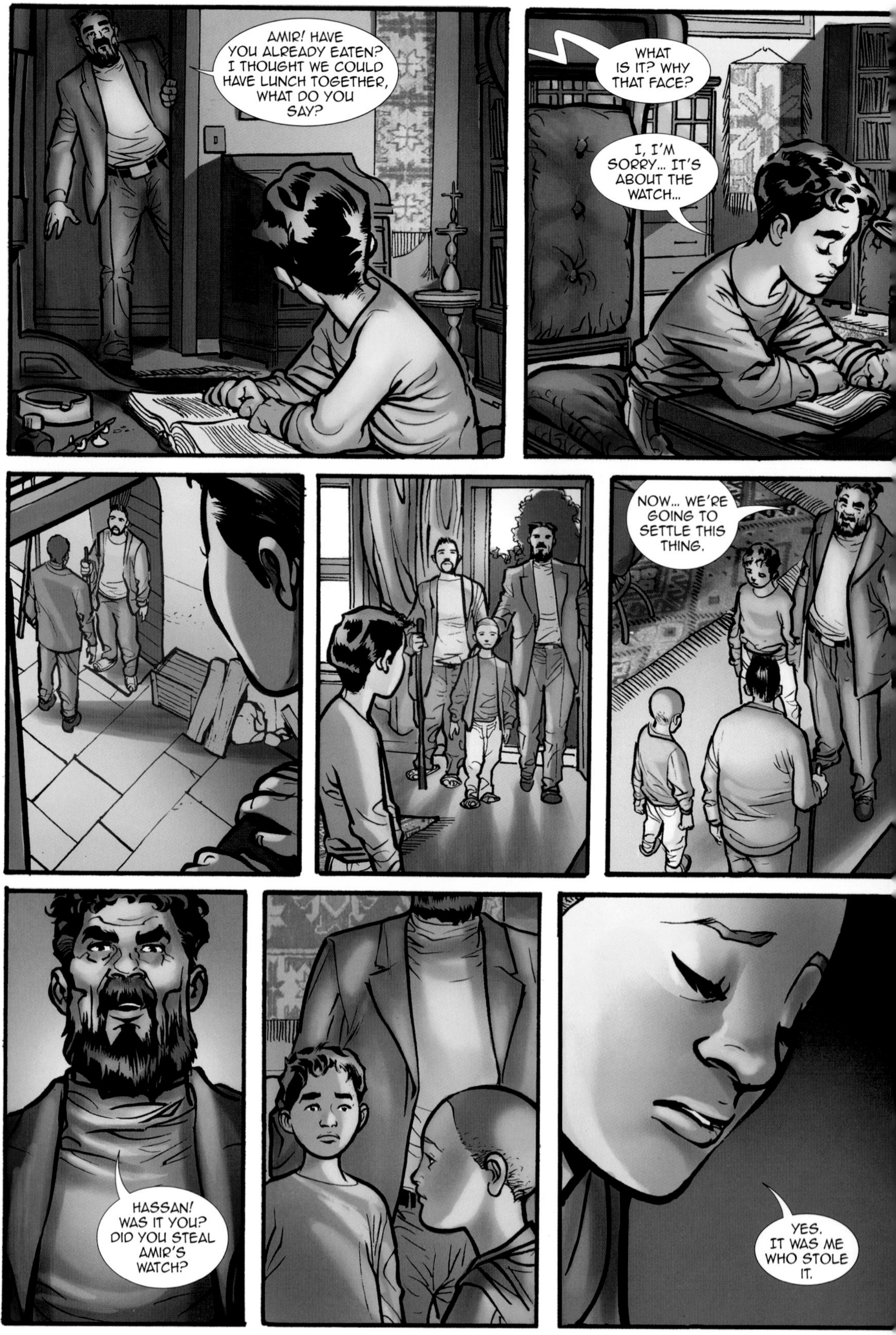
AMIR! HAVE YOU ALREADY EATEN? I THOUGHT WE COULD HAVE LUNCH TOGETHER, WHAT DO YOU SAY?
WHAT IS IT? WHY THAT FACE?
I, I'M SORRY... IT'S ABOUT THE WATCH...
NOW... WE'RE GOING TO SETTLE THIS THING.
HASSAN! WAS IT YOU? DID YOU STEAL AMIR'S WATCH?
YES. IT WAS ME WHO STOLE IT.

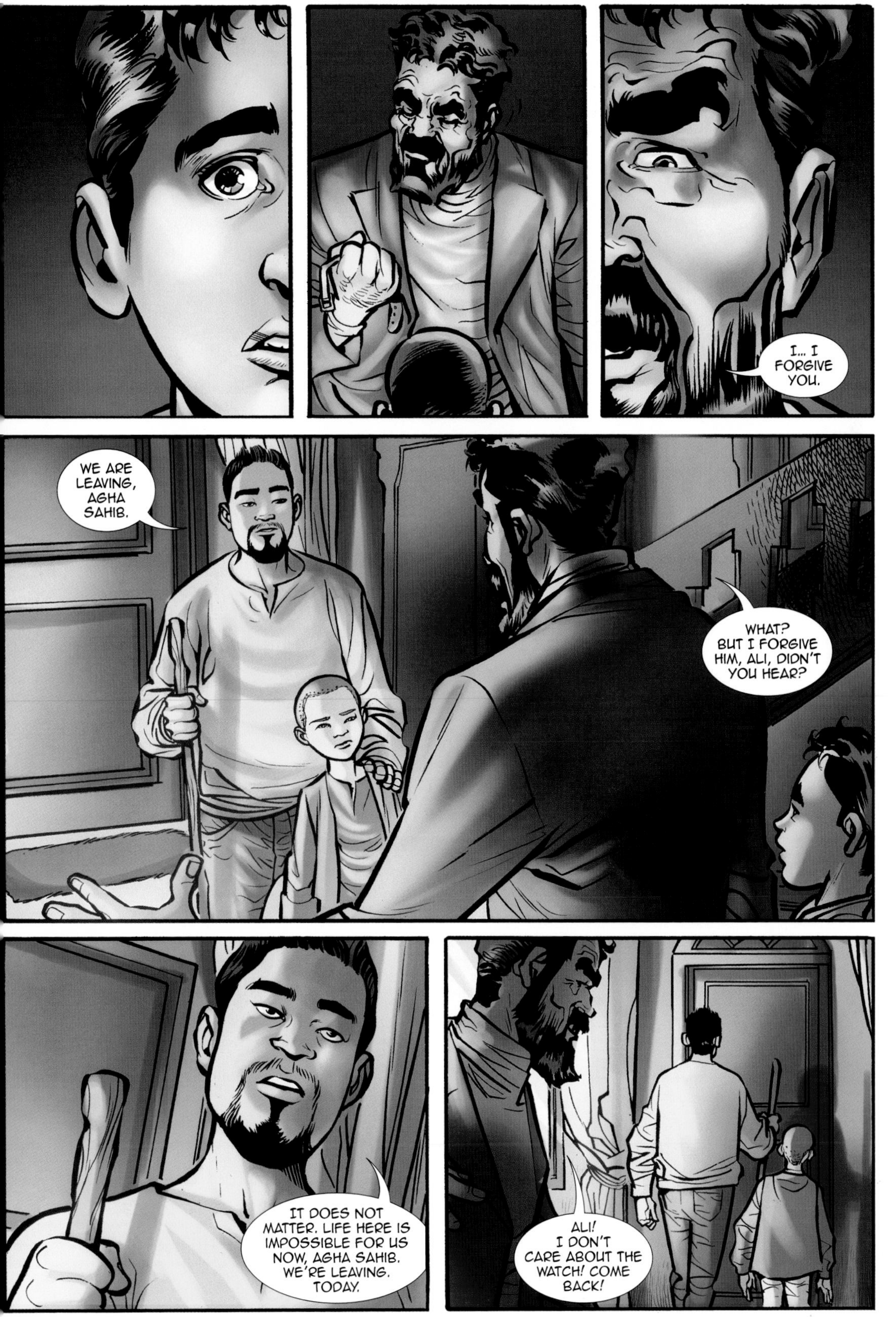
I... I FORGIVE YOU.
WE ARE LEAVING, AGHA SAHIB.
WHAT? BUT I FORGIVE HIM, ALI, DIDN'T YOU HEAR?
IT DOES NOT MATTER. LIFE HERE IS IMPOSSIBLE FOR US NOW, AGHA SAHIB. WE'RE LEAVING. TODAY.
ALI! I DON'T CARE ABOUT THE WATCH! COME BACK!

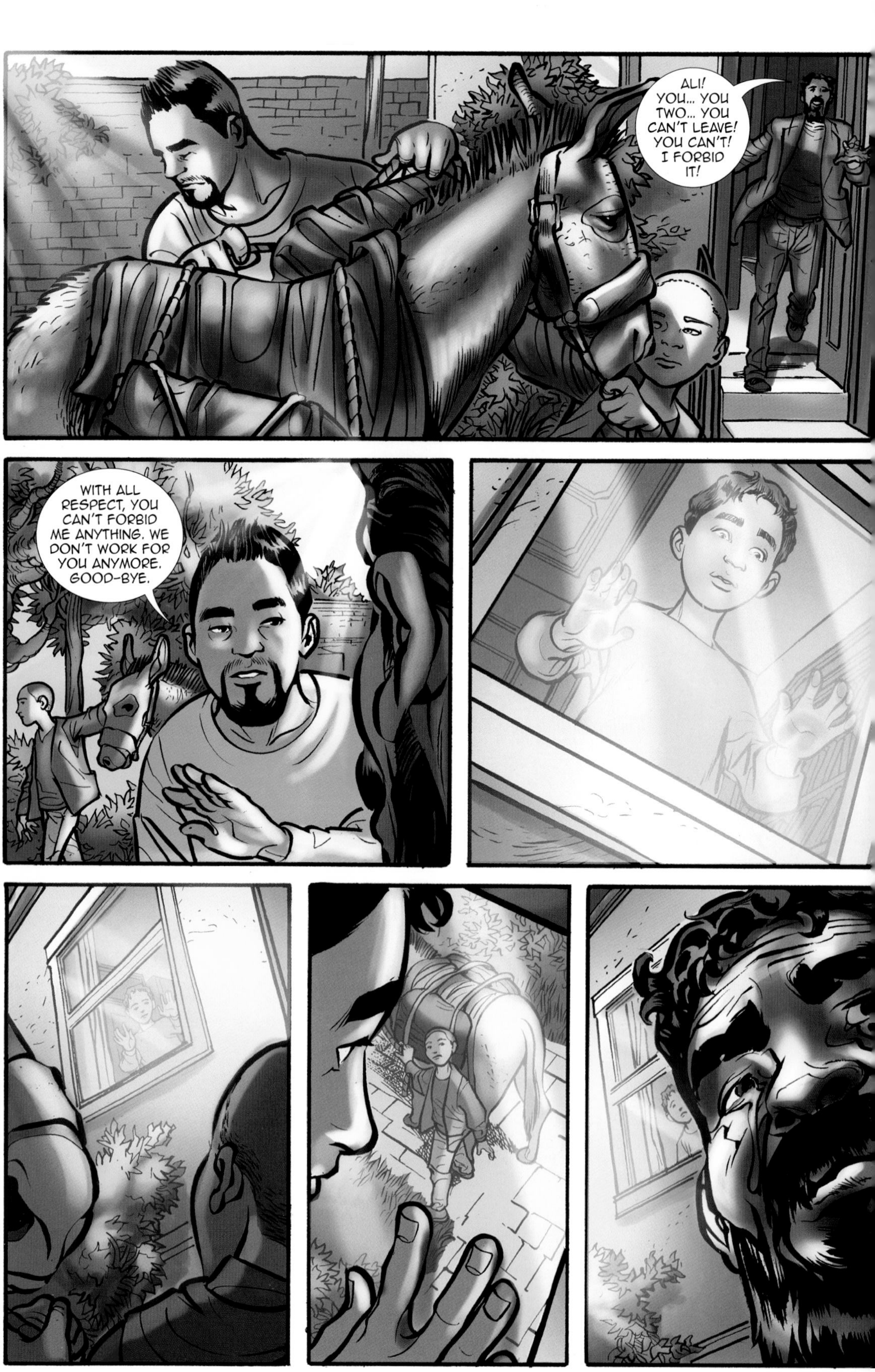
ALI! YOU... YOU TWO... YOU CAN'T LEAVE! YOU CAN'T! I FORBID IT!
WITH ALL RESPECT, YOU CAN'T FORBID ME ANYTHING. WE DON'T WORK FOR YOU ANYMORE. GOOD-BYE.

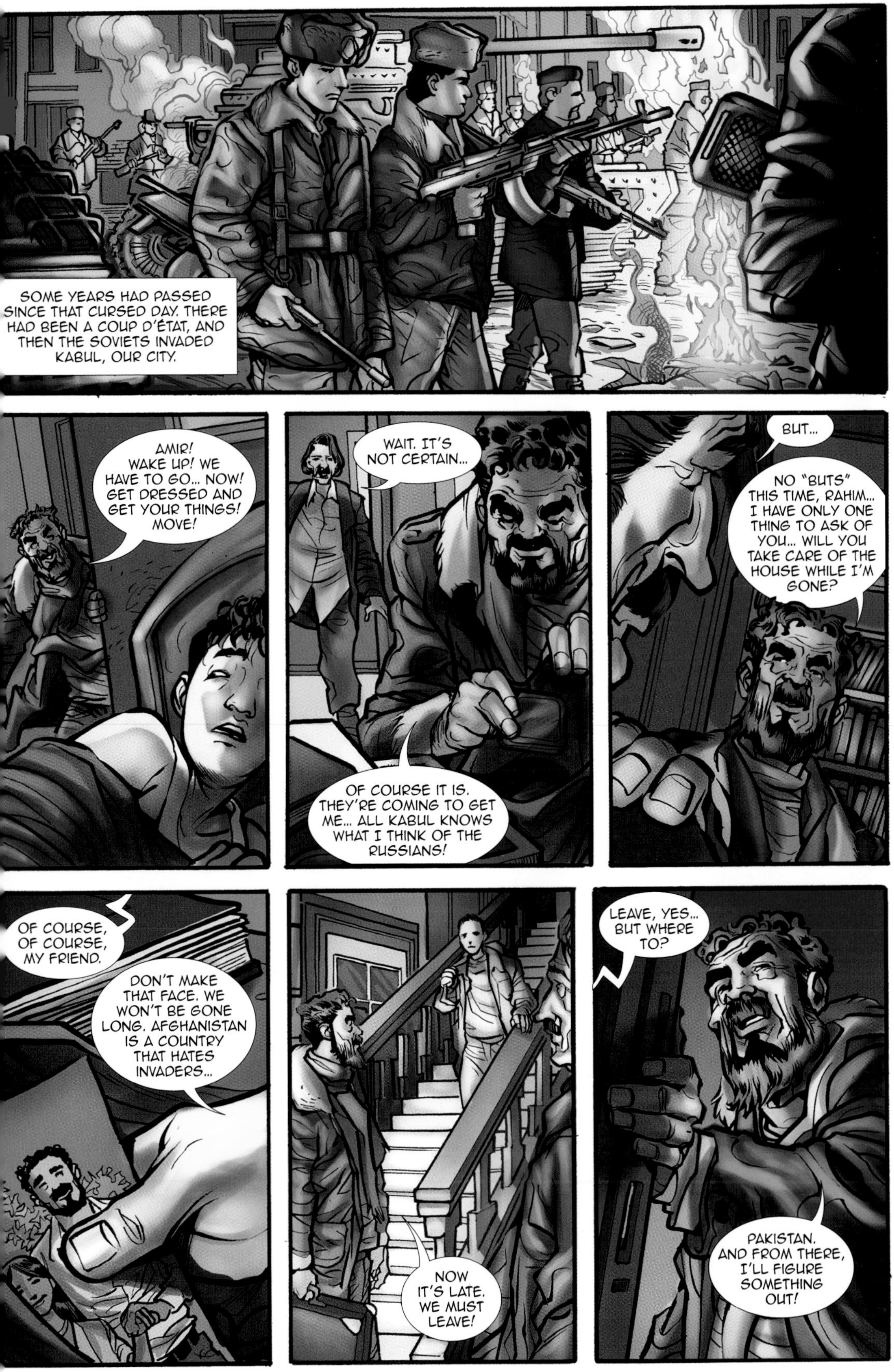
SOME YEARS HAD PASSED SINCE THAT CURSED DAY. THERE HAD BEEN A COUP D'ÉTAT, AND THEN THE SOVIETS INVADED KABUL, OUR CITY.
AMIR! WAKE UP! WE HAVE TO GO... NOW! GET DRESSED AND GET YOUR THINGS! MOVE!
WAIT. IT'S NOT CERTAIN...
OF COURSE IT IS. THEY'RE COMING TO GET ME... ALL KABUL KNOWS WHAT I THINK OF THE RUSSIANS!
BUT...
NO "BUTS" THIS TIME, RAHIM... I HAVE ONLY ONE THING TO ASK OF YOU... WILL YOU TAKE CARE OF THE HOUSE WHILE I'M GONE?
OF COURSE, OF COURSE, MY FRIEND.
DON'T MAKE THAT FACE. WE WON'T BE GONE LONG. AFGHANISTAN IS A COUNTRY THAT HATES INVADERS...
NOW IT'S LATE. WE MUST LEAVE!
LEAVE, YES... BUT WHERE TO?
PAKISTAN. AND FROM THERE, I'LL FIGURE SOMETHING OUT!

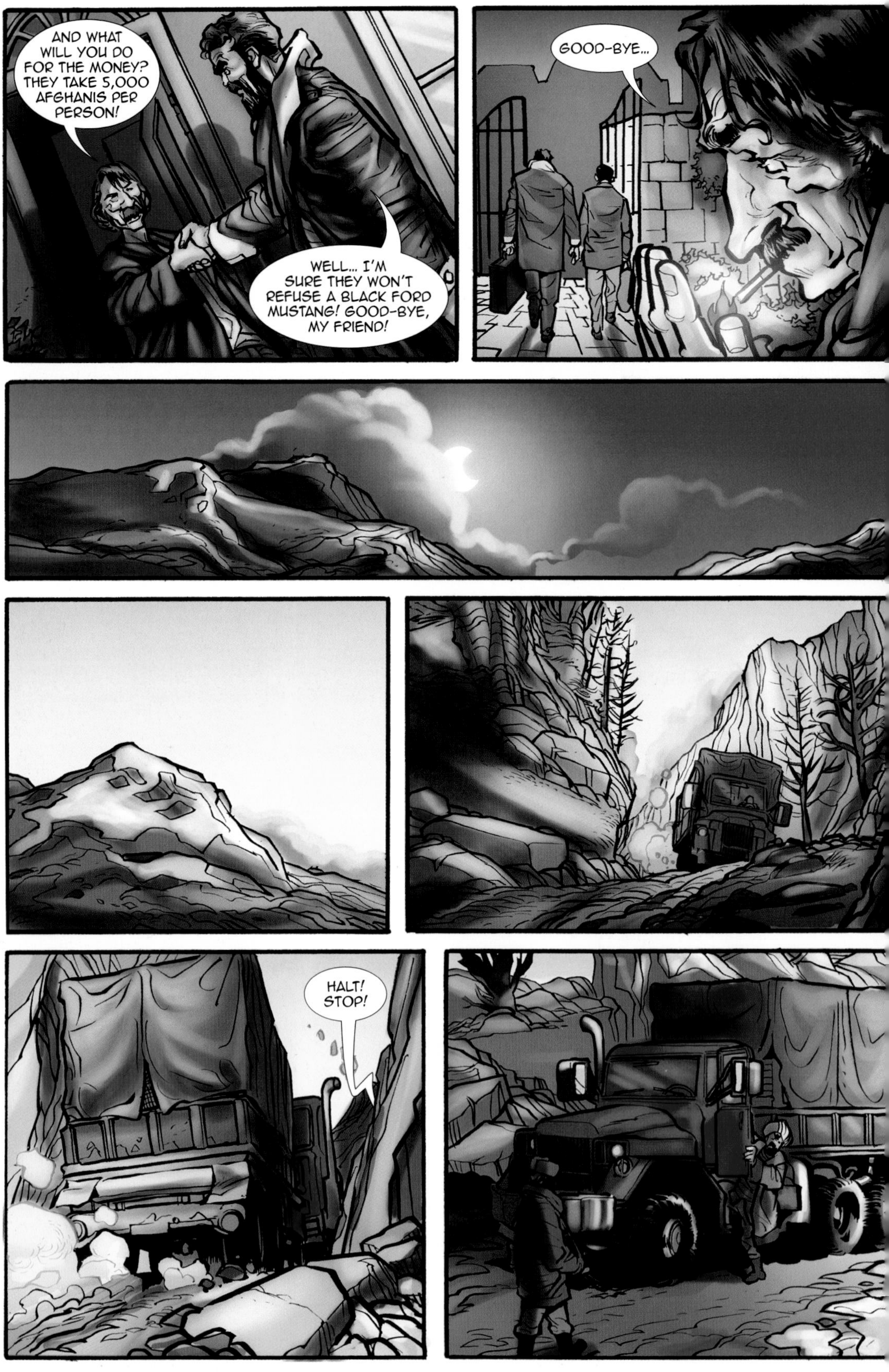
AND WHAT WILL YOU DO FOR THE MONEY? THEY TAKE 5,000 AFGHANIS PER PERSON!
WELL... I'M SURE THEY WON'T REFUSE A BLACK FORD MUSTANG! GOOD-BYE, MY FRIEND!
GOOD-BYE...
HALT! STOP!

HE... WANTS A HALF HOUR WITH THE LADY IN THE BACK OF THE TRUCK. IT'S HIS PRICE FOR LETTING US PASS.

WHY DON'T YOU INSTEAD ASK HIM WHERE HIS SHAME IS?!

WHAT IS HE SAYING?!

HE SAYS THIS IS WAR. THERE IS NO SHAME IN WAR.

TELL HIM HE'S WRONG. WAR DOESN'T NEGATE DECENCY.

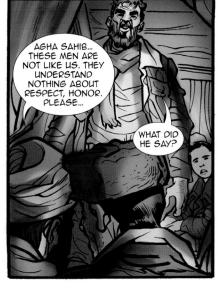

AGHA SAHIB... THESE MEN ARE NOT LIKE US. THEY UNDERSTAND NOTHING ABOUT RESPECT, HONOR. PLEASE...

WHAT DID HE SAY?

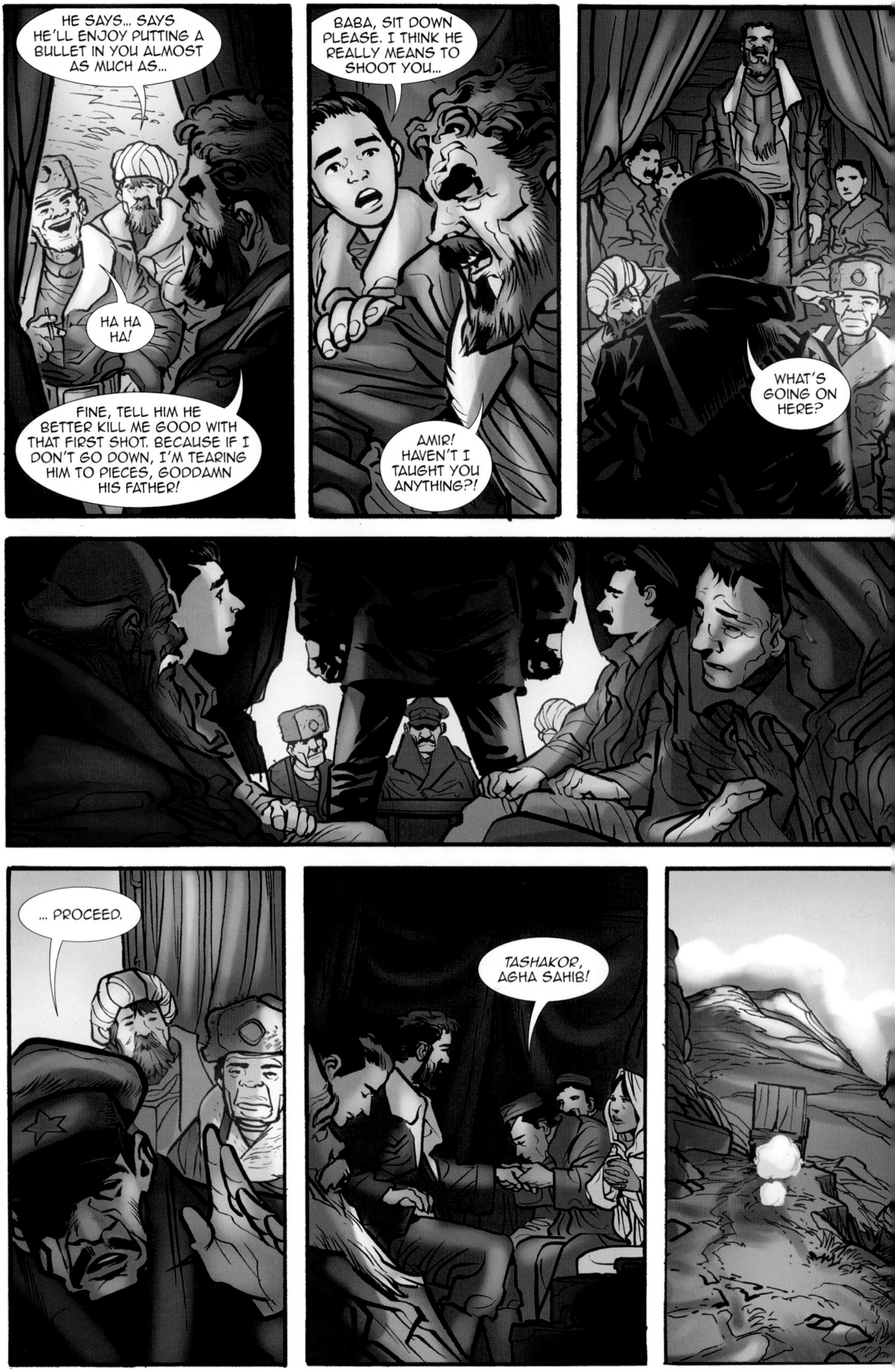
HE SAYS... SAYS HE'LL ENJOY PUTTING A BULLET IN YOU ALMOST AS MUCH AS...
HA HA HA!
FINE, TELL HIM HE BETTER KILL ME GOOD WITH THAT FIRST SHOT. BECAUSE IF I DON'T GO DOWN, I'M TEARING HIM TO PIECES, GODDAMN HIS FATHER!
BABA, SIT DOWN PLEASE. I THINK HE REALLY MEANS TO SHOOT YOU...
AMIR! HAVEN'T I TAUGHT YOU ANYTHING?!
WHAT'S GOING ON HERE?
... PROCEED.
TASHAKOR, AGHA SAHIB!

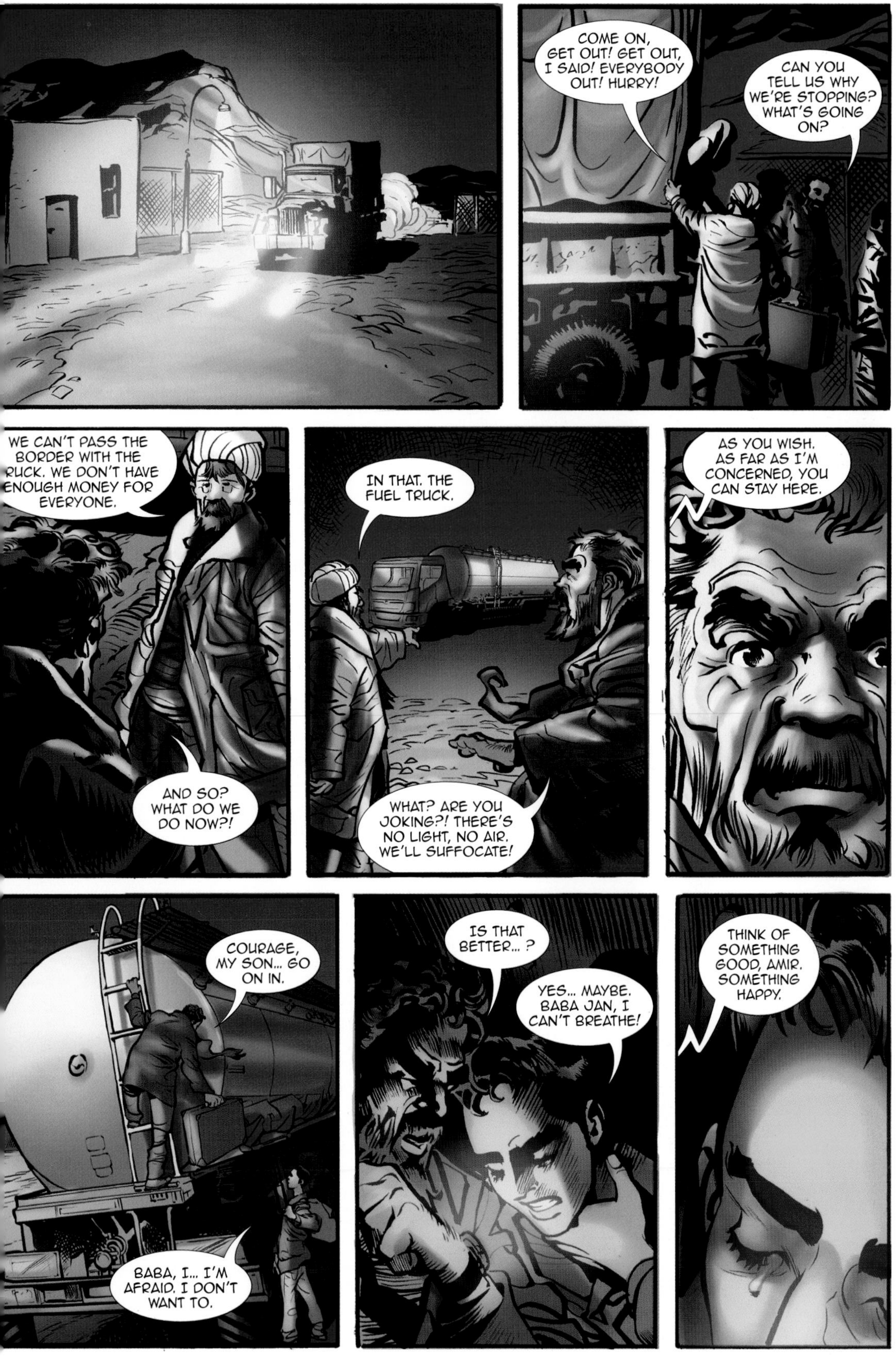
COME ON, GET OUT! GET OUT, I SAID! EVERYBODY OUT! HURRY!
CAN YOU TELL US WHY WE'RE STOPPING? WHAT'S GOING ON?
WE CAN'T PASS THE BORDER WITH THE RUCK. WE DON'T HAVE ENOUGH MONEY FOR EVERYONE.
AND SO? WHAT DO WE DO NOW?!
IN THAT. THE FUEL TRUCK.
WHAT? ARE YOU JOKING?! THERE'S NO LIGHT, NO AIR. WE'LL SUFFOCATE!
AS YOU WISH. AS FAR AS I'M CONCERNED, YOU CAN STAY HERE.
COURAGE, MY SON... GO ON IN.
BABA, I... I'M AFRAID. I DON'T WANT TO.
IS THAT BETTER... ?
YES... MAYBE. BABA JAN, I CAN'T BREATHE!
THINK OF SOMETHING GOOD, AMIR. SOMETHING HAPPY.

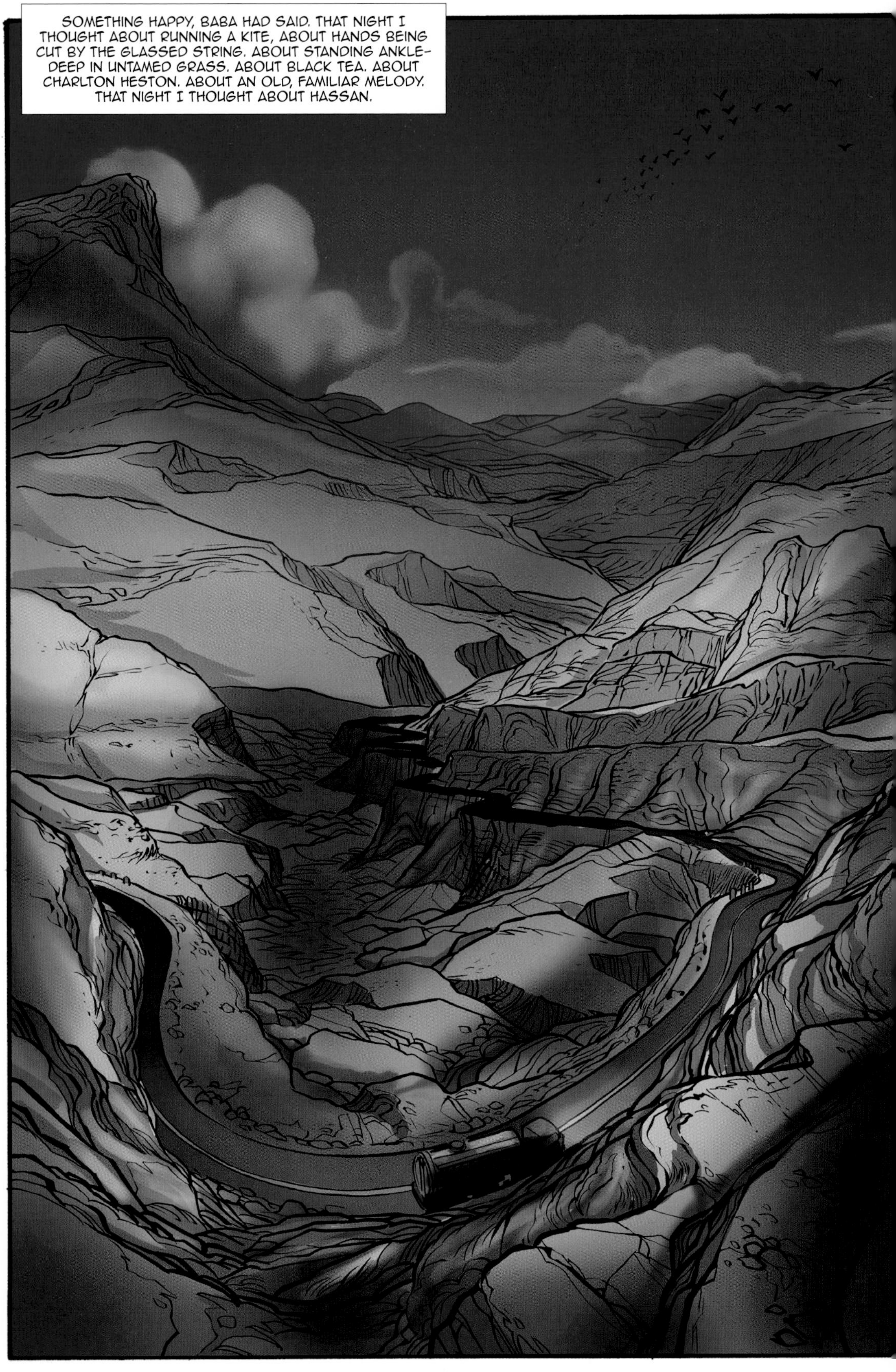
SOMETHING HAPPY, BABA HAD SAID. THAT NIGHT I THOUGHT ABOUT RUNNING A KITE, ABOUT HANDS BEING CUT BY THE GLASSED STRING. ABOUT STANDING ANKLE-DEEP IN UNTAMED GRASS. ABOUT BLACK TEA. ABOUT CHARLTON HESTON. ABOUT AN OLD, FAMILIAR MELODY. THAT NIGHT I THOUGHT ABOUT HASSAN.

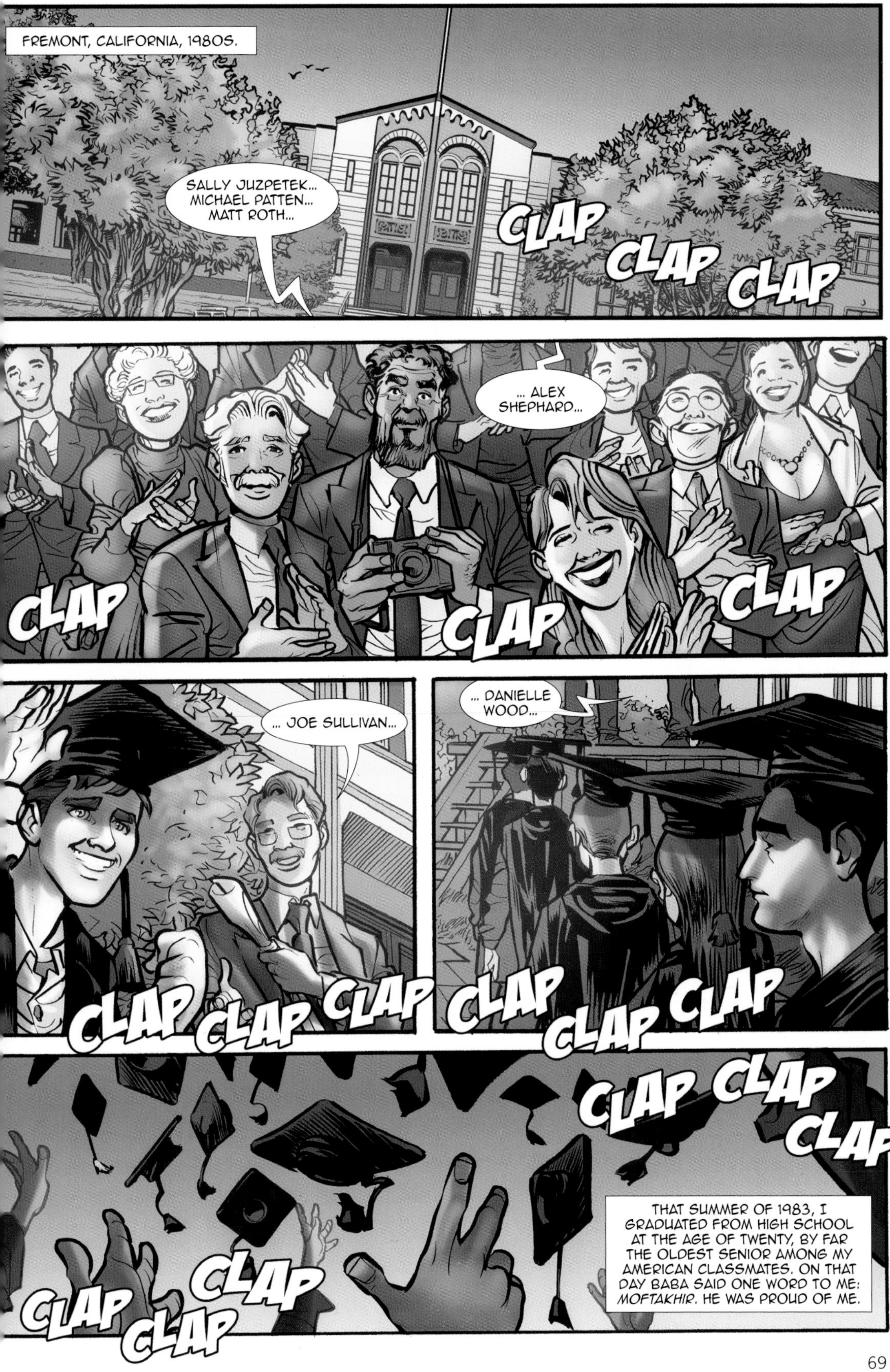
FREMONT, CALIFORNIA, 1980S.
SALLY JUZPETEK... MICHAEL PATTEN... MATT ROTH...
CLAP
CLAP
CLAP
... ALEX SHEPHARD...
CLAP
CLAP
CLAP
... JOE SULLIVAN...
CLAP
CLAP
CLAP
... DANIELLE WOOD...
CLAP
CLAP
CLAP
CLAP
CLAP
CLAP
THAT SUMMER OF 1983, I GRADUATED FROM HIGH SCHOOL AT THE AGE OF TWENTY, BY FAR THE OLDEST SENIOR AMONG MY AMERICAN CLASSMATES. ON THAT DAY BABA SAID ONE WORD TO ME: *MOFTAKHIR*. HE WAS PROUD OF ME.
CLAP
CLAP
CLAP

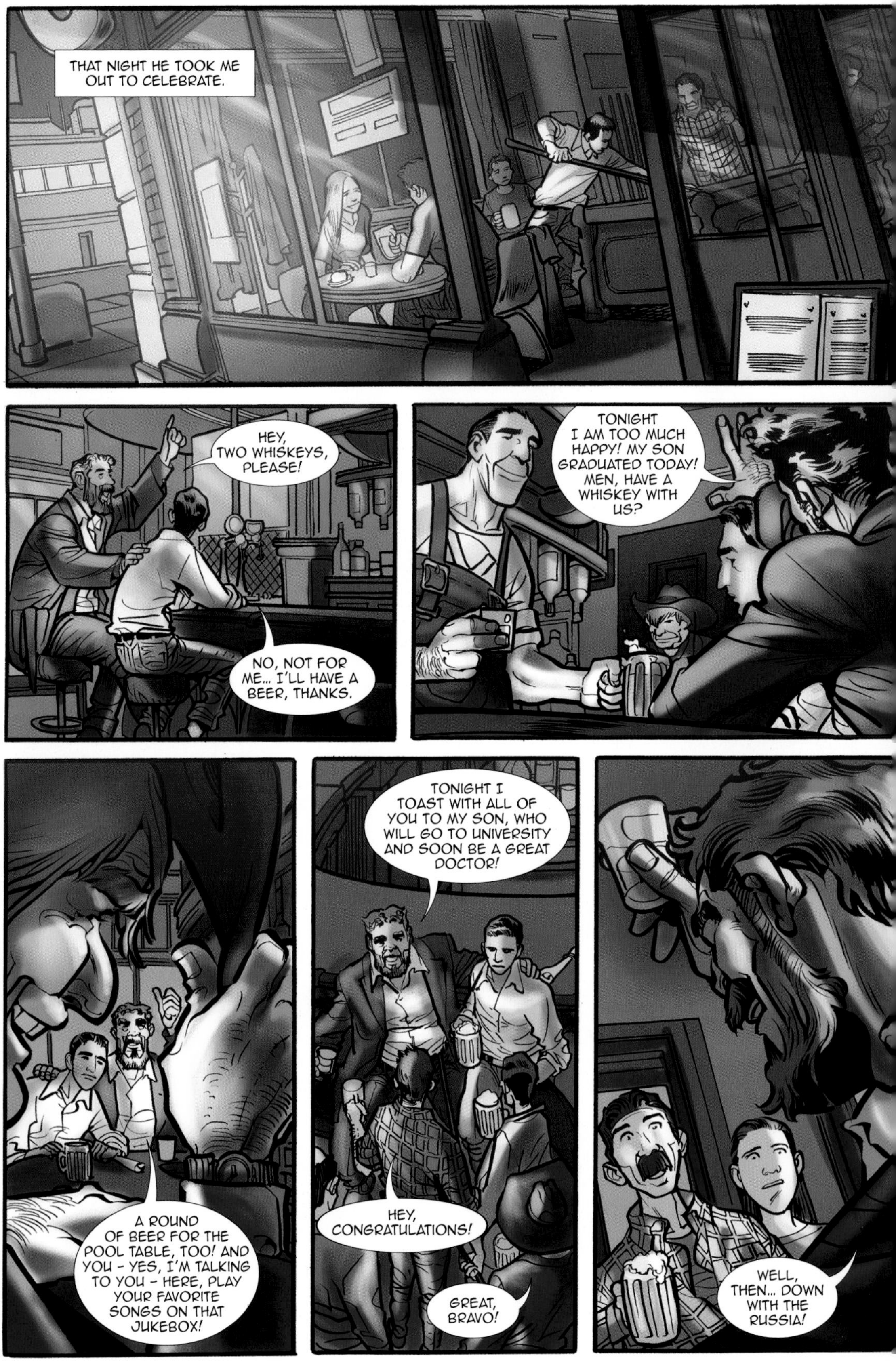
THAT NIGHT HE TOOK ME OUT TO CELEBRATE.
HEY, TWO WHISKEYS, PLEASE!
NO, NOT FOR ME... I'LL HAVE A BEER, THANKS.
TONIGHT I AM TOO MUCH HAPPY! MY SON GRADUATED TODAY! MEN, HAVE A WHISKEY WITH US?
A ROUND OF BEER FOR THE POOL TABLE, TOO! AND YOU - YES, I'M TALKING TO YOU - HERE, PLAY YOUR FAVORITE SONGS ON THAT JUKEBOX!
TONIGHT I TOAST WITH ALL OF YOU TO MY SON, WHO WILL GO TO UNIVERSITY AND SOON BE A GREAT DOCTOR!
HEY, CONGRATULATIONS!
GREAT, BRAVO!
WELL, THEN... DOWN WITH THE RUSSIA!

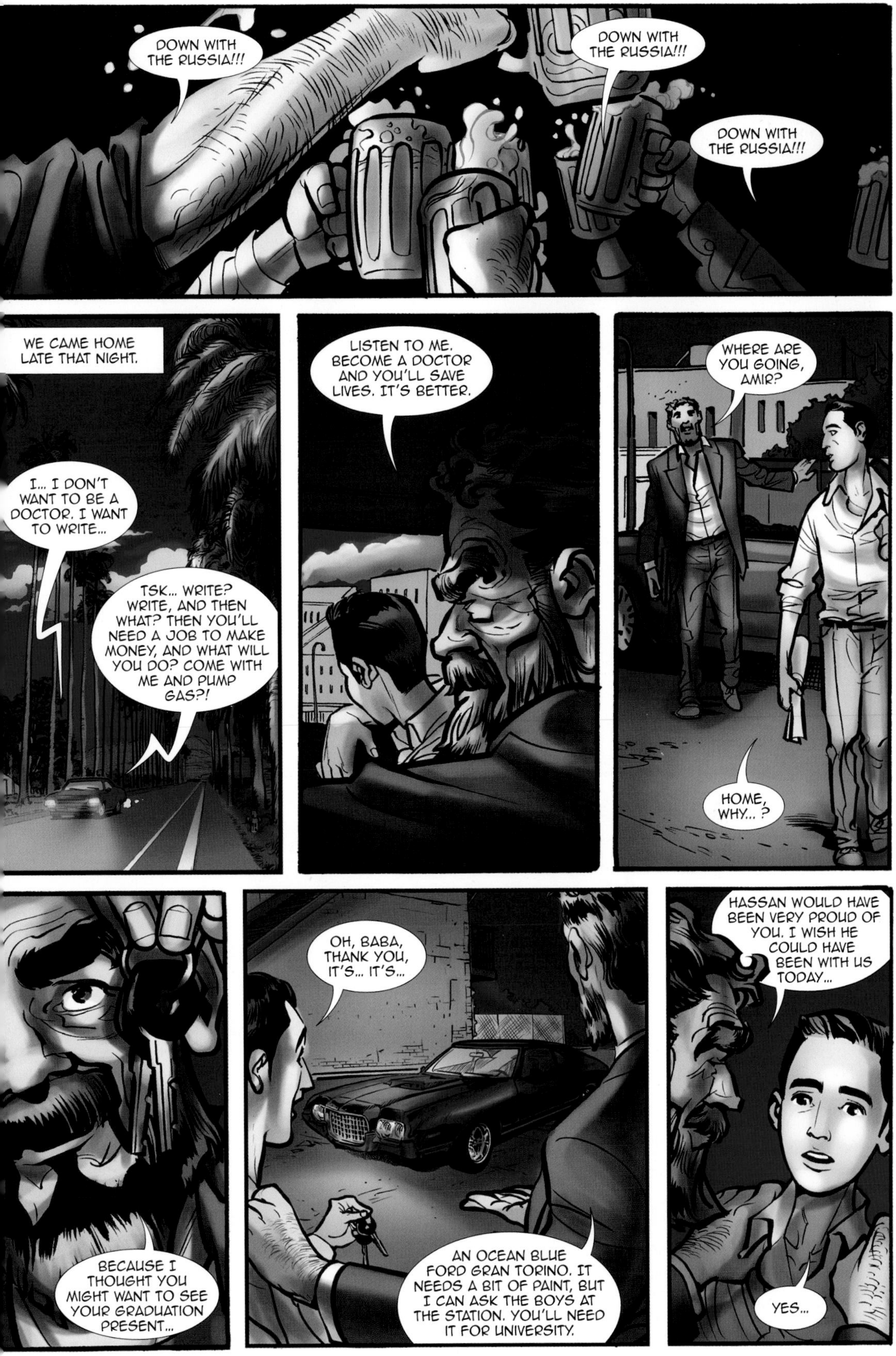
DOWN WITH THE RUSSIA!!!
DOWN WITH THE RUSSIA!!!
DOWN WITH THE RUSSIA!!!
WE CAME HOME LATE THAT NIGHT.
I... I DON'T WANT TO BE A DOCTOR. I WANT TO WRITE...
TSK... WRITE? WRITE, AND THEN WHAT? THEN YOU'LL NEED A JOB TO MAKE MONEY, AND WHAT WILL YOU DO? COME WITH ME AND PUMP GAS?!
LISTEN TO ME. BECOME A DOCTOR AND YOU'LL SAVE LIVES. IT'S BETTER.
WHERE ARE YOU GOING, AMIR?
HOME, WHY... ?
BECAUSE I THOUGHT YOU MIGHT WANT TO SEE YOUR GRADUATION PRESENT...
OH, BABA, THANK YOU, IT'S... IT'S...
AN OCEAN BLUE FORD GRAN TORINO. IT NEEDS A BIT OF PAINT, BUT I CAN ASK THE BOYS AT THE STATION. YOU'LL NEED IT FOR UNIVERSITY.
HASSAN WOULD HAVE BEEN VERY PROUD OF YOU. I WISH HE COULD HAVE BEEN WITH US TODAY...
YES...

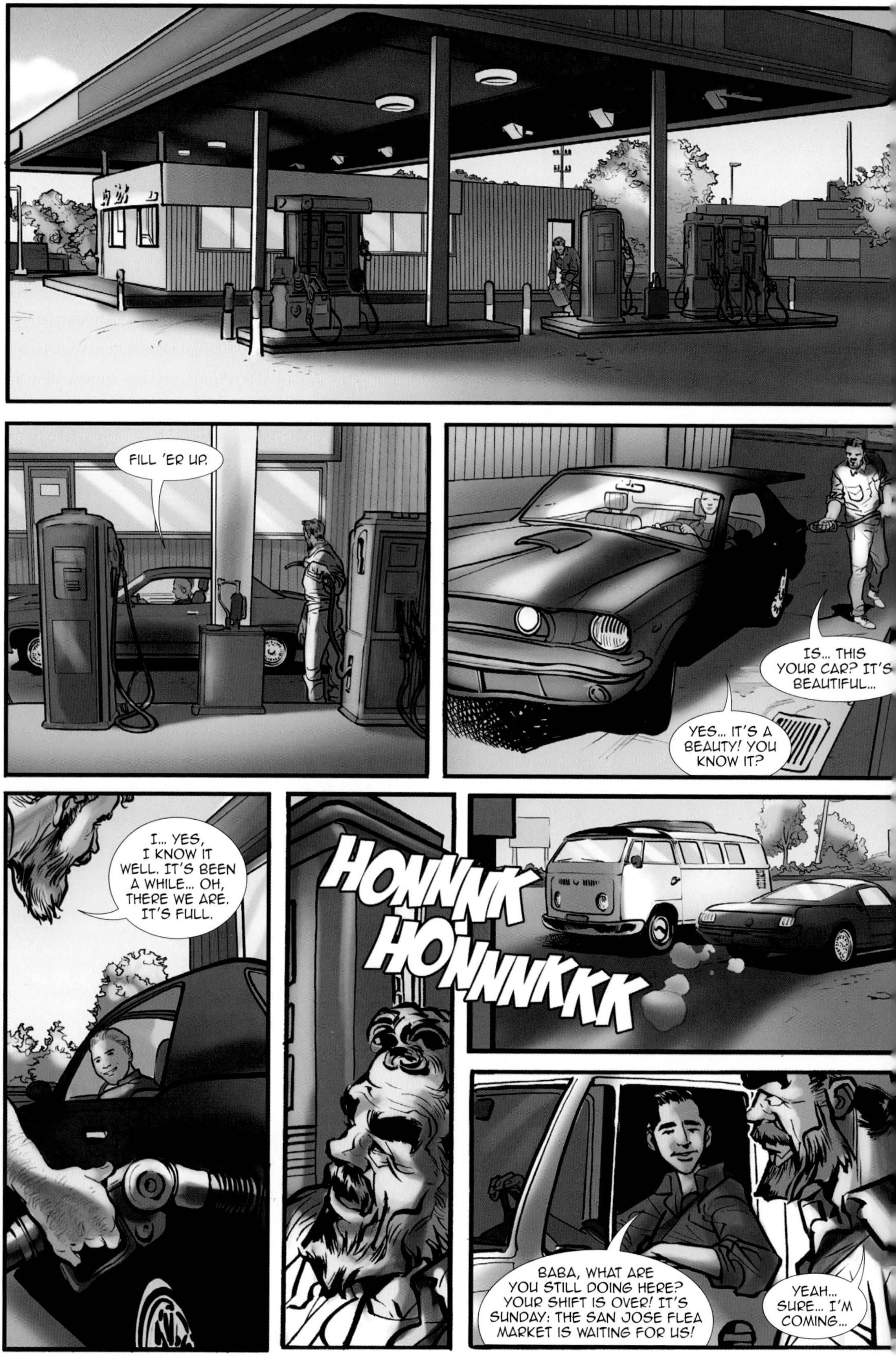
FILL 'ER UP.
IS... THIS YOUR CAR? IT'S BEAUTIFUL...
YES... IT'S A BEAUTY! YOU KNOW IT?
I... YES, I KNOW IT WELL. IT'S BEEN A WHILE... OH, THERE WE ARE. IT'S FULL.
HONNNK HONNNKKK
BABA, WHAT ARE YOU STILL DOING HERE? YOUR SHIFT IS OVER! IT'S SUNDAY: THE SAN JOSE FLEA MARKET IS WAITING FOR US!
YEAH... SURE... I'M COMING...

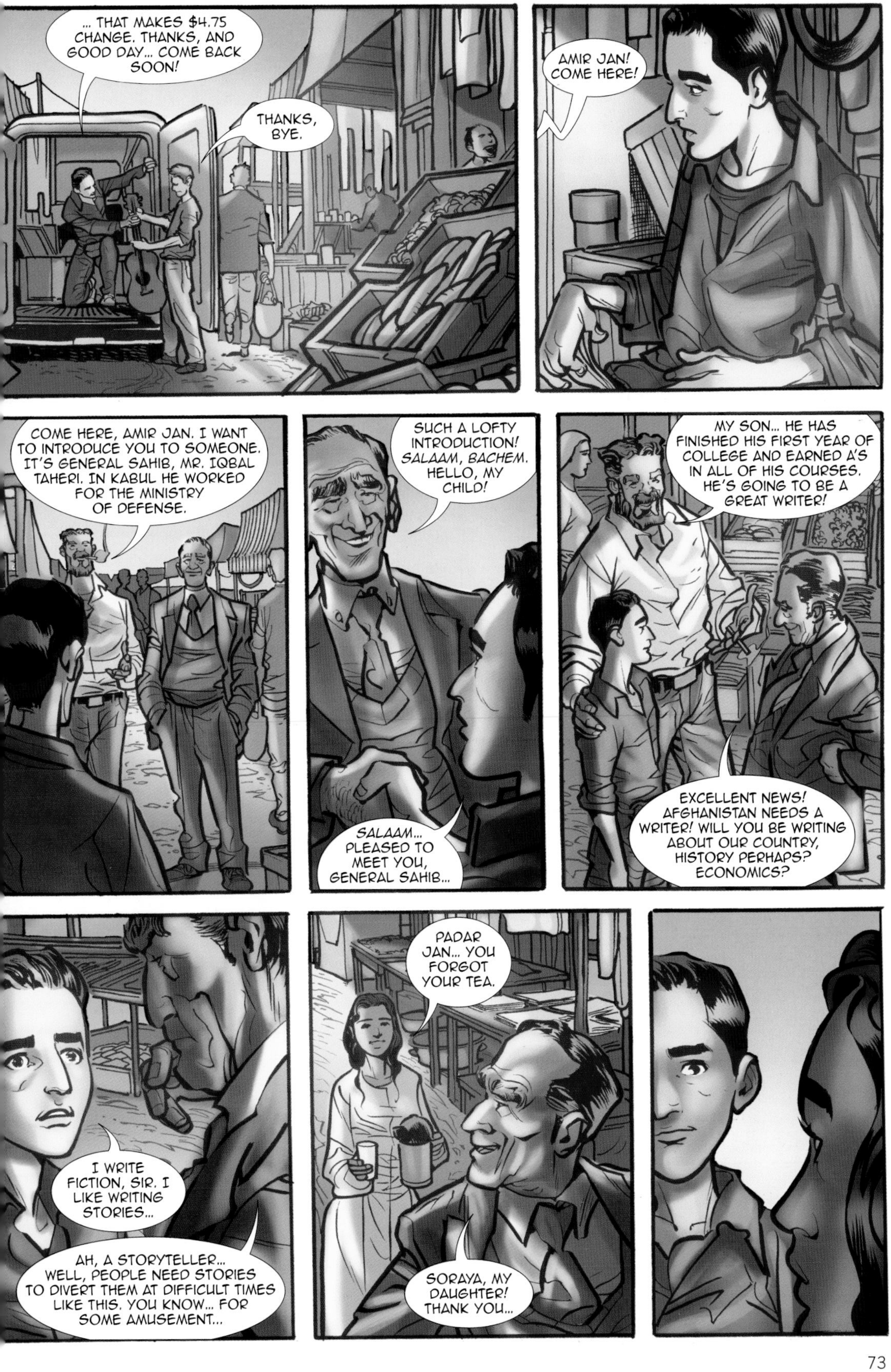
... THAT MAKES $4.75 CHANGE. THANKS, AND GOOD DAY... COME BACK SOON!
THANKS, BYE.
AMIR JAN! COME HERE!
COME HERE, AMIR JAN. I WANT TO INTRODUCE YOU TO SOMEONE. IT'S GENERAL SAHIB, MR. IQBAL TAHERI. IN KABUL HE WORKED FOR THE MINISTRY OF DEFENSE.
SUCH A LOFTY INTRODUCTION! SALAAM, BACHEM. HELLO, MY CHILD!
SALAAM... PLEASED TO MEET YOU, GENERAL SAHIB...
MY SON... HE HAS FINISHED HIS FIRST YEAR OF COLLEGE AND EARNED A'S IN ALL OF HIS COURSES. HE'S GOING TO BE A GREAT WRITER!
EXCELLENT NEWS! AFGHANISTAN NEEDS A WRITER! WILL YOU BE WRITING ABOUT OUR COUNTRY, HISTORY PERHAPS? ECONOMICS?
I WRITE FICTION, SIR. I LIKE WRITING STORIES...
AH, A STORYTELLER... WELL, PEOPLE NEED STORIES TO DIVERT THEM AT DIFFICULT TIMES LIKE THIS. YOU KNOW... FOR SOME AMUSEMENT...
PADAR JAN... YOU FORGOT YOUR TEA.
SORAYA, MY DAUGHTER! THANK YOU...

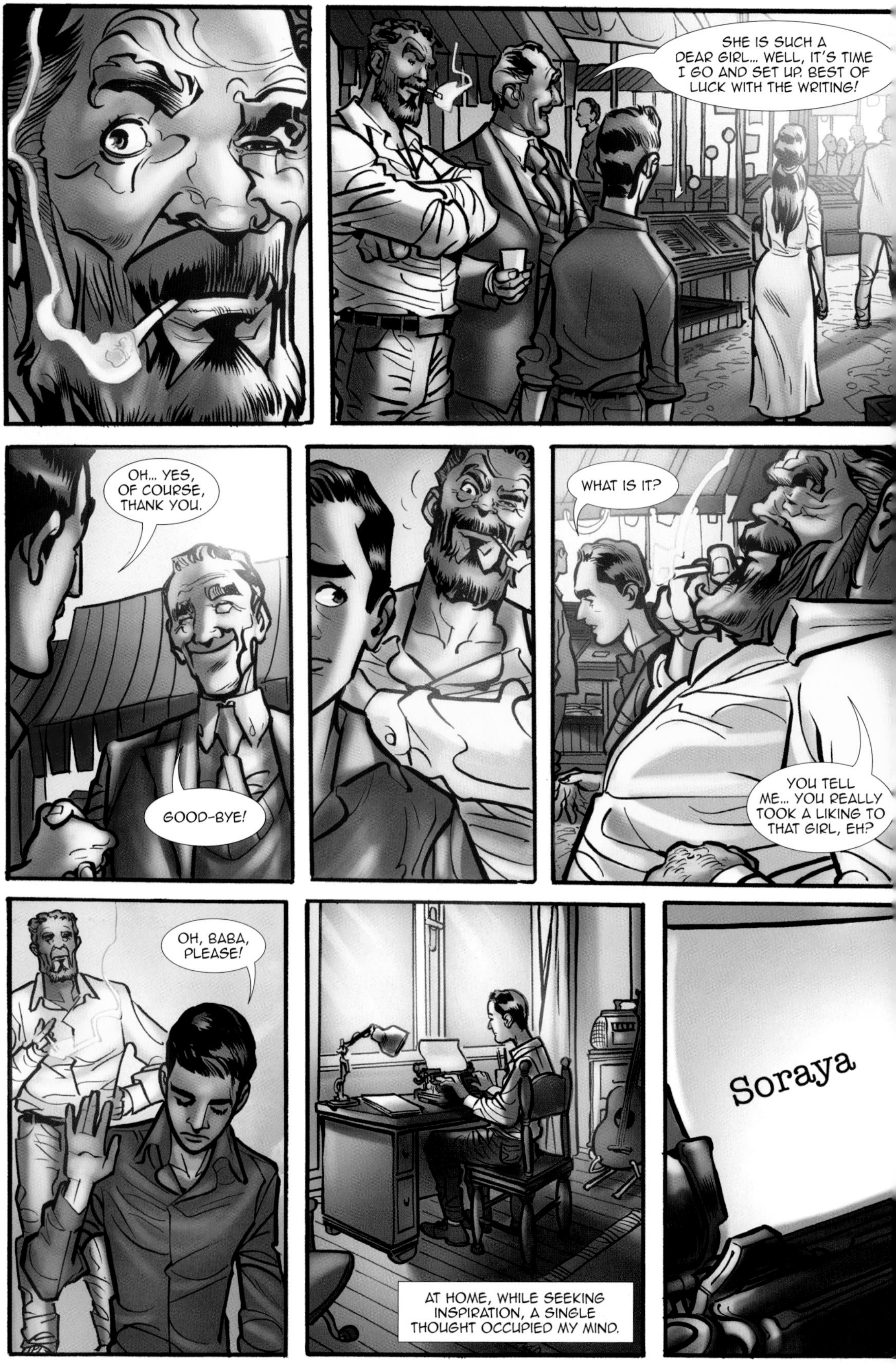
SHE IS SUCH A DEAR GIRL... WELL, IT'S TIME I GO AND SET UP. BEST OF LUCK WITH THE WRITING!
OH... YES, OF COURSE, THANK YOU.
GOOD-BYE!
WHAT IS IT?
YOU TELL ME... YOU REALLY TOOK A LIKING TO THAT GIRL, EH?
OH, BABA, PLEASE!
AT HOME, WHILE SEEKING INSPIRATION, A SINGLE THOUGHT OCCUPIED MY MIND.
Soraya

I FINISHED THE FIRST YEAR OF UNIVERSITY WITH TOP GRADES IN NEARLY ALL SUBJECTS.

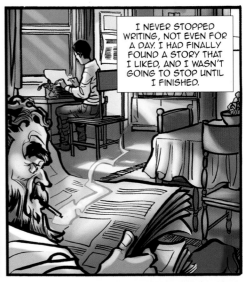

I NEVER STOPPED WRITING, NOT EVEN FOR A DAY. I HAD FINALLY FOUND A STORY THAT I LIKED, AND I WASN'T GOING TO STOP UNTIL I FINISHED.

EVERY WEEK I WAITED FOR SUNDAY TO ARRIVE. IT WAS THE ONLY DAY I WAS ABLE TO SEE HER. THE SWEET AND BEAUTIFUL SORAYA.

HEY, BABA, WOULD YOU LIKE A COKE?

YES, THANKS... BUT BE CAREFUL, AMIR.

OF WHAT, BABA?

... OF GENERAL TAHERI. HE IS A PASHTUN TO THE ROOT. HONOR AND PRIDE.

I TOLD YOU... I'M ONLY GOING TO GET US DRINKS.

JUST DON'T EMBARRASS ME, THAT'S ALL I ASK. PLEASE!

I WON'T. GOD, BABA.

COUGH COUGH COUGH

DAMNED COUGH!

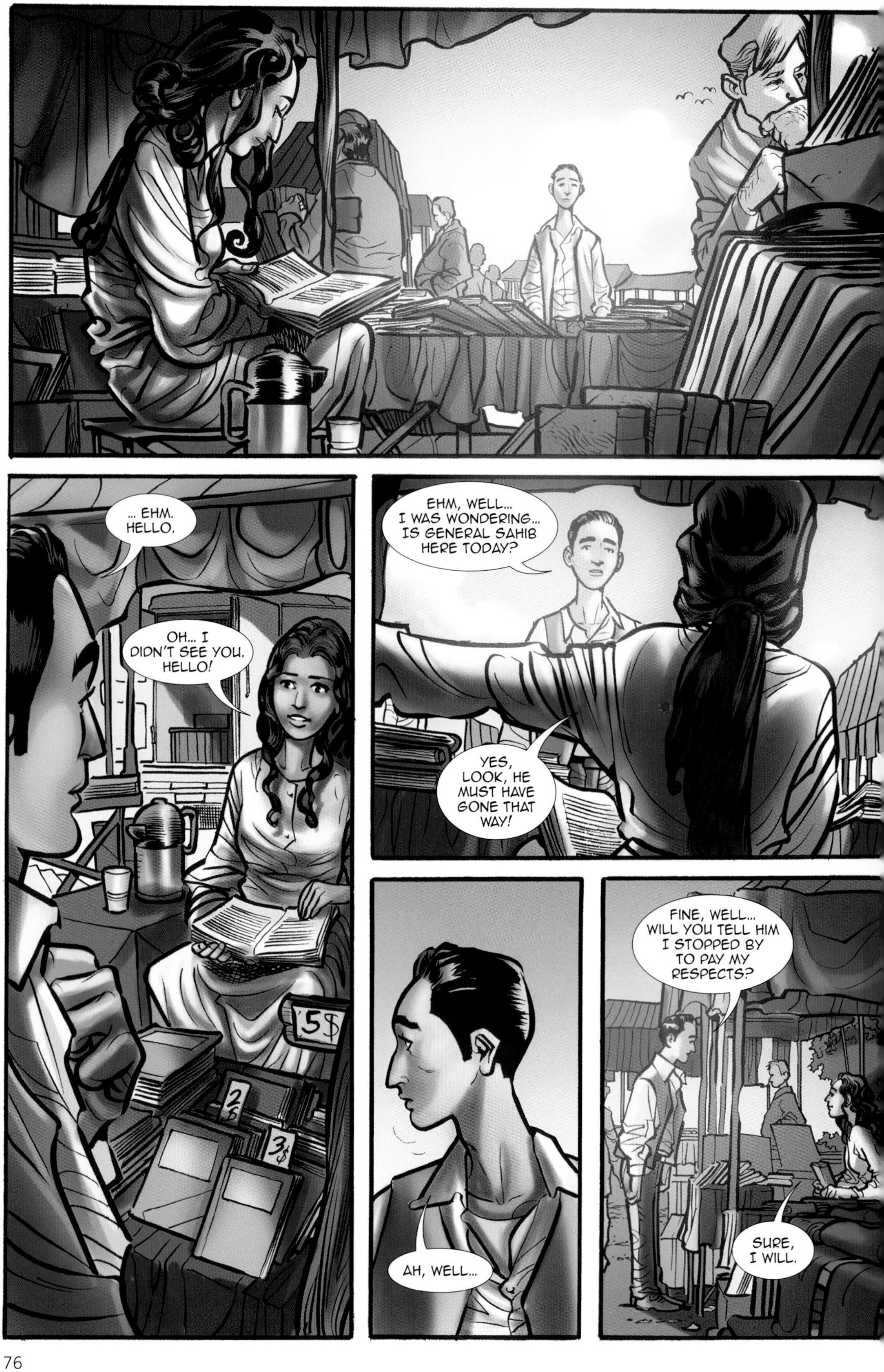
... EHM. HELLO.
OH... I DIDN'T SEE YOU. HELLO!
5$
2$
3$
EHM, WELL... I WAS WONDERING... IS GENERAL SAHIB HERE TODAY?
YES, LOOK, HE MUST HAVE GONE THAT WAY!
AH, WELL...
FINE, WELL... WILL YOU TELL HIM I STOPPED BY TO PAY MY RESPECTS?
SURE, I WILL.

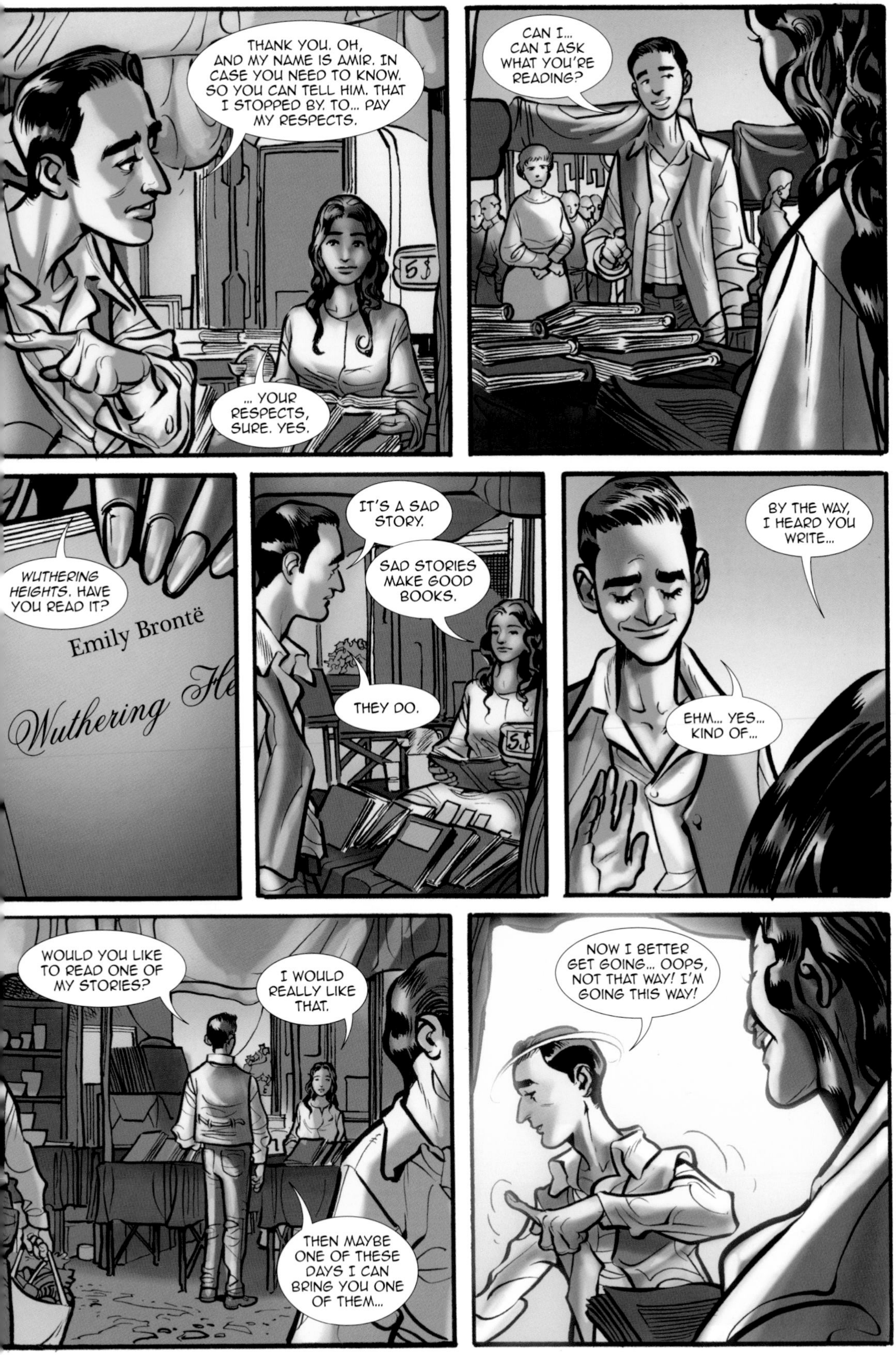
THANK YOU. OH, AND MY NAME IS AMIR. IN CASE YOU NEED TO KNOW. SO YOU CAN TELL HIM. THAT I STOPPED BY. TO... PAY MY RESPECTS.
... YOUR RESPECTS, SURE. YES.
CAN I... CAN I ASK WHAT YOU'RE READING?
WUTHERING HEIGHTS. HAVE YOU READ IT?
Emily Brontë
Wuthering He
IT'S A SAD STORY.
SAD STORIES MAKE GOOD BOOKS.
THEY DO.
BY THE WAY, I HEARD YOU WRITE...
EHM... YES... KIND OF...
WOULD YOU LIKE TO READ ONE OF MY STORIES?
I WOULD REALLY LIKE THAT.
THEN MAYBE ONE OF THESE DAYS I CAN BRING YOU ONE OF THEM...
NOW I BETTER GET GOING... OOPS, NOT THAT WAY! I'M GOING THIS WAY!

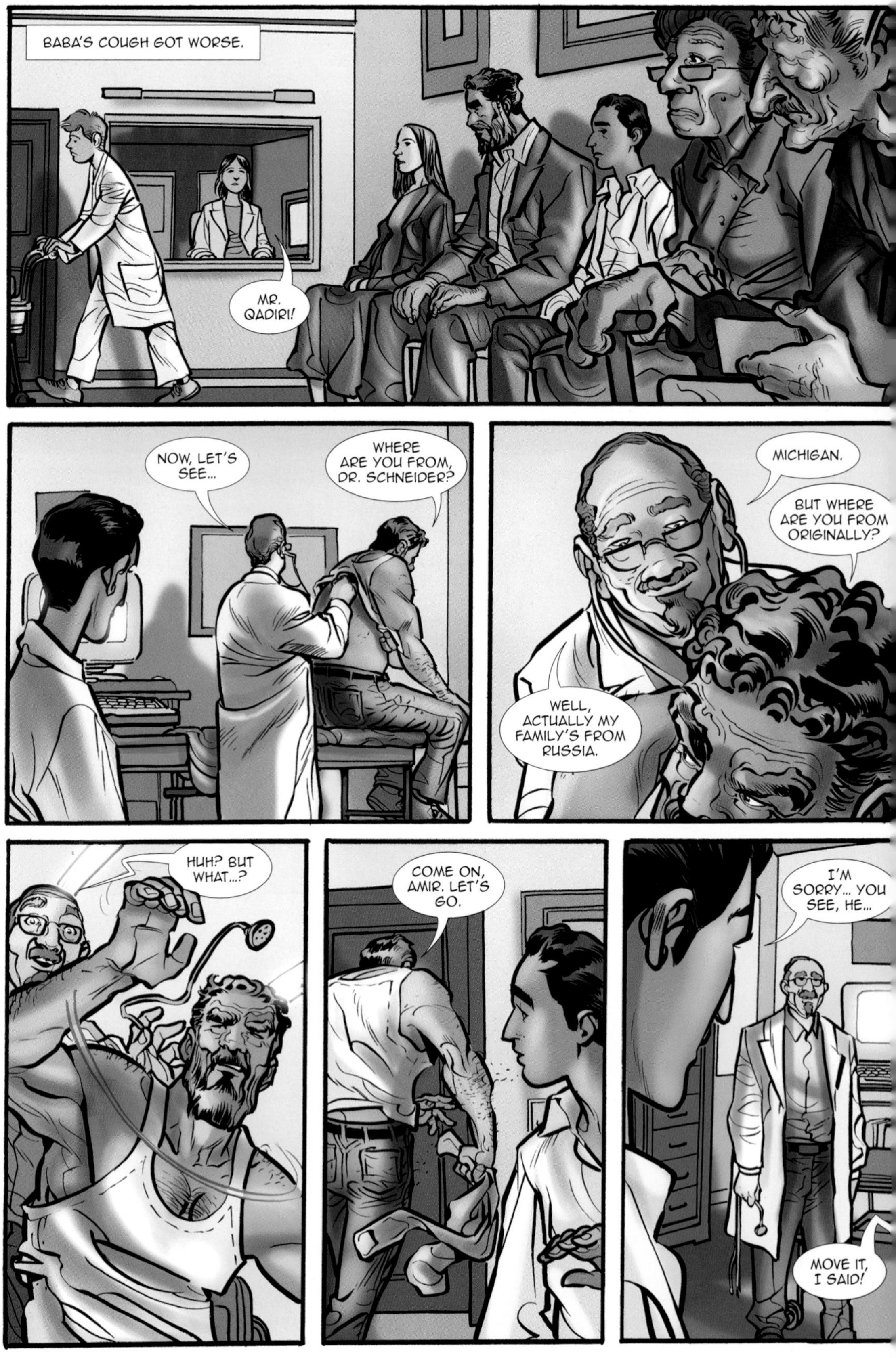
BABA'S COUGH GOT WORSE.
MR. QADIRI!
NOW, LET'S SEE...
WHERE ARE YOU FROM, DR. SCHNEIDER?
MICHIGAN.
BUT WHERE ARE YOU FROM ORIGINALLY?
WELL, ACTUALLY MY FAMILY'S FROM RUSSIA.
HUH? BUT WHAT...?
COME ON, AMIR. LET'S GO.
I'M SORRY... YOU SEE, HE...
MOVE IT, I SAID!

DO YOU LIKE BARGAINING? I HATE IT!

NO, I DON'T LIKE IT EITHER... EHM... I BROUGHT YOU THIS. IT'S ONE OF MY... YES, ONE OF MY STORIES.

OH, YOU REMEMB—

AMIR JAN, OUR INSPIRING STORYTELLER. WHAT A PLEASURE!

SALAAM, GENERAL SAHIB. HOW ARE YOU?

THEY SAY IT WILL RAIN THIS WEEK.

HARD TO BELIEVE, ISN'T IT?

YOU KNOW, BACHEM, I HAVE GROWN RATHER FOND OF YOU. YOU ARE A DECENT BOY, BUT EVEN DECENT BOYS NEED REMINDING SOMETIMES: YOU ARE AMONG PEERS IN THIS FLEA MARKET...

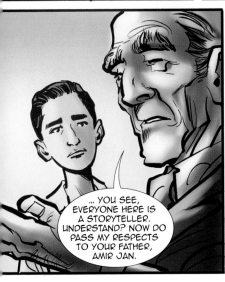

... YOU SEE, EVERYONE HERE IS A STORYTELLER. UNDERSTAND? NOW DO PASS MY RESPECTS TO YOUR FATHER, AMIR JAN.

... AND SO HE SENT YOU BACK HERE, EH? JUST AS I THOUGHT. HONOR AND PRIDE, I TOLD YOU SO.

YES, BUT...

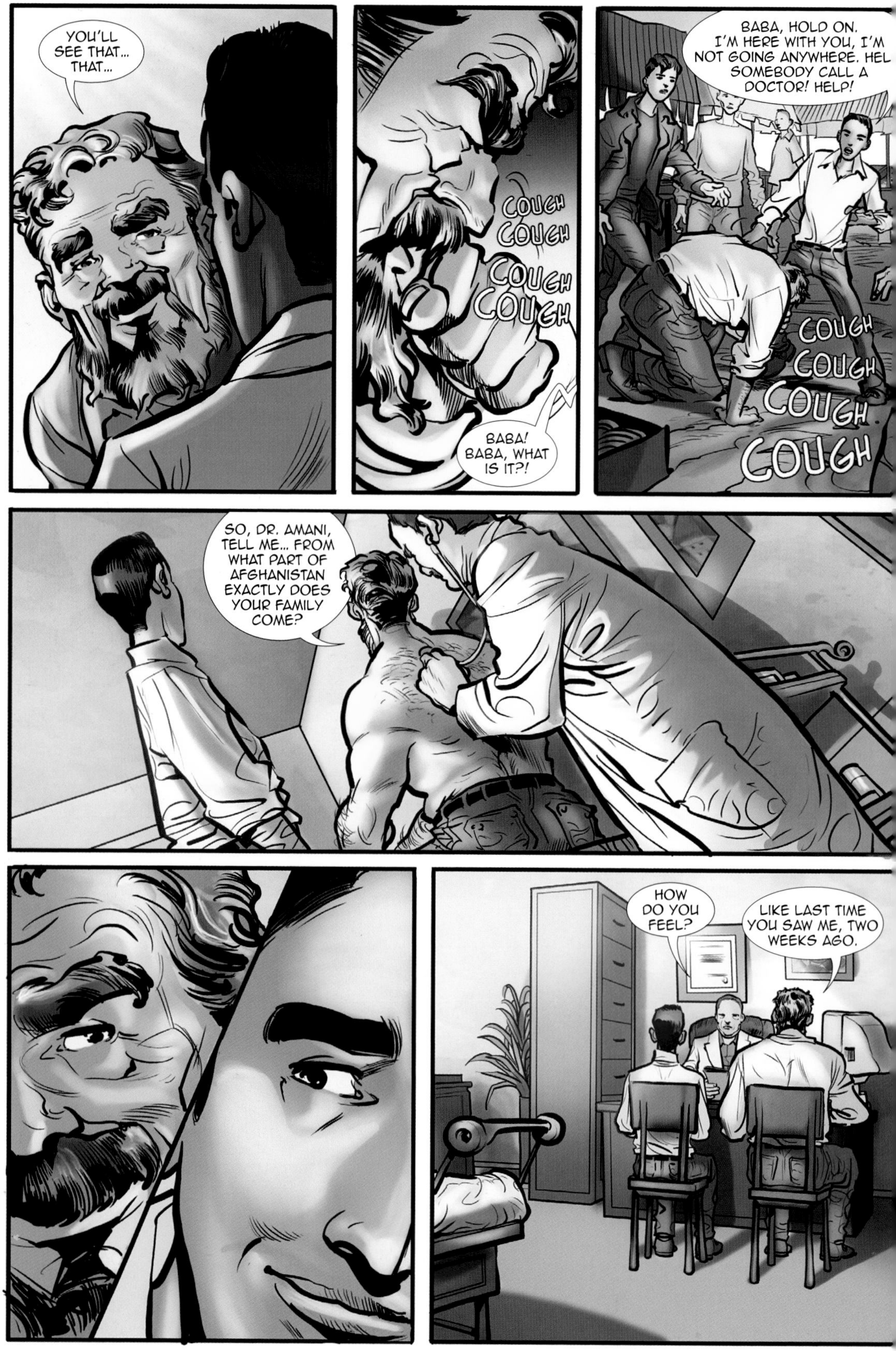
YOU'LL SEE THAT... THAT...
COUGH COUGH COUGH COUGH
BABA! BABA, WHAT IS IT?!
BABA, HOLD ON. I'M HERE WITH YOU, I'M NOT GOING ANYWHERE. HEL SOMEBODY CALL A DOCTOR! HELP!
COUGH COUGH COUGH COUGH
SO, DR. AMANI, TELL ME... FROM WHAT PART OF AFGHANISTAN EXACTLY DOES YOUR FAMILY COME?
HOW DO YOU FEEL?
LIKE LAST TIME YOU SAW ME, TWO WEEKS AGO.

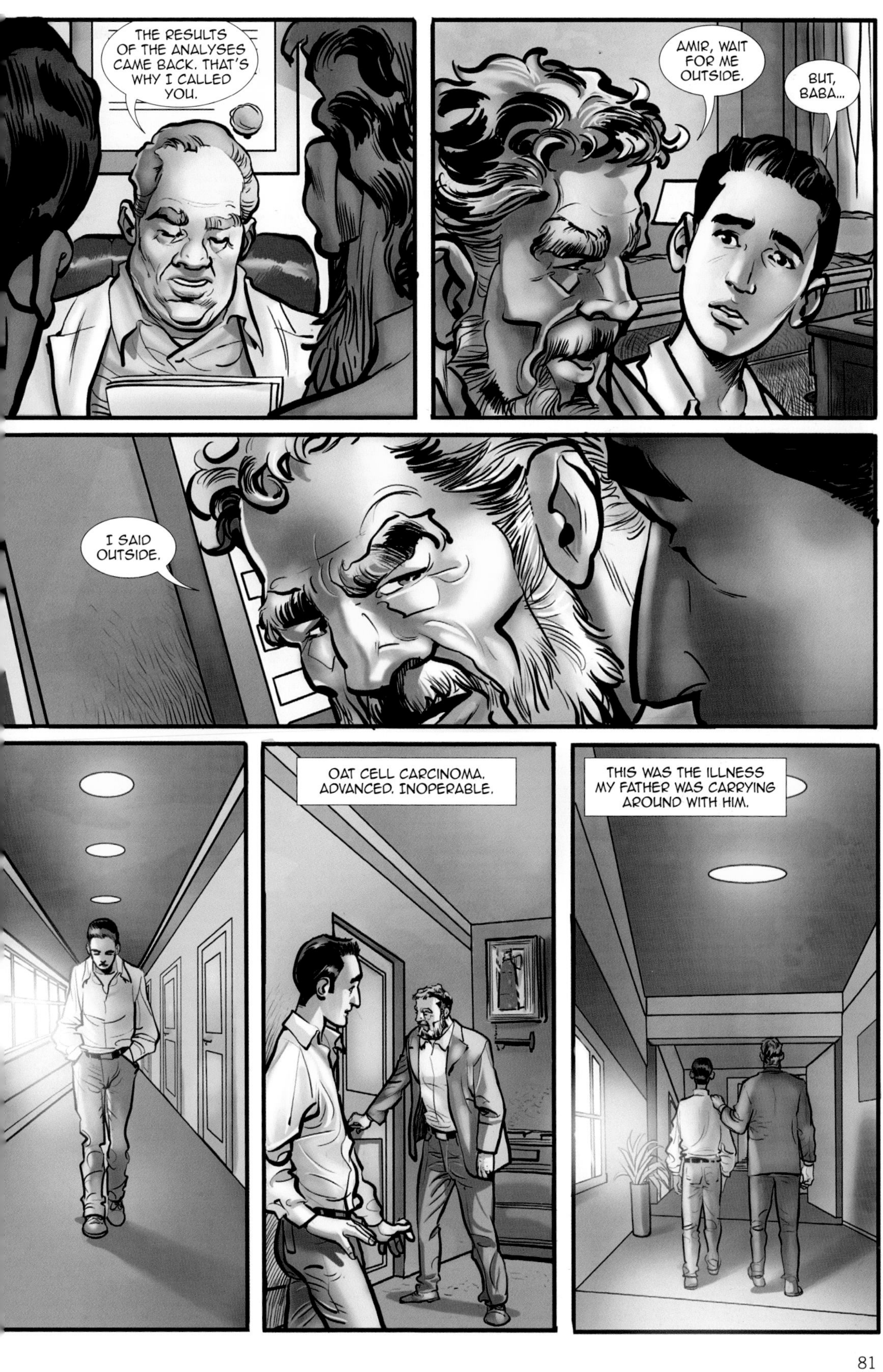
THE RESULTS OF THE ANALYSES CAME BACK. THAT'S WHY I CALLED YOU.
AMIR, WAIT FOR ME OUTSIDE.
BUT, BABA...
I SAID OUTSIDE.
OAT CELL CARCINOMA. ADVANCED. INOPERABLE.
THIS WAS THE ILLNESS MY FATHER WAS CARRYING AROUND WITH HIM.

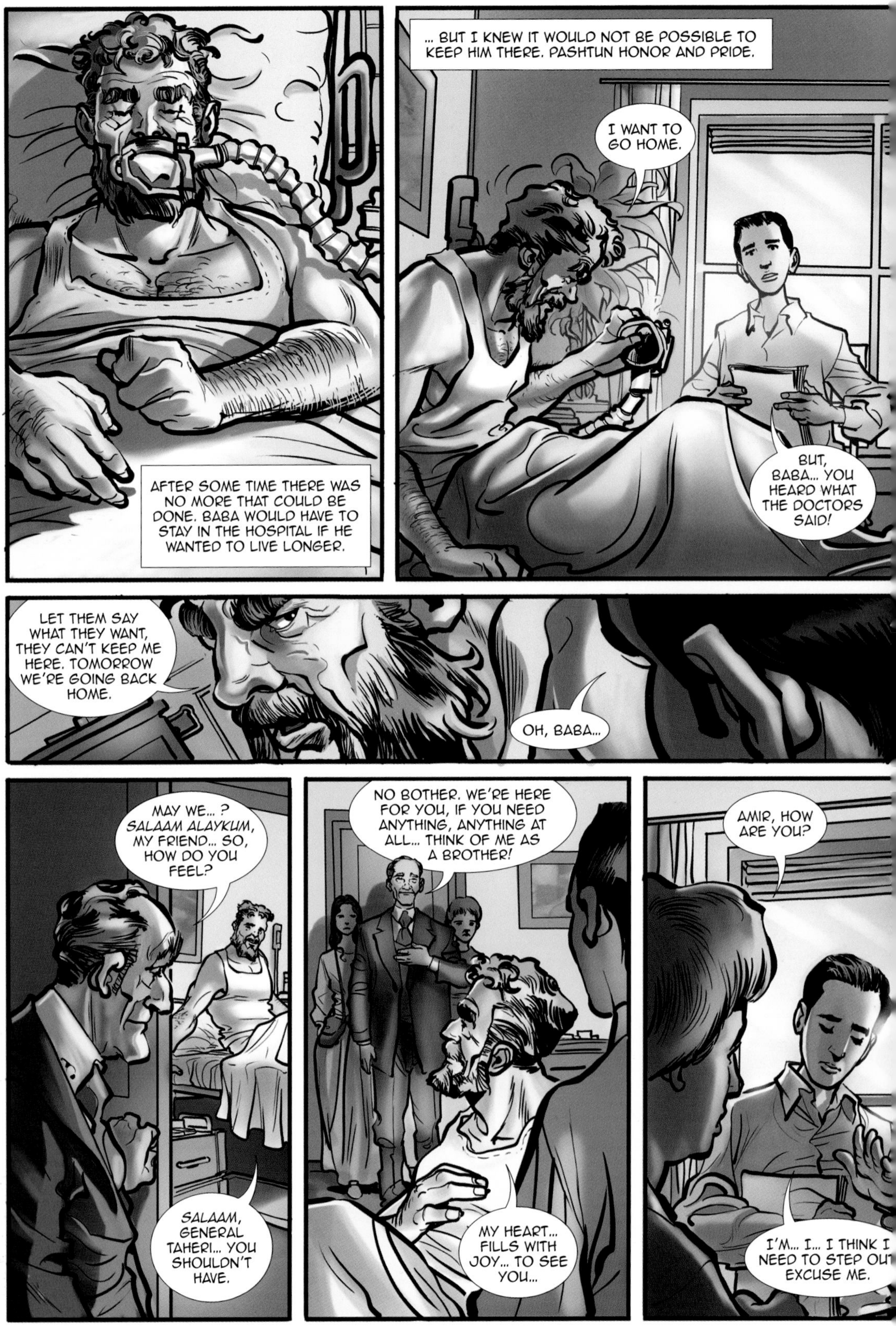
AFTER SOME TIME THERE WAS NO MORE THAT COULD BE DONE. BABA WOULD HAVE TO STAY IN THE HOSPITAL IF HE WANTED TO LIVE LONGER.
... BUT I KNEW IT WOULD NOT BE POSSIBLE TO KEEP HIM THERE. PASHTUN HONOR AND PRIDE.
I WANT TO GO HOME.
BUT, BABA... YOU HEARD WHAT THE DOCTORS SAID!
LET THEM SAY WHAT THEY WANT, THEY CAN'T KEEP ME HERE. TOMORROW WE'RE GOING BACK HOME.
OH, BABA...
MAY WE... ? *SALAAM ALAYKUM*, MY FRIEND... SO, HOW DO YOU FEEL?
SALAAM, GENERAL TAHERI... YOU SHOULDN'T HAVE.
NO BOTHER. WE'RE HERE FOR YOU, IF YOU NEED ANYTHING, ANYTHING AT ALL... THINK OF ME AS A BROTHER!
MY HEART... FILLS WITH JOY... TO SEE YOU...
AMIR, HOW ARE YOU?
I'M... I... I THINK I NEED TO STEP OUT EXCUSE ME.

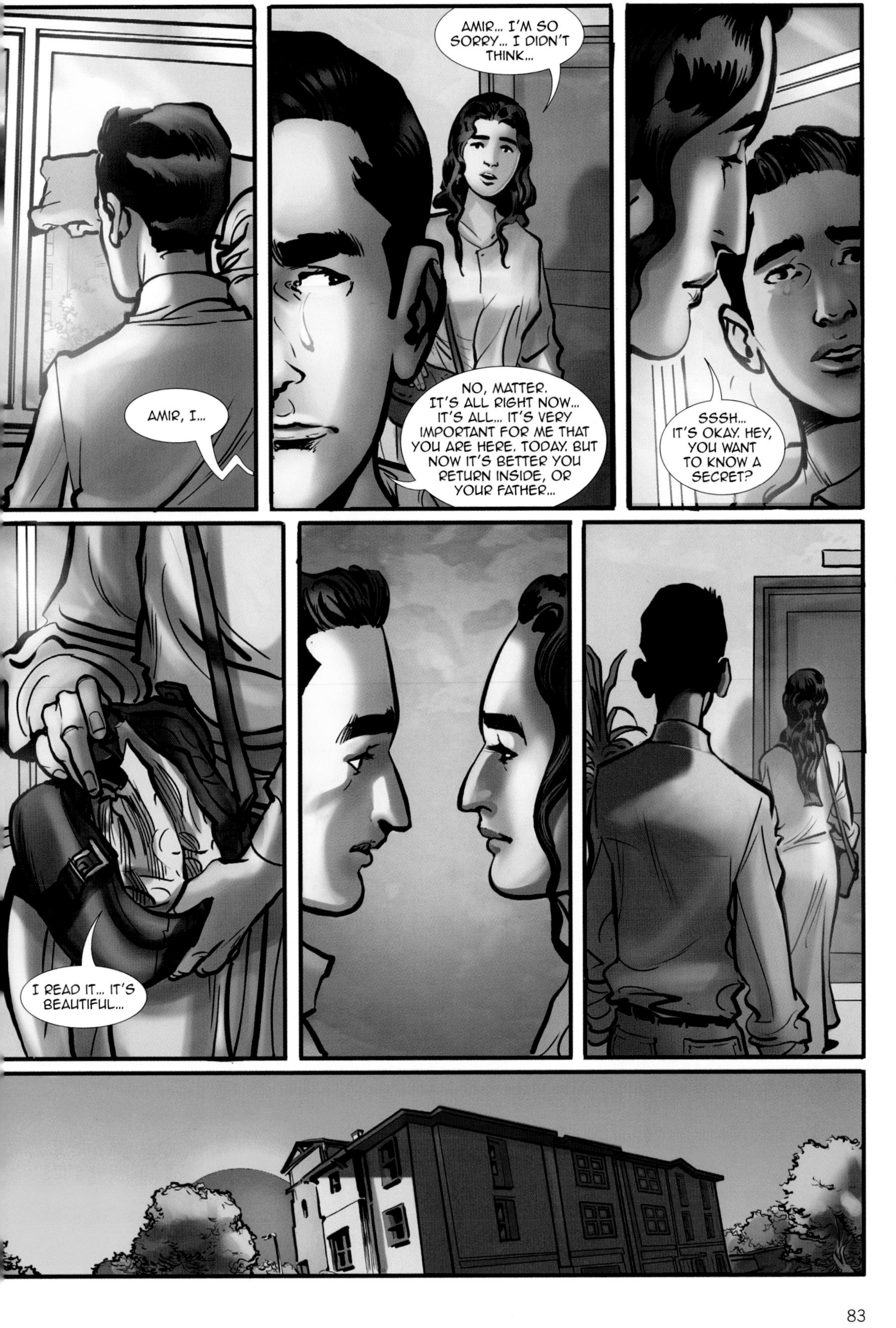
AMIR, I...
AMIR... I'M SO SORRY... I DIDN'T THINK...
NO, MATTER. IT'S ALL RIGHT NOW... IT'S ALL... IT'S VERY IMPORTANT FOR ME THAT YOU ARE HERE. TODAY. BUT NOW IT'S BETTER YOU RETURN INSIDE, OR YOUR FATHER...
SSSH... IT'S OKAY. HEY, YOU WANT TO KNOW A SECRET?
I READ IT... IT'S BEAUTIFUL...

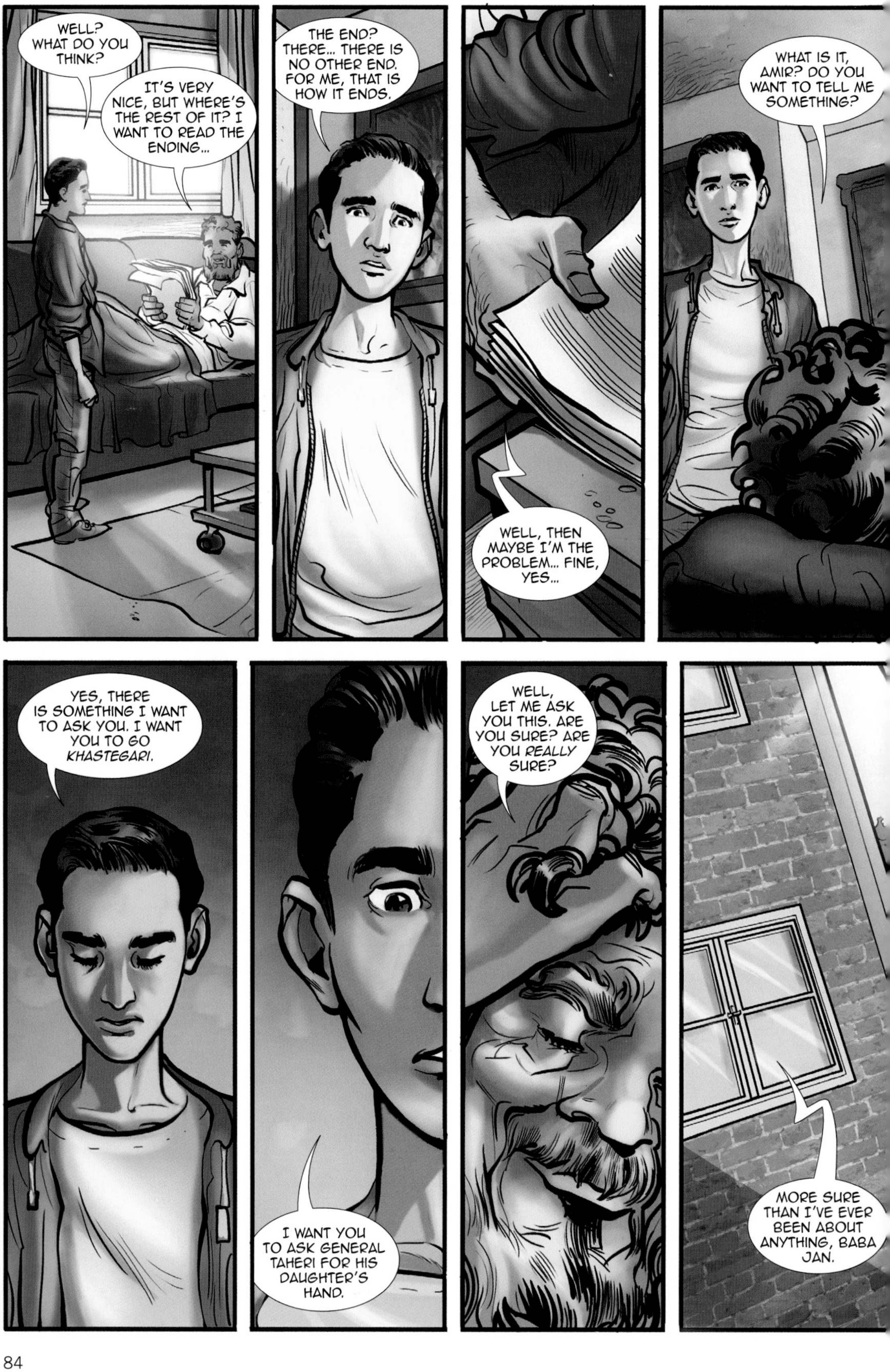
WELL? WHAT DO YOU THINK?
IT'S VERY NICE, BUT WHERE'S THE REST OF IT? I WANT TO READ THE ENDING...
THE END? THERE... THERE IS NO OTHER END. FOR ME, THAT IS HOW IT ENDS.
WELL, THEN MAYBE I'M THE PROBLEM... FINE, YES...
WHAT IS IT, AMIR? DO YOU WANT TO TELL ME SOMETHING?
YES, THERE IS SOMETHING I WANT TO ASK YOU. I WANT YOU TO GO *KHASTEGARI*.
I WANT YOU TO ASK GENERAL TAHERI FOR HIS DAUGHTER'S HAND.
WELL, LET ME ASK YOU THIS. ARE YOU SURE? ARE YOU *REALLY* SURE?
MORE SURE THAN I'VE EVER BEEN ABOUT ANYTHING, BABA JAN.

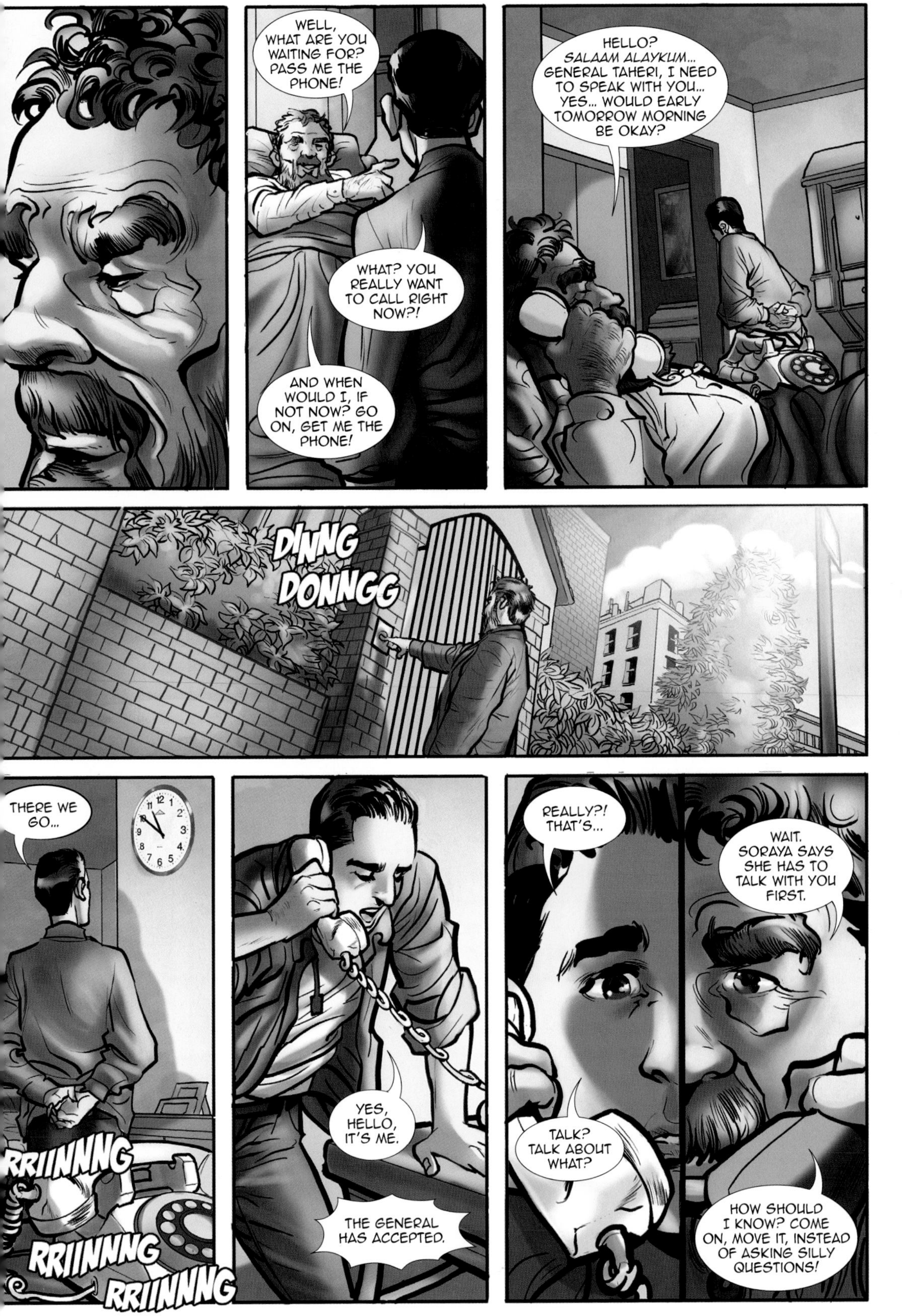
WELL, WHAT ARE YOU WAITING FOR? PASS ME THE PHONE!
WHAT? YOU REALLY WANT TO CALL RIGHT NOW?!
AND WHEN WOULD I, IF NOT NOW? GO ON, GET ME THE PHONE!
HELLO? SALAAM ALAYKUM... GENERAL TAHERI, I NEED TO SPEAK WITH YOU... YES... WOULD EARLY TOMORROW MORNING BE OKAY?
DINNG
DONNGG
THERE WE GO...
RRIINNNG
RRIINNNG
RRIINNNG
YES, HELLO, IT'S ME.
THE GENERAL HAS ACCEPTED.
REALLY?! THAT'S...
WAIT. SORAYA SAYS SHE HAS TO TALK WITH YOU FIRST.
TALK? TALK ABOUT WHAT?
HOW SHOULD I KNOW? COME ON, MOVE IT, INSTEAD OF ASKING SILLY QUESTIONS!

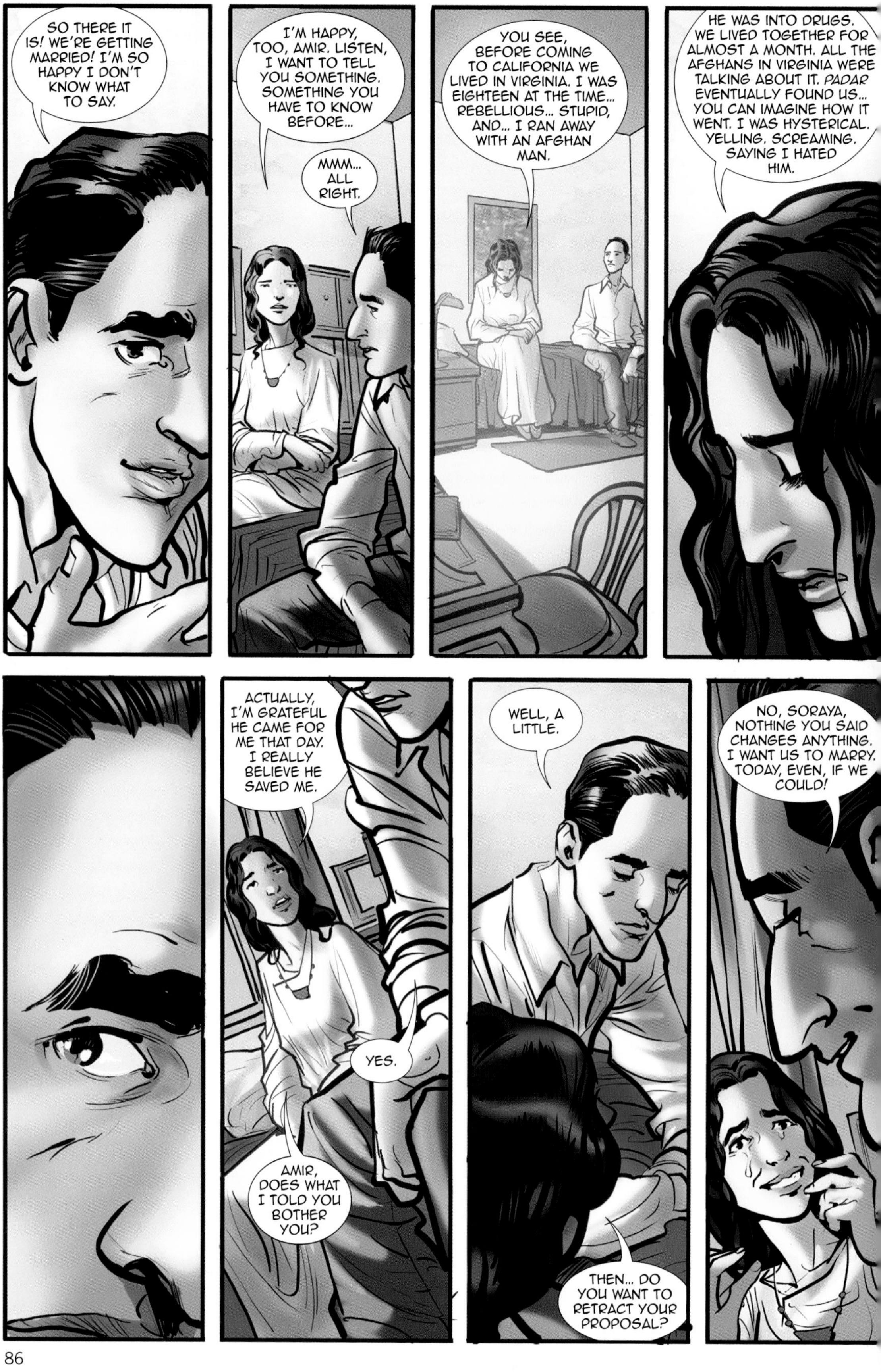
SO THERE IT IS! WE'RE GETTING MARRIED! I'M SO HAPPY I DON'T KNOW WHAT TO SAY.
I'M HAPPY, TOO, AMIR. LISTEN, I WANT TO TELL YOU SOMETHING. SOMETHING YOU HAVE TO KNOW BEFORE...
MMM... ALL RIGHT.
YOU SEE, BEFORE COMING TO CALIFORNIA WE LIVED IN VIRGINIA. I WAS EIGHTEEN AT THE TIME... REBELLIOUS... STUPID, AND... I RAN AWAY WITH AN AFGHAN MAN.
HE WAS INTO DRUGS. WE LIVED TOGETHER FOR ALMOST A MONTH. ALL THE AFGHANS IN VIRGINIA WERE TALKING ABOUT IT. *PADAR* EVENTUALLY FOUND US... YOU CAN IMAGINE HOW IT WENT. I WAS HYSTERICAL. YELLING. SCREAMING. SAYING I HATED HIM.
ACTUALLY, I'M GRATEFUL HE CAME FOR ME THAT DAY. I REALLY BELIEVE HE SAVED ME.
AMIR, DOES WHAT I TOLD YOU BOTHER YOU?
YES.
WELL, A LITTLE.
THEN... DO YOU WANT TO RETRACT YOUR PROPOSAL?
NO, SORAYA, NOTHING YOU SAID CHANGES ANYTHING. I WANT US TO MARRY. TODAY, EVEN, IF WE COULD!

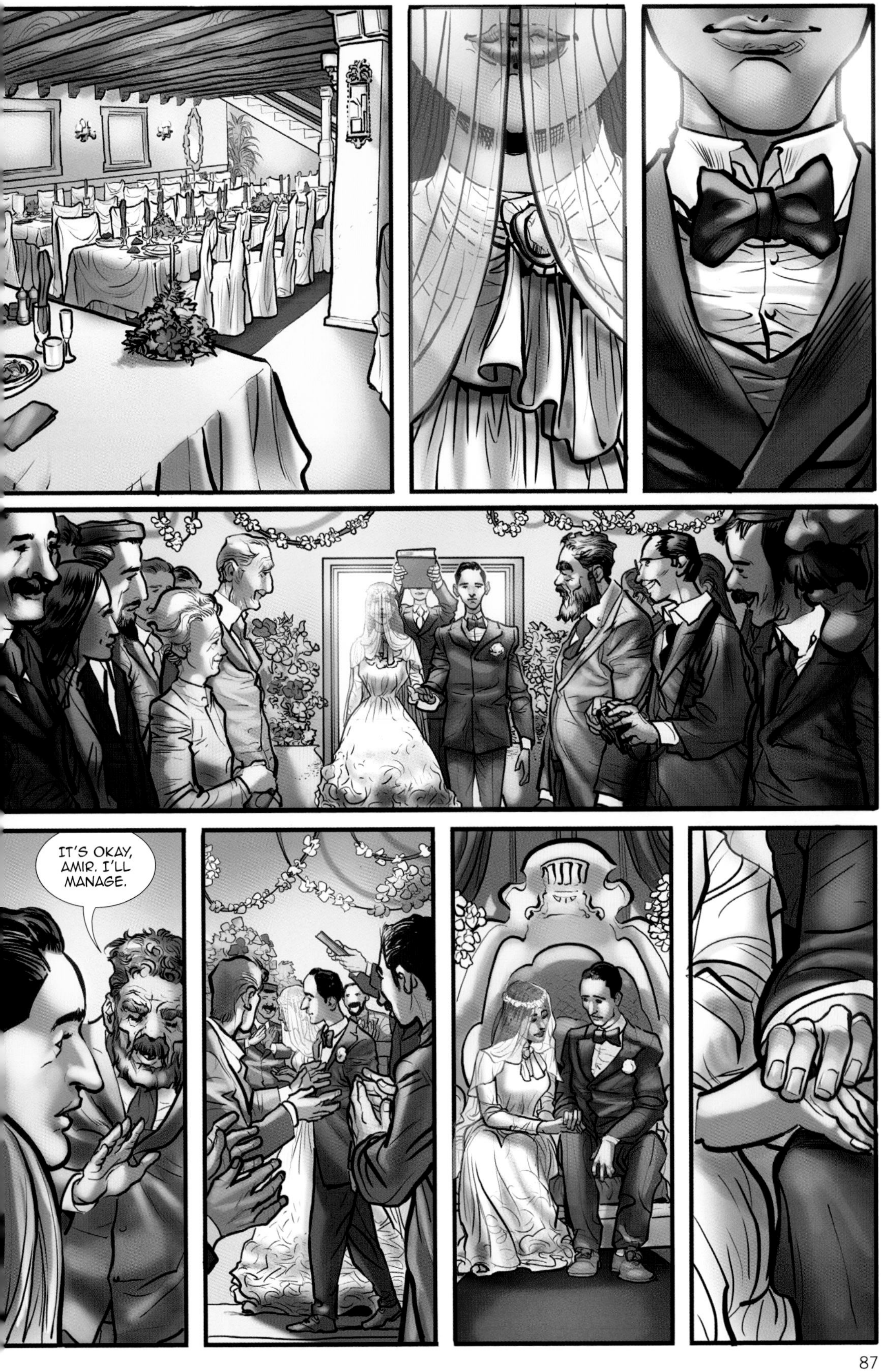
IT'S OKAY, AMIR. I'LL MANAGE.

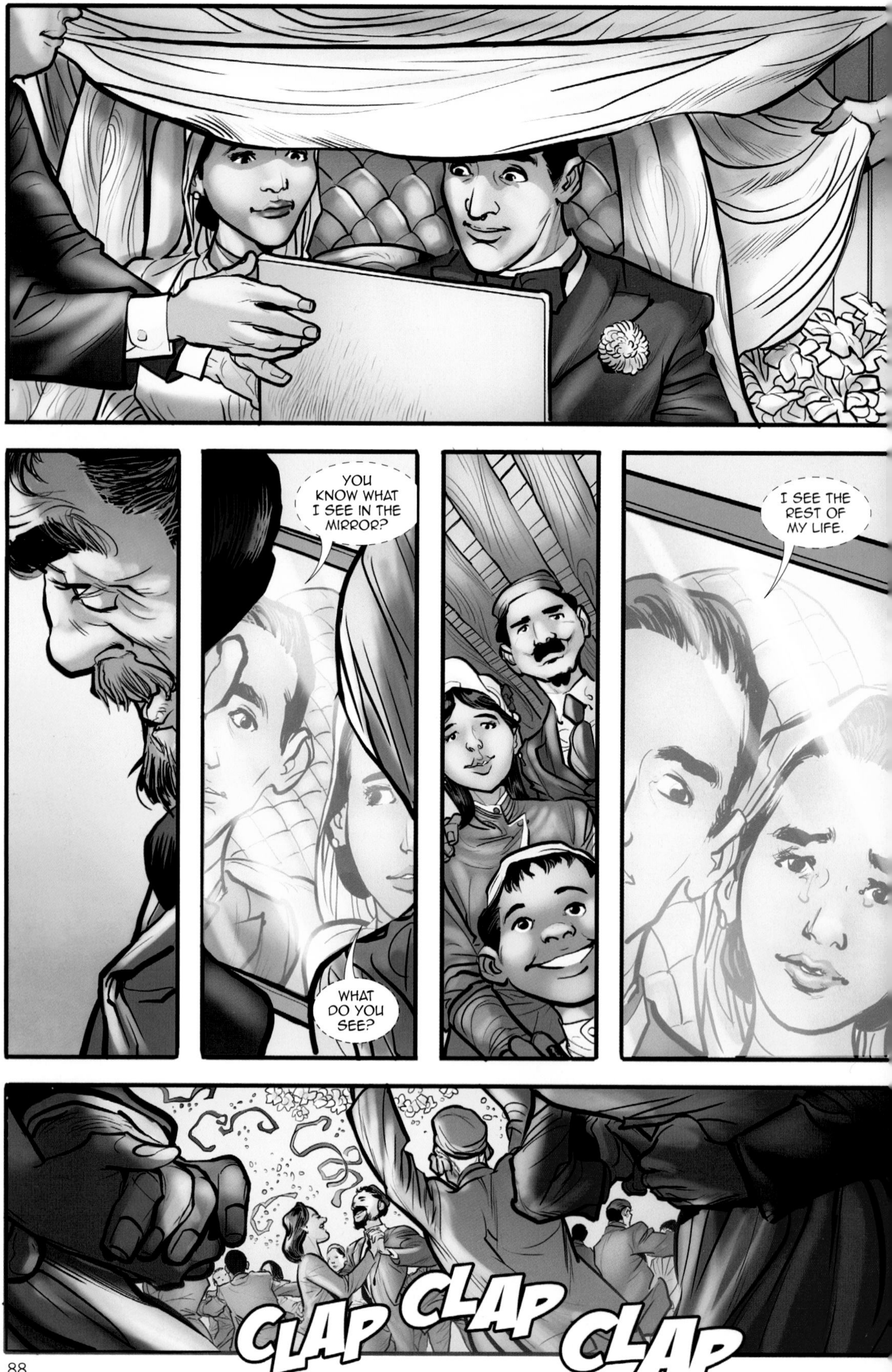

YOU KNOW WHAT I SEE IN THE MIRROR?
WHAT DO YOU SEE?
I SEE THE REST OF MY LIFE.
CLAP CLAP CLAP

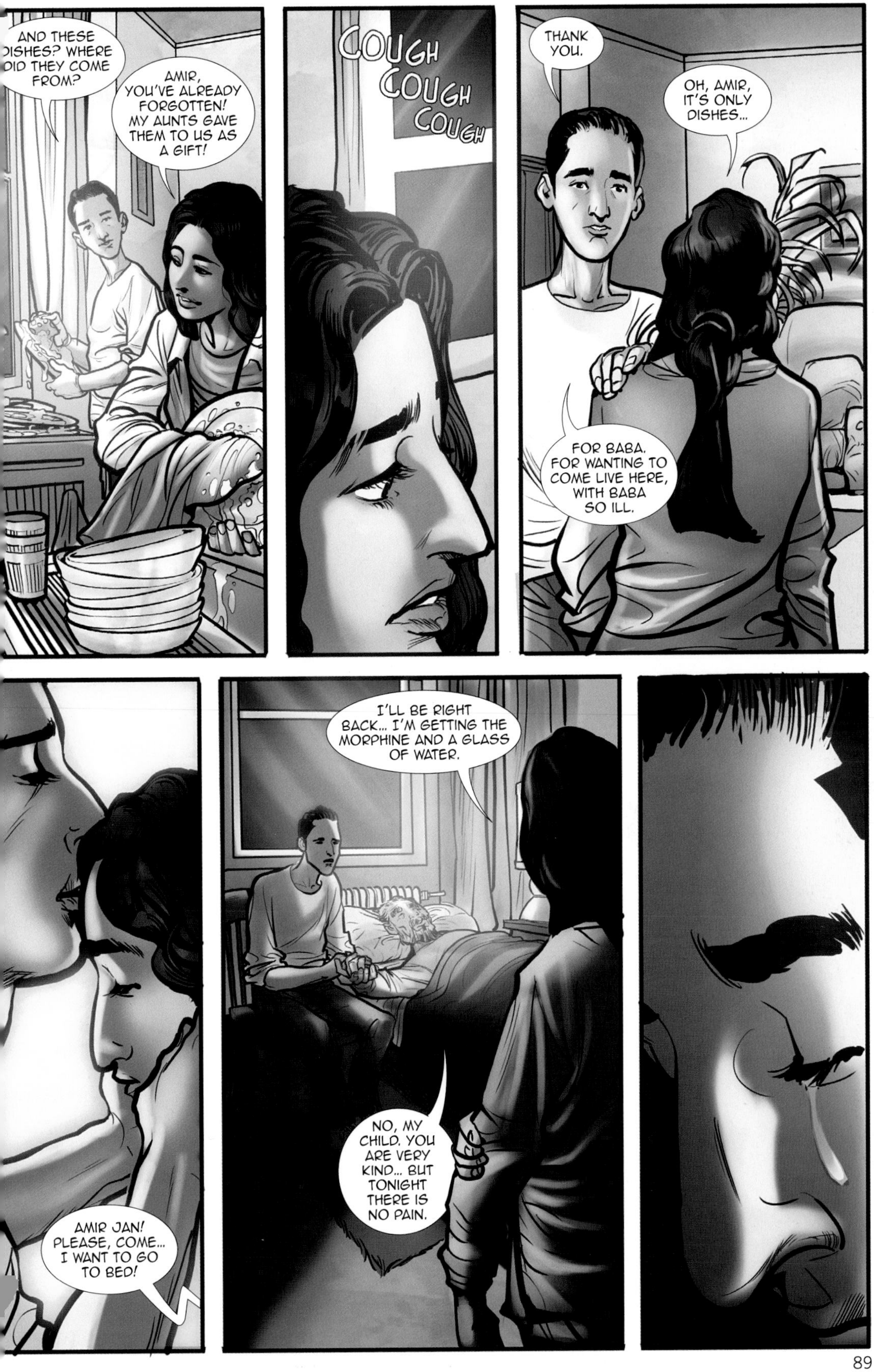
AND THESE DISHES? WHERE DID THEY COME FROM?
AMIR, YOU'VE ALREADY FORGOTTEN! MY AUNTS GAVE THEM TO US AS A GIFT!
COUGH COUGH COUGH
THANK YOU.
OH, AMIR, IT'S ONLY DISHES...
FOR BABA. FOR WANTING TO COME LIVE HERE, WITH BABA SO ILL.
AMIR JAN! PLEASE, COME... I WANT TO GO TO BED!
I'LL BE RIGHT BACK... I'M GETTING THE MORPHINE AND A GLASS OF WATER.
NO, MY CHILD. YOU ARE VERY KIND... BUT TONIGHT THERE IS NO PAIN.

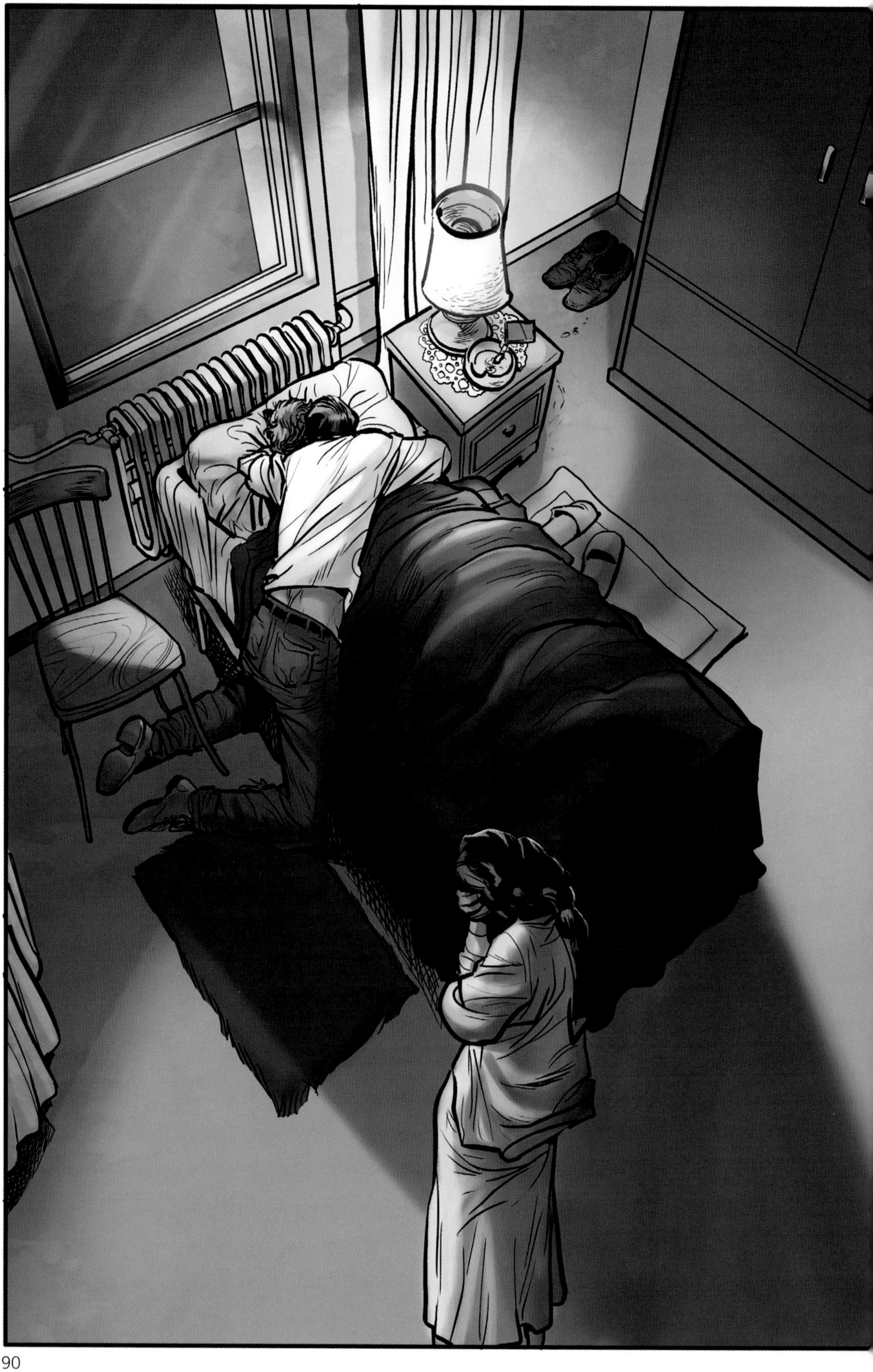

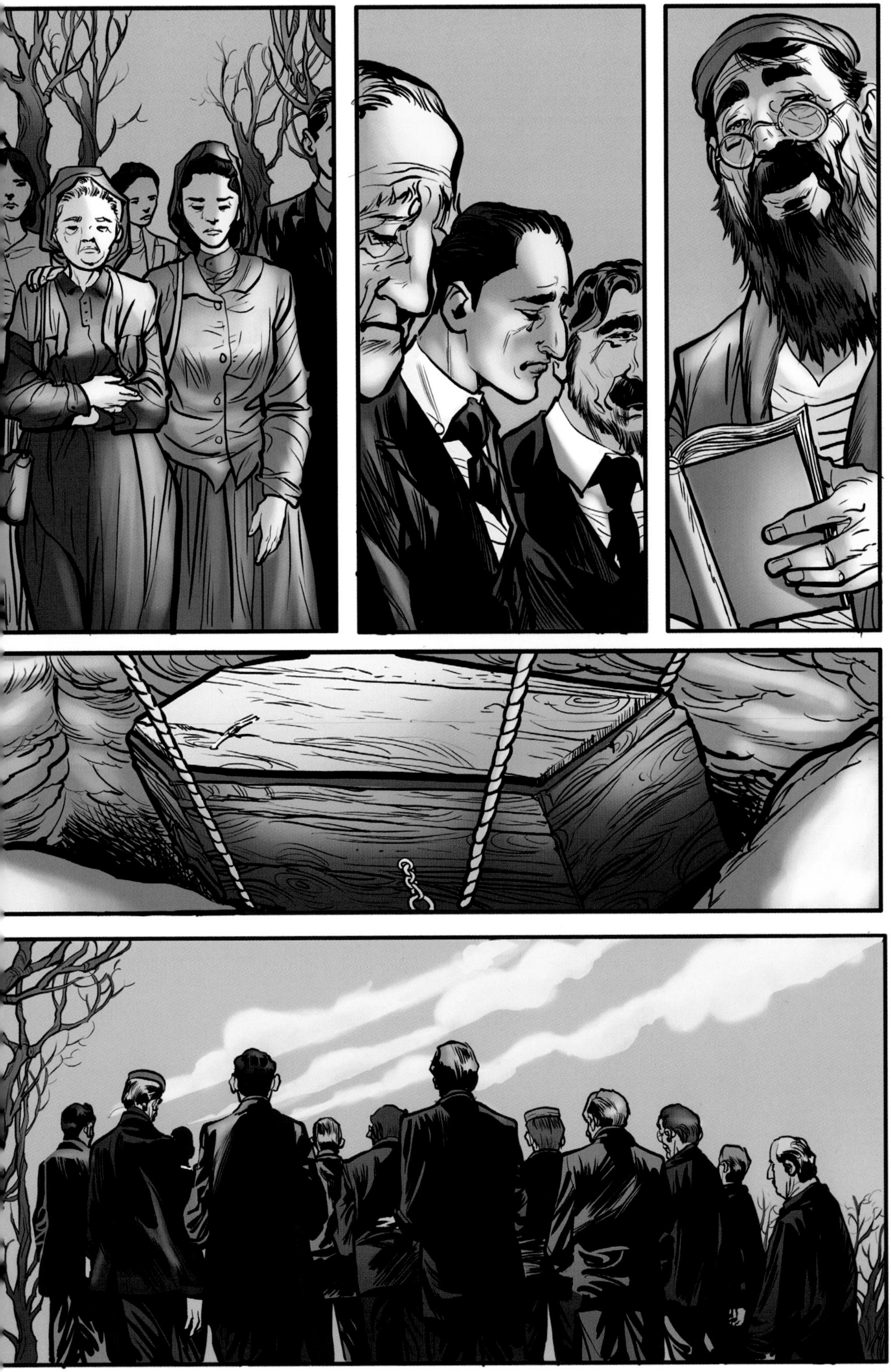

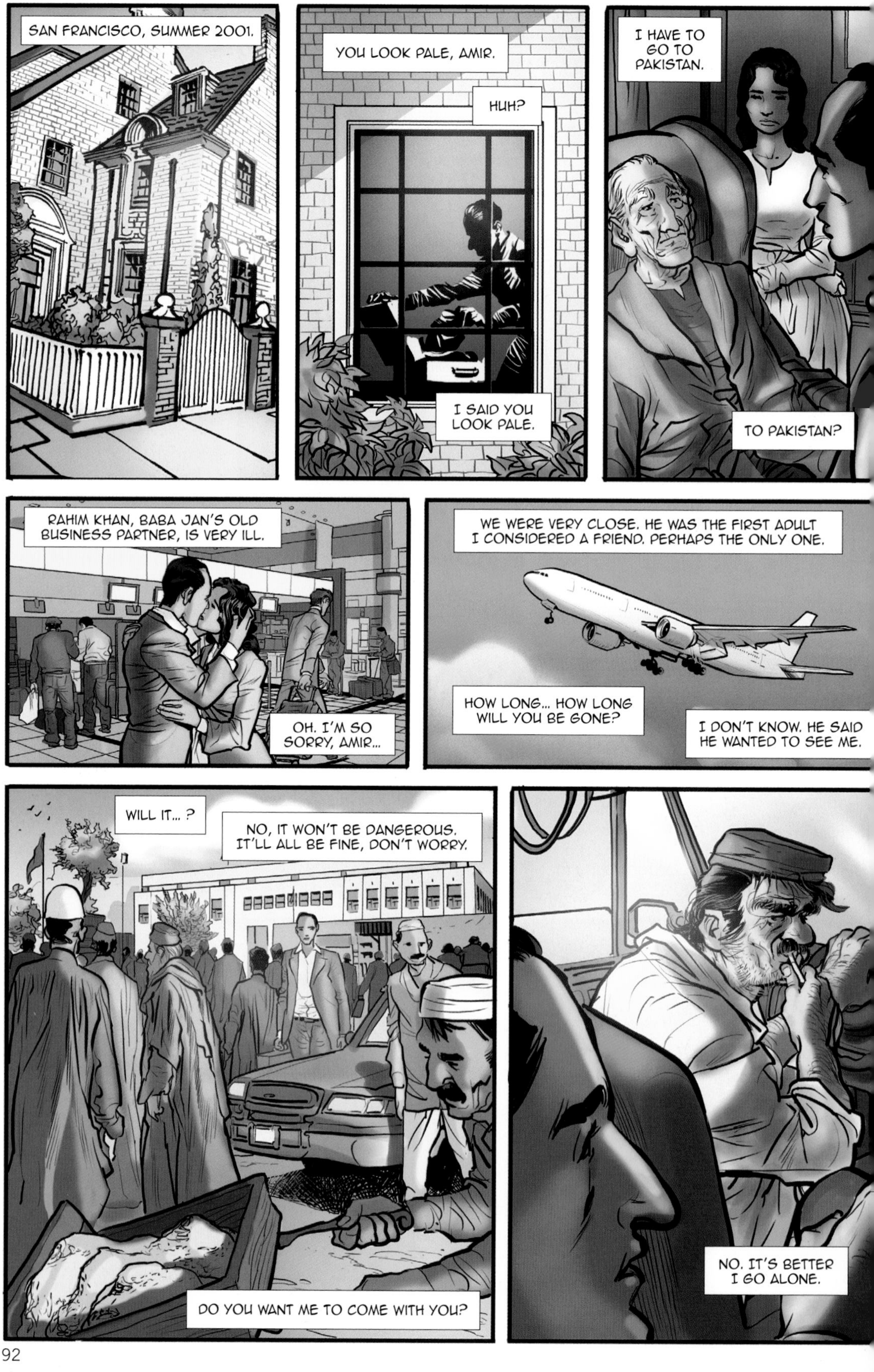
SAN FRANCISCO, SUMMER 2001.
YOU LOOK PALE, AMIR.
HUH?
I SAID YOU LOOK PALE.
I HAVE TO GO TO PAKISTAN.
TO PAKISTAN?
RAHIM KHAN, BABA JAN'S OLD BUSINESS PARTNER, IS VERY ILL.
OH. I'M SO SORRY, AMIR...
WE WERE VERY CLOSE. HE WAS THE FIRST ADULT I CONSIDERED A FRIEND. PERHAPS THE ONLY ONE.
HOW LONG... HOW LONG WILL YOU BE GONE?
I DON'T KNOW. HE SAID HE WANTED TO SEE ME.
WILL IT... ?
NO, IT WON'T BE DANGEROUS. IT'LL ALL BE FINE, DON'T WORRY.
DO YOU WANT ME TO COME WITH YOU?
NO. IT'S BETTER I GO ALONE.

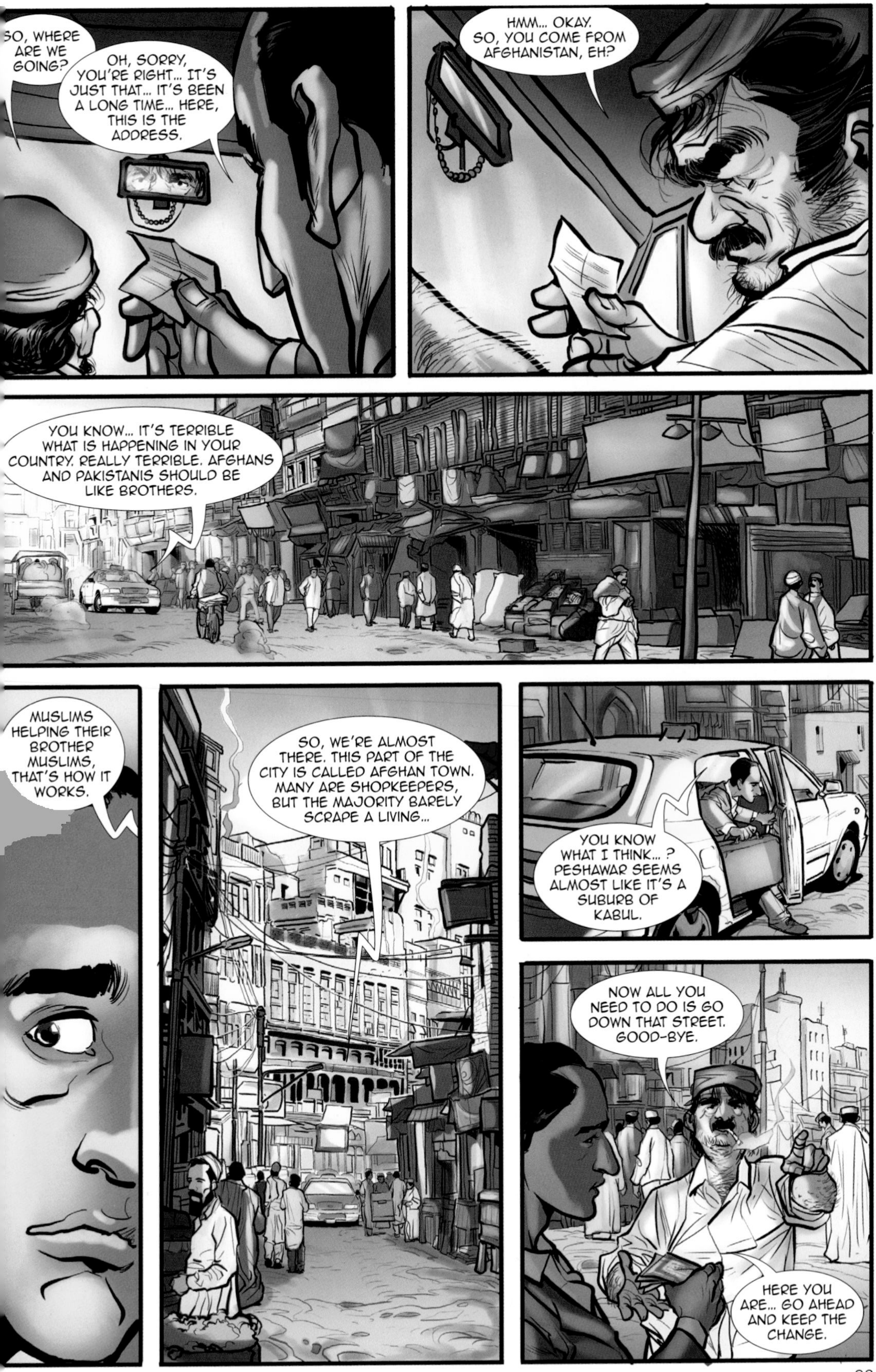
SO, WHERE ARE WE GOING?
OH, SORRY, YOU'RE RIGHT... IT'S JUST THAT... IT'S BEEN A LONG TIME... HERE, THIS IS THE ADDRESS.
HMM... OKAY. SO, YOU COME FROM AFGHANISTAN, EH?
YOU KNOW... IT'S TERRIBLE WHAT IS HAPPENING IN YOUR COUNTRY. REALLY TERRIBLE. AFGHANS AND PAKISTANIS SHOULD BE LIKE BROTHERS.
MUSLIMS HELPING THEIR BROTHER MUSLIMS, THAT'S HOW IT WORKS.
SO, WE'RE ALMOST THERE. THIS PART OF THE CITY IS CALLED AFGHAN TOWN. MANY ARE SHOPKEEPERS, BUT THE MAJORITY BARELY SCRAPE A LIVING...
YOU KNOW WHAT I THINK... ? PESHAWAR SEEMS ALMOST LIKE IT'S A SUBURB OF KABUL.
NOW ALL YOU NEED TO DO IS GO DOWN THAT STREET. GOOD-BYE.
HERE YOU ARE... GO AHEAD AND KEEP THE CHANGE.

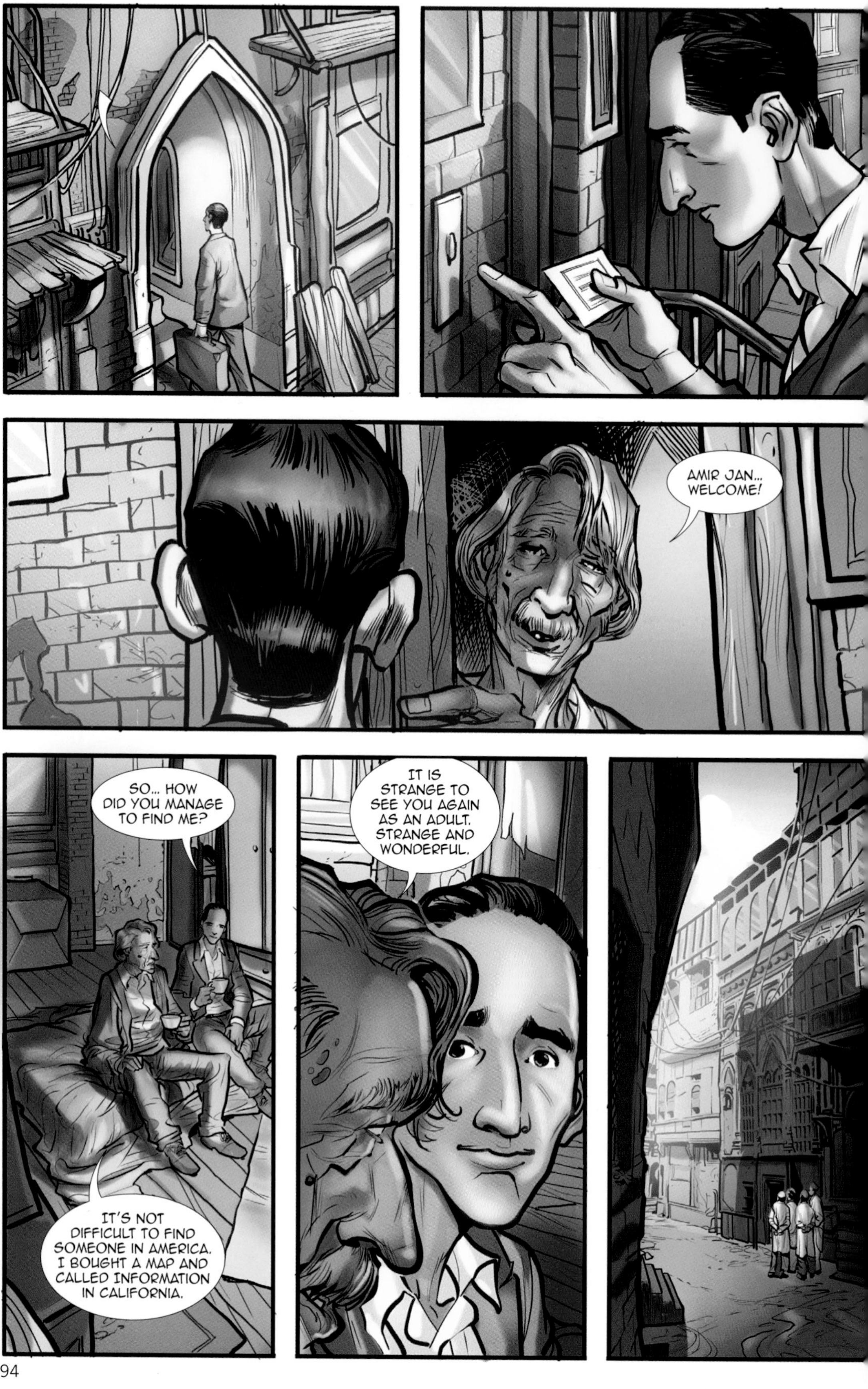
AMIR JAN... WELCOME!
SO... HOW DID YOU MANAGE TO FIND ME?
IT'S NOT DIFFICULT TO FIND SOMEONE IN AMERICA. I BOUGHT A MAP AND CALLED INFORMATION IN CALIFORNIA.
IT IS STRANGE TO SEE YOU AGAIN AS AN ADULT. STRANGE AND WONDERFUL.

UHM... YES... I REMEMBER GENERAL TAHERI, A MAN OF CONVICTIONS! AND SO YOU MARRIED HIS DAUGHTER, EH...? TELL ME, ANY CHILDREN?

WE... DON'T HAVE ANY CHILDREN.

OH...

WAIT, I HAVE SOMETHING FOR YOU! I ALMOST FORGOT.

THIS IS THE LAST NOVEL I WROTE. IT'S JUST COME OUT.

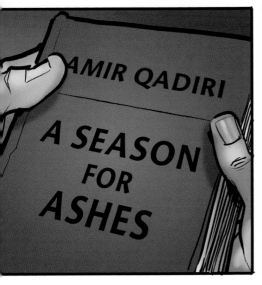

AMIR QADIRI

A SEASON FOR ASHES

AMIR JAN... THIS IS AN HONOR.

YOU KNOW, I WENT ON FOR YEARS WRITING IN BOUND NOTEBOOKS LIKE THE ONE YOU GAVE ME.

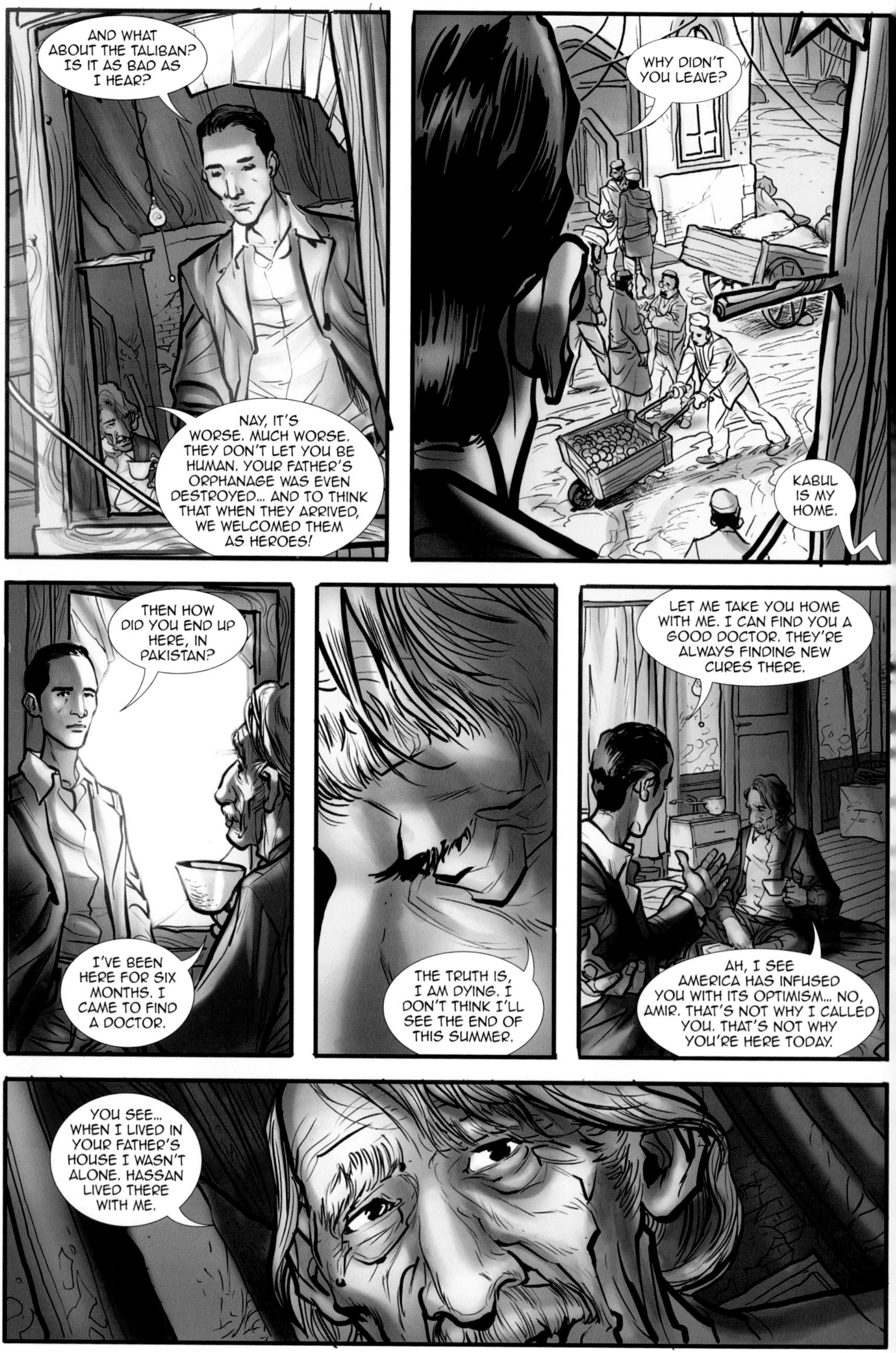
AND WHAT ABOUT THE TALIBAN? IS IT AS BAD AS I HEAR?
NAY, IT'S WORSE. MUCH WORSE. THEY DON'T LET YOU BE HUMAN. YOUR FATHER'S ORPHANAGE WAS EVEN DESTROYED... AND TO THINK THAT WHEN THEY ARRIVED, WE WELCOMED THEM AS HEROES!
WHY DIDN'T YOU LEAVE?
KABUL IS MY HOME.
THEN HOW DID YOU END UP HERE, IN PAKISTAN?
I'VE BEEN HERE FOR SIX MONTHS. I CAME TO FIND A DOCTOR.
THE TRUTH IS, I AM DYING. I DON'T THINK I'LL SEE THE END OF THIS SUMMER.
LET ME TAKE YOU HOME WITH ME. I CAN FIND YOU A GOOD DOCTOR. THEY'RE ALWAYS FINDING NEW CURES THERE.
AH, I SEE AMERICA HAS INFUSED YOU WITH ITS OPTIMISM... NO, AMIR. THAT'S NOT WHY I CALLED YOU. THAT'S NOT WHY YOU'RE HERE TODAY.
YOU SEE... WHEN I LIVED IN YOUR FATHER'S HOUSE I WASN'T ALONE. HASSAN LIVED THERE WITH ME.

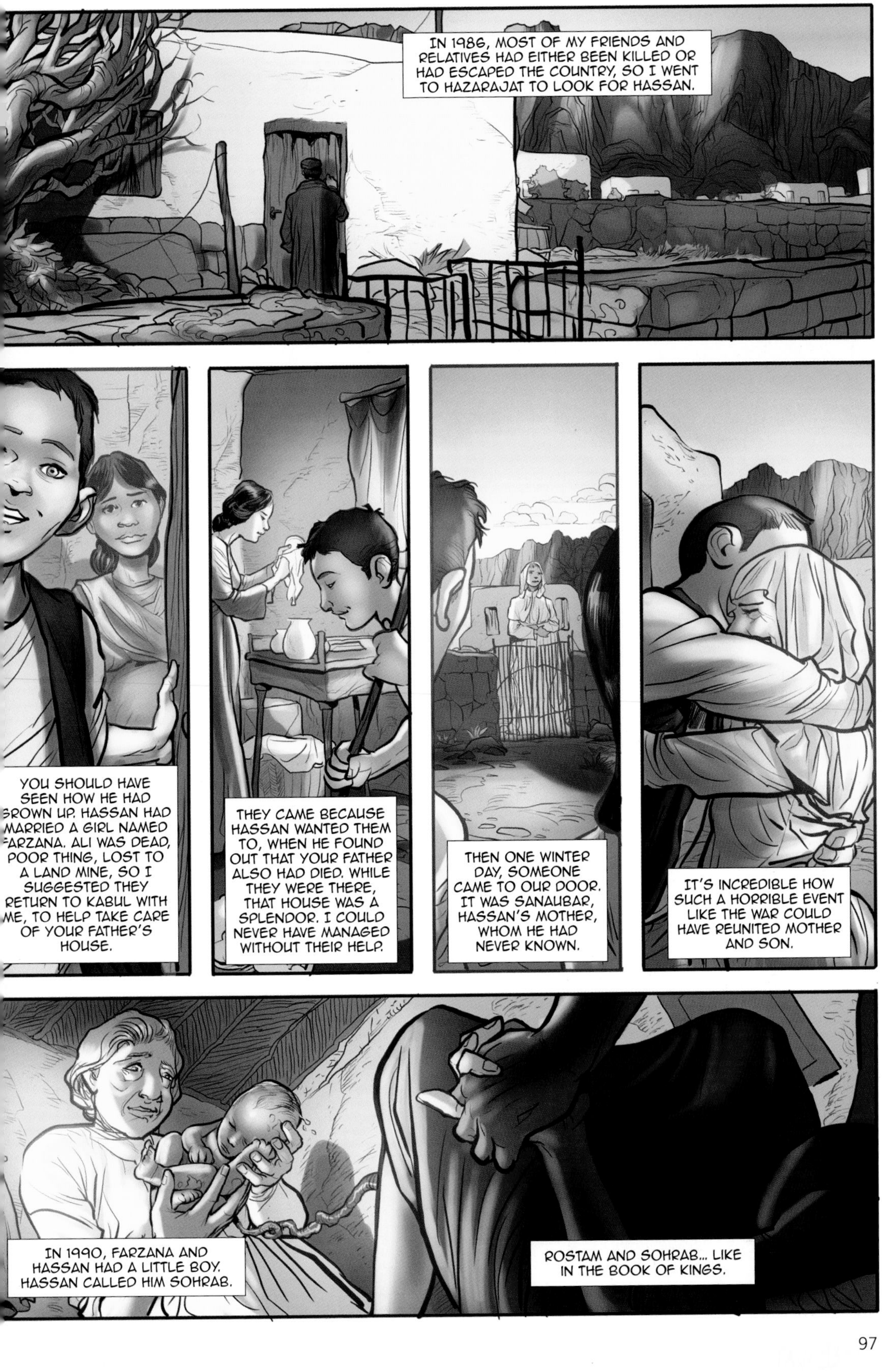
IN 1986, MOST OF MY FRIENDS AND RELATIVES HAD EITHER BEEN KILLED OR HAD ESCAPED THE COUNTRY, SO I WENT TO HAZARAJAT TO LOOK FOR HASSAN.
YOU SHOULD HAVE SEEN HOW HE HAD GROWN UP. HASSAN HAD MARRIED A GIRL NAMED FARZANA. ALI WAS DEAD, POOR THING, LOST TO A LAND MINE, SO I SUGGESTED THEY RETURN TO KABUL WITH ME, TO HELP TAKE CARE OF YOUR FATHER'S HOUSE.
THEY CAME BECAUSE HASSAN WANTED THEM TO, WHEN HE FOUND OUT THAT YOUR FATHER ALSO HAD DIED. WHILE THEY WERE THERE, THAT HOUSE WAS A SPLENDOR. I COULD NEVER HAVE MANAGED WITHOUT THEIR HELP.
THEN ONE WINTER DAY, SOMEONE CAME TO OUR DOOR. IT WAS SANAUBAR, HASSAN'S MOTHER, WHOM HE HAD NEVER KNOWN.
IT'S INCREDIBLE HOW SUCH A HORRIBLE EVENT LIKE THE WAR COULD HAVE REUNITED MOTHER AND SON.
IN 1990, FARZANA AND HASSAN HAD A LITTLE BOY. HASSAN CALLED HIM SOHRAB.
ROSTAM AND SOHRAB... LIKE IN THE BOOK OF KINGS.

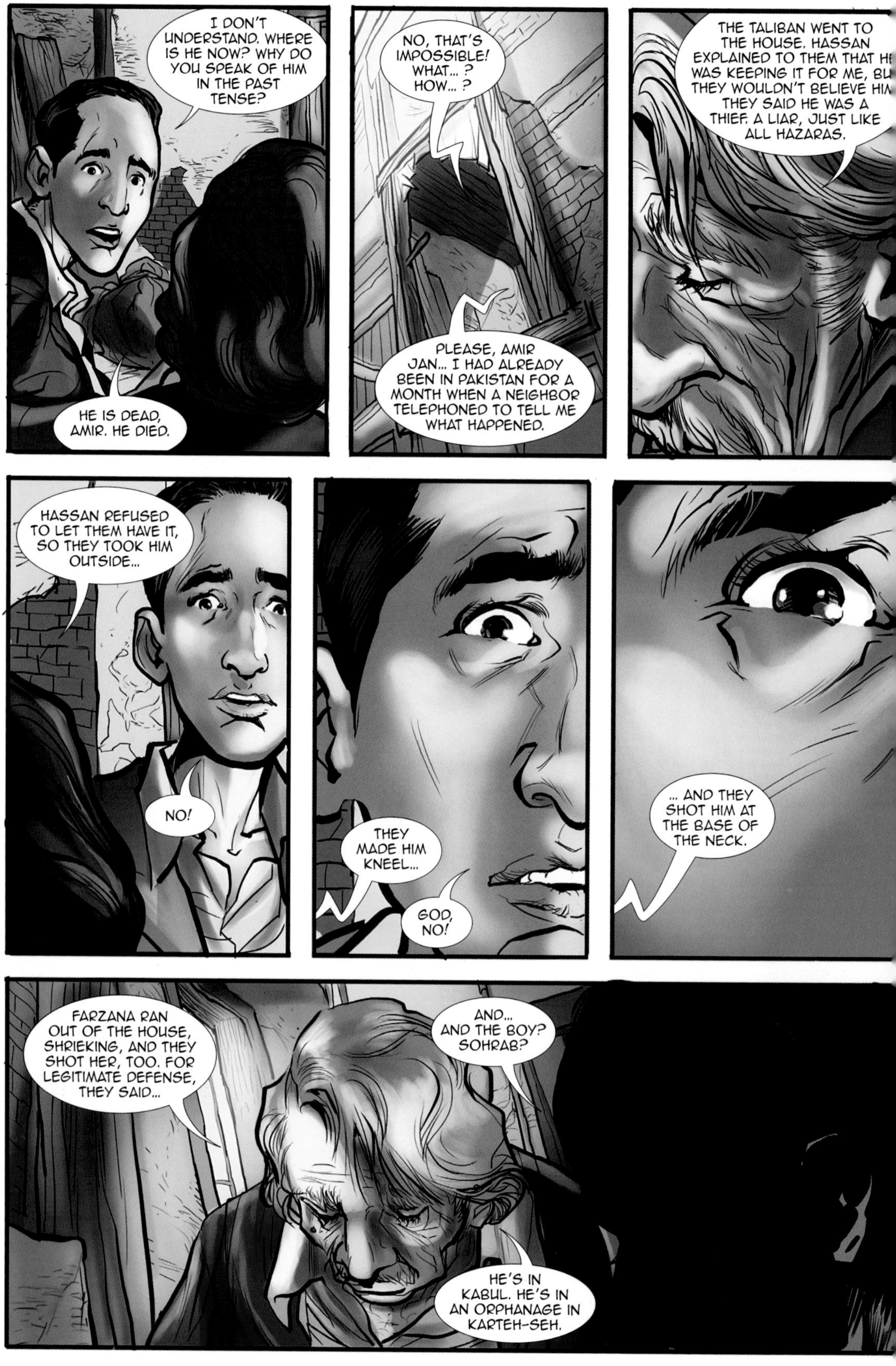

I DON'T UNDERSTAND. WHERE IS HE NOW? WHY DO YOU SPEAK OF HIM IN THE PAST TENSE?
HE IS DEAD, AMIR. HE DIED.
NO, THAT'S IMPOSSIBLE! WHAT... ? HOW... ?
PLEASE, AMIR JAN... I HAD ALREADY BEEN IN PAKISTAN FOR A MONTH WHEN A NEIGHBOR TELEPHONED TO TELL ME WHAT HAPPENED.
THE TALIBAN WENT TO THE HOUSE. HASSAN EXPLAINED TO THEM THAT HE WAS KEEPING IT FOR ME, BUT THEY WOULDN'T BELIEVE HIM. THEY SAID HE WAS A THIEF. A LIAR, JUST LIKE ALL HAZARAS.
HASSAN REFUSED TO LET THEM HAVE IT, SO THEY TOOK HIM OUTSIDE...
NO!
THEY MADE HIM KNEEL...
GOD, NO!
... AND THEY SHOT HIM AT THE BASE OF THE NECK.
FARZANA RAN OUT OF THE HOUSE, SHRIEKING, AND THEY SHOT HER, TOO. FOR LEGITIMATE DEFENSE, THEY SAID...
AND... AND THE BOY? SOHRAB?
HE'S IN KABUL. HE'S IN AN ORPHANAGE IN KARTEH-SEH.

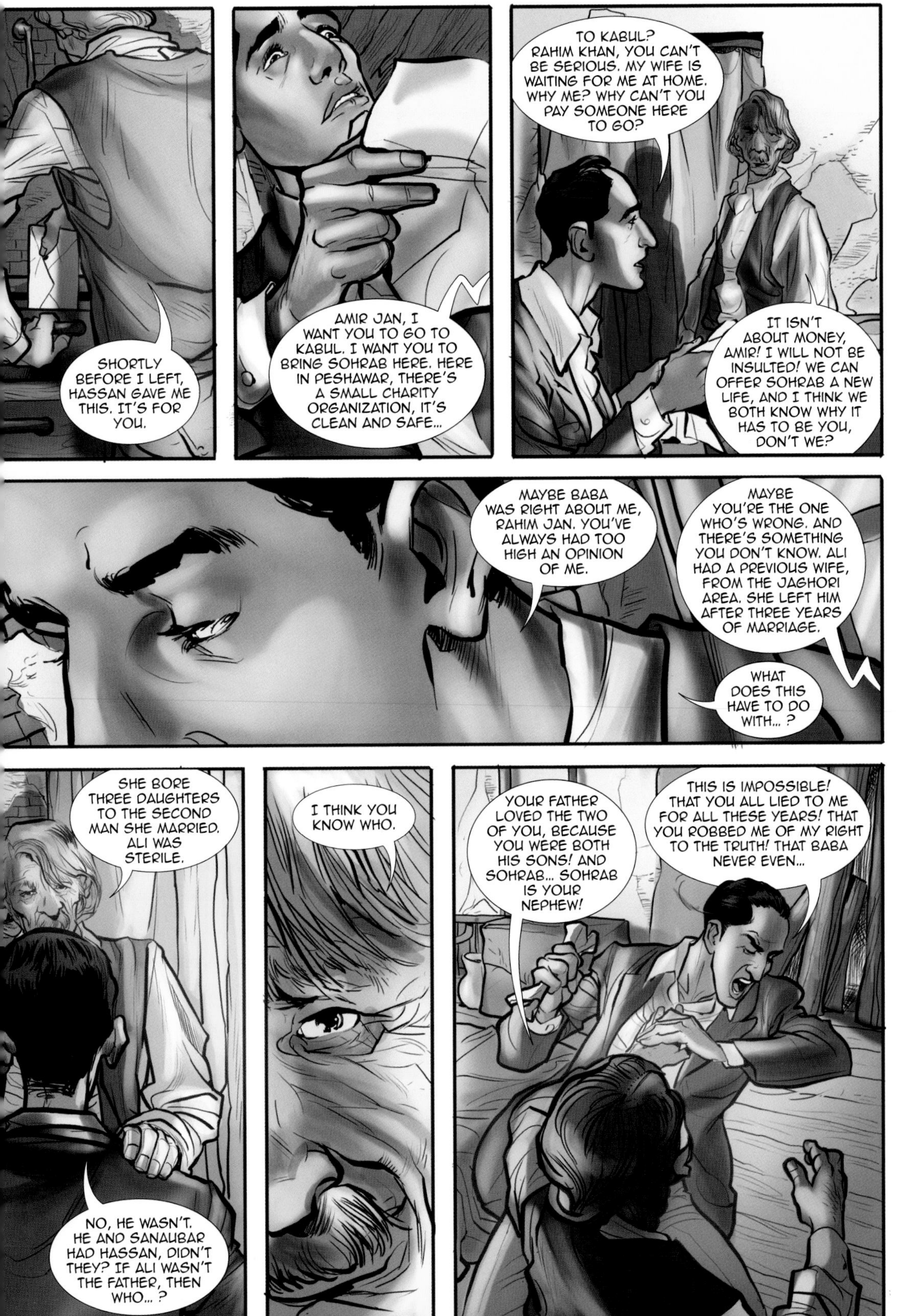
SHORTLY BEFORE I LEFT, HASSAN GAVE ME THIS. IT'S FOR YOU.
AMIR JAN, I WANT YOU TO GO TO KABUL. I WANT YOU TO BRING SOHRAB HERE. HERE IN PESHAWAR, THERE'S A SMALL CHARITY ORGANIZATION, IT'S CLEAN AND SAFE...
TO KABUL? RAHIM KHAN, YOU CAN'T BE SERIOUS. MY WIFE IS WAITING FOR ME AT HOME. WHY ME? WHY CAN'T YOU PAY SOMEONE HERE TO GO?
IT ISN'T ABOUT MONEY, AMIR! I WILL NOT BE INSULTED! WE CAN OFFER SOHRAB A NEW LIFE, AND I THINK WE BOTH KNOW WHY IT HAS TO BE YOU, DON'T WE?
MAYBE BABA WAS RIGHT ABOUT ME, RAHIM JAN. YOU'VE ALWAYS HAD TOO HIGH AN OPINION OF ME.
MAYBE YOU'RE THE ONE WHO'S WRONG. AND THERE'S SOMETHING YOU DON'T KNOW. ALI HAD A PREVIOUS WIFE, FROM THE JAGHORI AREA. SHE LEFT HIM AFTER THREE YEARS OF MARRIAGE.
WHAT DOES THIS HAVE TO DO WITH... ?
SHE BORE THREE DAUGHTERS TO THE SECOND MAN SHE MARRIED. ALI WAS STERILE.
NO, HE WASN'T. HE AND SANAUBAR HAD HASSAN, DIDN'T THEY? IF ALI WASN'T THE FATHER, THEN WHO... ?
I THINK YOU KNOW WHO.
YOUR FATHER LOVED THE TWO OF YOU, BECAUSE YOU WERE BOTH HIS SONS! AND SOHRAB... SOHRAB IS YOUR NEPHEW!
THIS IS IMPOSSIBLE! THAT YOU ALL LIED TO ME FOR ALL THESE YEARS! THAT YOU ROBBED ME OF MY RIGHT TO THE TRUTH! THAT BABA NEVER EVEN...

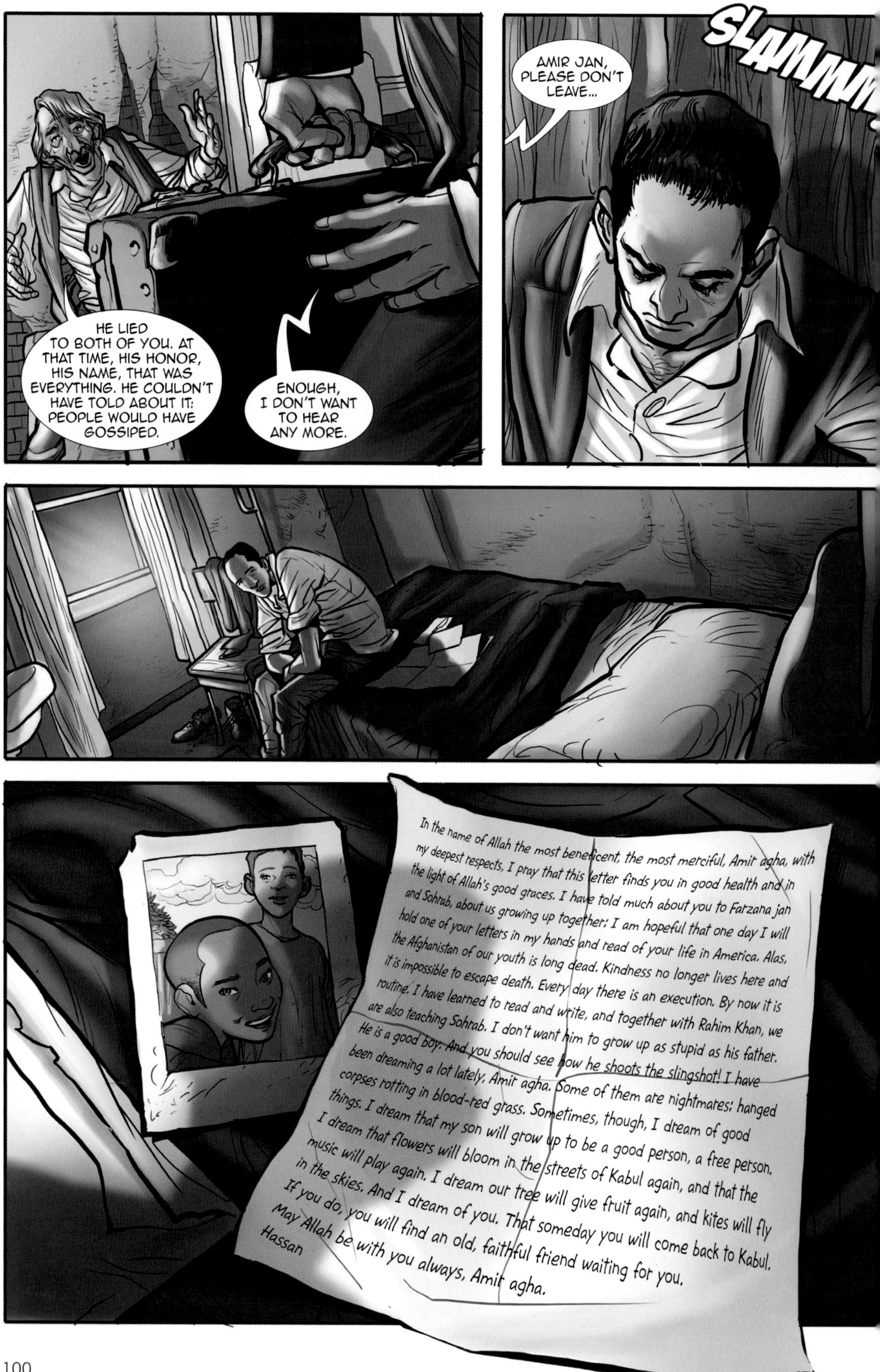
HE LIED TO BOTH OF YOU. AT THAT TIME, HIS HONOR, HIS NAME, THAT WAS EVERYTHING. HE COULDN'T HAVE TOLD ABOUT IT: PEOPLE WOULD HAVE GOSSIPED.
ENOUGH, I DON'T WANT TO HEAR ANY MORE.
AMIR JAN, PLEASE DON'T LEAVE...
SLAMMM
In the name of Allah the most beneficent, the most merciful, Amir agha, with my deepest respects, I pray that this letter finds you in good health and in the light of Allah's good graces. I have told much about you to Farzana jan and Sohrab, about us growing up together; I am hopeful that one day I will hold one of your letters in my hands and read of your life in America. Alas, the Afghanistan of our youth is long dead. Kindness no longer lives here and it is impossible to escape death. Every day there is an execution. By now it is routine. I have learned to read and write, and together with Rahim Khan, we are also teaching Sohrab. I don't want him to grow up as stupid as his father. He is a good boy. And you should see how he shoots the slingshot! I have been dreaming a lot lately, Amir agha. Some of them are nightmares; hanged corpses rotting in blood-red grass. Sometimes, though, I dream of good things. I dream that my son will grow up to be a good person, a free person. I dream that flowers will bloom in the streets of Kabul again, and that the music will play again. I dream our tree will give fruit again, and kites will fly in the skies. And I dream of you. That someday you will come back to Kabul. If you do, you will find an old, faithful friend waiting for you. May Allah be with you always, Amir agha.
Hassan

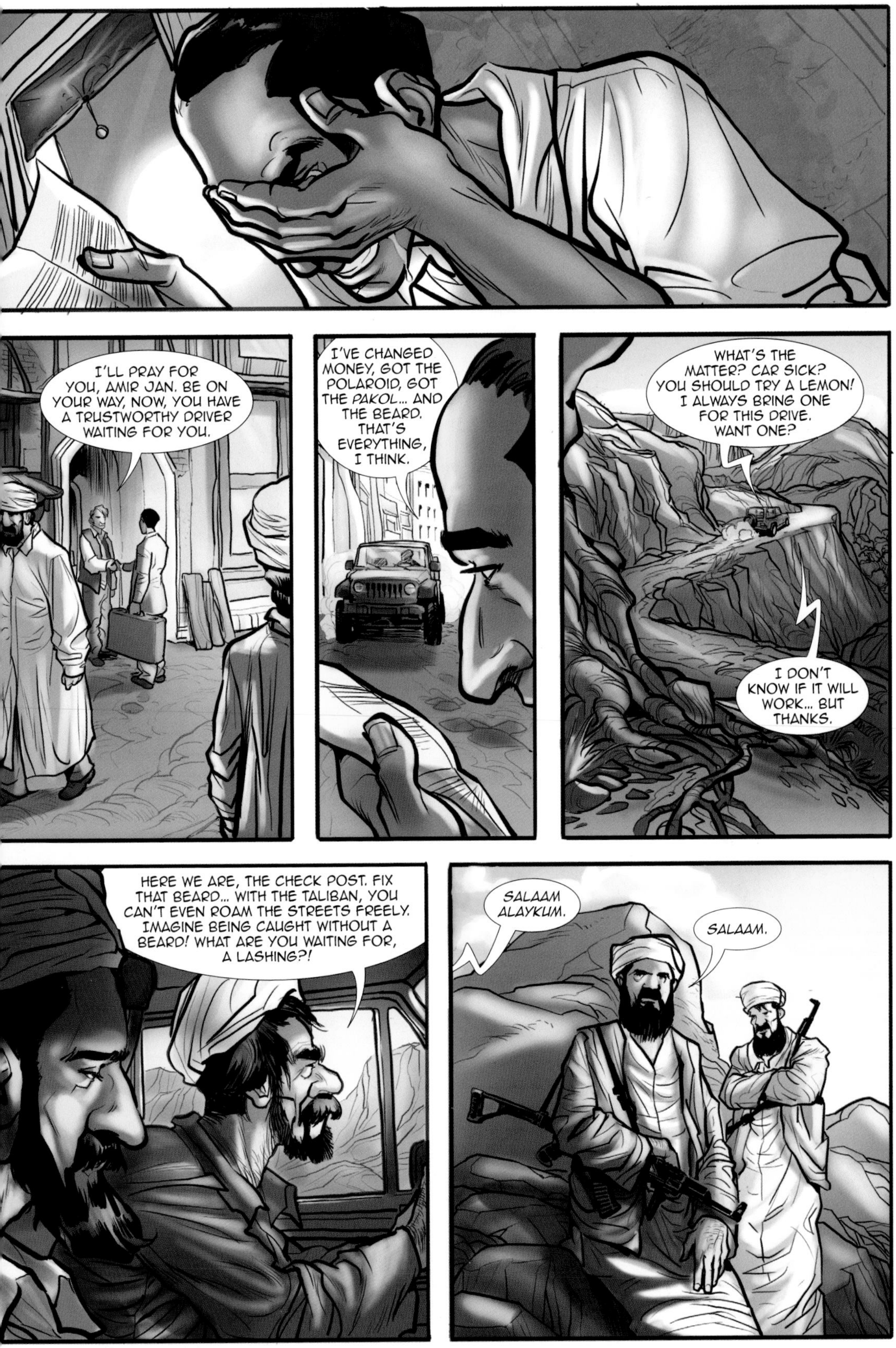
I'LL PRAY FOR YOU, AMIR JAN. BE ON YOUR WAY, NOW, YOU HAVE A TRUSTWORTHY DRIVER WAITING FOR YOU.
I'VE CHANGED MONEY, GOT THE POLAROID, GOT THE *PAKOL*... AND THE BEARD. THAT'S EVERYTHING, I THINK.
WHAT'S THE MATTER? CAR SICK? YOU SHOULD TRY A LEMON! I ALWAYS BRING ONE FOR THIS DRIVE. WANT ONE?
I DON'T KNOW IF IT WILL WORK... BUT THANKS.
HERE WE ARE, THE CHECK POST. FIX THAT BEARD... WITH THE TALIBAN, YOU CAN'T EVEN ROAM THE STREETS FREELY. IMAGINE BEING CAUGHT WITHOUT A BEARD! WHAT ARE YOU WAITING FOR, A LASHING?!
SALAAM ALAYKUM.
SALAAM.

WHY SUCH A FRIGHTENED FACE, MR. AMIR?

IT'S... IT'S JUST THAT... I DON'T...

NOT USED TO IT? IF YOU WANT TO SURVIVE, YOU HAVE TO STOP BEING AFRAID: AN AFGHAN WHO IS AFRAID OF DYING IS AN AFGHAN WHO IS ALREADY DEAD... HE JUST DOESN'T KNOW IT YET.

WHAT ARE YOU SAYING, I'M NOT A REAL AFGHAN? I WAS RAISED HERE, EVEN IF I DID LEAVE TWENTY YEARS AGO.

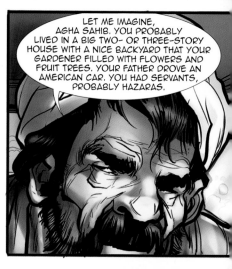

LET ME IMAGINE, AGHA SAHIB. YOU PROBABLY LIVED IN A BIG TWO- OR THREE-STORY HOUSE WITH A NICE BACKYARD THAT YOUR GARDENER FILLED WITH FLOWERS AND FRUIT TREES. YOUR FATHER DROVE AN AMERICAN CAR. YOU HAD SERVANTS, PROBABLY HAZARAS.

THAT'S NOT THE REAL AFGHANISTAN, AGHA SAHIB. YOU'VE ALWAYS BEEN A TOURIST HERE, YOU JUST DIDN'T KNOW IT.

YOU'RE A WRITER? MAYBE YOU SHOULD TELL THE REST OF THE WORLD WHAT THE TALIBAN ARE DOING TO OUR COUNTRY.

NO, I... WRITE STORIES. NOVELS. THE LAST ONE IS CALLED A SEASON FOR ASHES.

PFFF... AND WHAT BRINGS YOU BACK HERE? SELL THIS LAND, SELL THAT HOUSE, COLLECT THE MONEY, AND RUN AWAY LIKE A MOUSE, RIGHT?

BAS! IS THAT HOW YOU TREAT A GUEST, MY BROTHER? EXCUSE US, AGHA SAHIB.

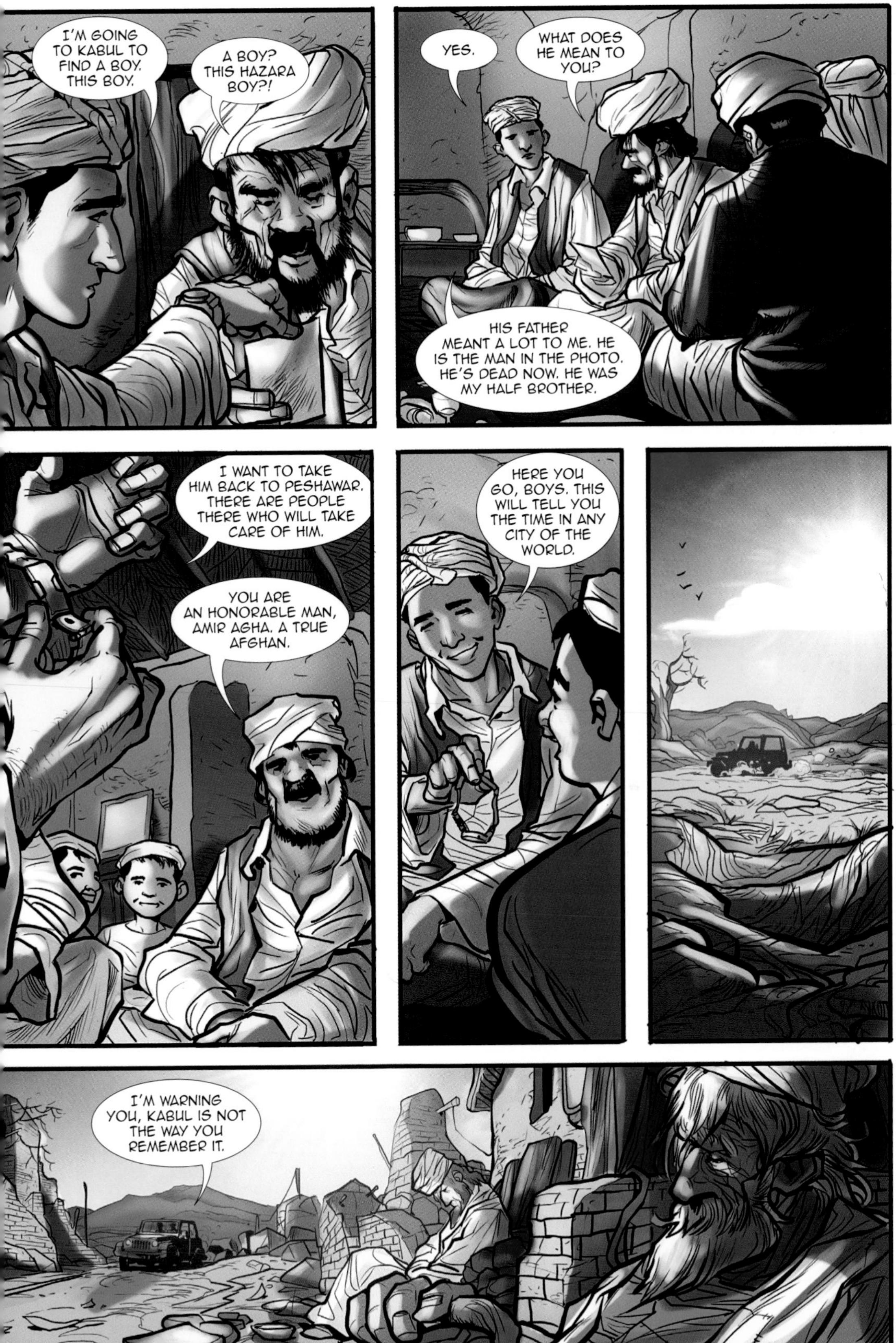
I'M GOING TO KABUL TO FIND A BOY. THIS BOY.
A BOY? THIS HAZARA BOY?!
YES.
WHAT DOES HE MEAN TO YOU?
HIS FATHER MEANT A LOT TO ME. HE IS THE MAN IN THE PHOTO. HE'S DEAD NOW. HE WAS MY HALF BROTHER.
I WANT TO TAKE HIM BACK TO PESHAWAR. THERE ARE PEOPLE THERE WHO WILL TAKE CARE OF HIM.
YOU ARE AN HONORABLE MAN, AMIR AGHA. A TRUE AFGHAN.
HERE YOU GO, BOYS. THIS WILL TELL YOU THE TIME IN ANY CITY OF THE WORLD.
I'M WARNING YOU, KABUL IS NOT THE WAY YOU REMEMBER IT.

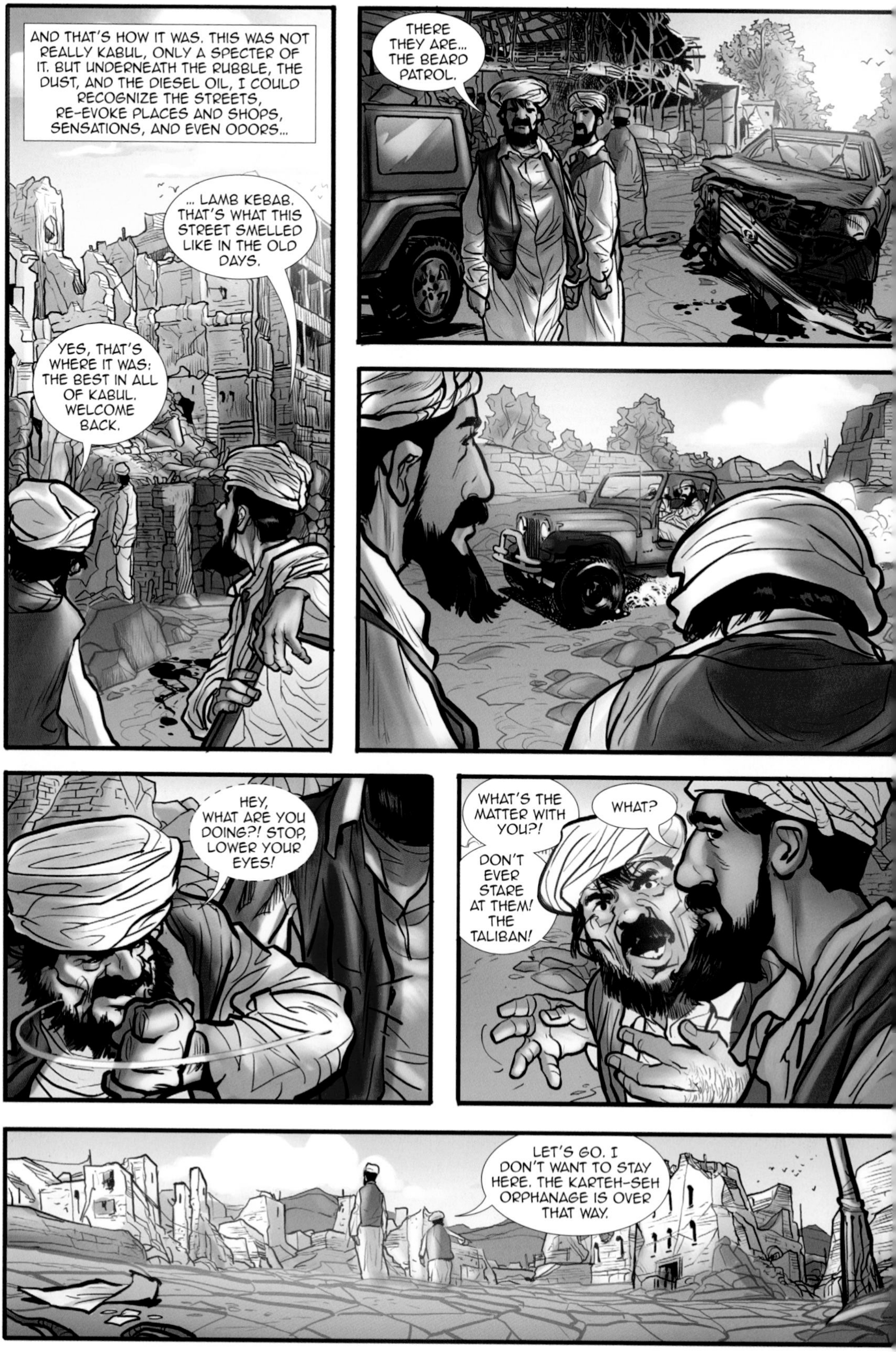
AND THAT'S HOW IT WAS. THIS WAS NOT REALLY KABUL, ONLY A SPECTER OF IT. BUT UNDERNEATH THE RUBBLE, THE DUST, AND THE DIESEL OIL, I COULD RECOGNIZE THE STREETS, RE-EVOKE PLACES AND SHOPS, SENSATIONS, AND EVEN ODORS...
... LAMB KEBAB. THAT'S WHAT THIS STREET SMELLED LIKE IN THE OLD DAYS.
YES, THAT'S WHERE IT WAS: THE BEST IN ALL OF KABUL. WELCOME BACK.
THERE THEY ARE... THE BEARD PATROL.
HEY, WHAT ARE YOU DOING?! STOP, LOWER YOUR EYES!
WHAT'S THE MATTER WITH YOU?!
WHAT?
DON'T EVER STARE AT THEM! THE TALIBAN!
LET'S GO. I DON'T WANT TO STAY HERE. THE KARTEH-SEH ORPHANAGE IS OVER THAT WAY.

SALAAM ALAYKUM.

ALAYKUM SALAAM.

WE'RE SEARCHING FOR THIS BOY.

I AM SORRY. I HAVE NEVER SEEN HIM.

WHY NOT TAKE A CLOSER LOOK?

I KNOW ALL THE CHILDREN IN THE ORPHANAGE, AND I'VE NEVER SEEN THAT ONE.

LOTFAN. PLEASE. HIS NAME IS SOHRAB. HIS FATHER HASSAN WAS MY BROTHER. HE KNOWS HOW TO READ AND WRITE. AND HE'S GOOD WITH THE SLINGSHOT. I'M HIS UNCLE... I CAN TAKE HIM WITH ME TO PAKISTAN!

YOU WERE WRONG ABOUT ONE THING. HE'S NOT GOOD WITH THE SLINGSHOT, HE'S GREAT. I'LL TAKE YOU TO MY OFFICE.

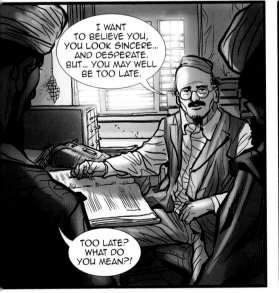

I WANT TO BELIEVE YOU, YOU LOOK SINCERE... AND DESPERATE. BUT... YOU MAY WELL BE TOO LATE.

TOO LATE? WHAT DO YOU MEAN?!

THERE IS A TALIB OFFICIAL. HE VISITS ONCE EVERY MONTH OR TWO. HE BRINGS CASH WITH HIM, NOT A LOT... BUT BETTER THAN NOTHING AT ALL.

USUALLY HE'LL TAKE A GIRL. BUT NOT ALWAYS.

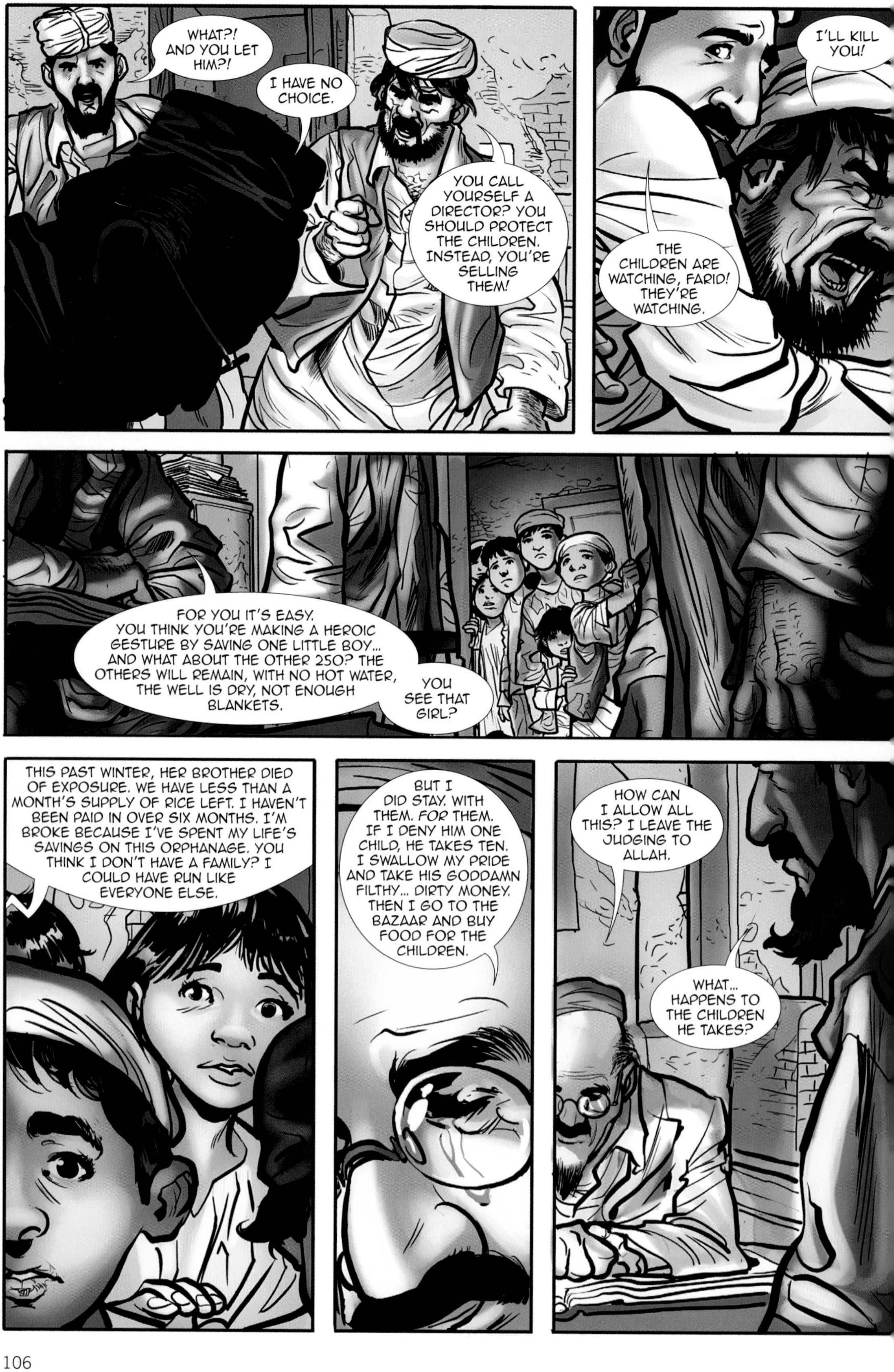
WHAT?! AND YOU LET HIM?!
I HAVE NO CHOICE.
YOU CALL YOURSELF A DIRECTOR? YOU SHOULD PROTECT THE CHILDREN. INSTEAD, YOU'RE SELLING THEM!
I'LL KILL YOU!
THE CHILDREN ARE WATCHING, FARID! THEY'RE WATCHING.
FOR YOU IT'S EASY. YOU THINK YOU'RE MAKING A HEROIC GESTURE BY SAVING ONE LITTLE BOY... AND WHAT ABOUT THE OTHER 250? THE OTHERS WILL REMAIN, WITH NO HOT WATER, THE WELL IS DRY, NOT ENOUGH BLANKETS.
YOU SEE THAT GIRL?
THIS PAST WINTER, HER BROTHER DIED OF EXPOSURE. WE HAVE LESS THAN A MONTH'S SUPPLY OF RICE LEFT. I HAVEN'T BEEN PAID IN OVER SIX MONTHS. I'M BROKE BECAUSE I'VE SPENT MY LIFE'S SAVINGS ON THIS ORPHANAGE. YOU THINK I DON'T HAVE A FAMILY? I COULD HAVE RUN LIKE EVERYONE ELSE.
BUT I DID STAY. WITH THEM. *FOR* THEM. IF I DENY HIM ONE CHILD, HE TAKES TEN. I SWALLOW MY PRIDE AND TAKE HIS GODDAMN FILTHY... DIRTY MONEY. THEN I GO TO THE BAZAAR AND BUY FOOD FOR THE CHILDREN.
HOW CAN I ALLOW ALL THIS? I LEAVE THE JUDGING TO ALLAH.
WHAT... HAPPENS TO THE CHILDREN HE TAKES?

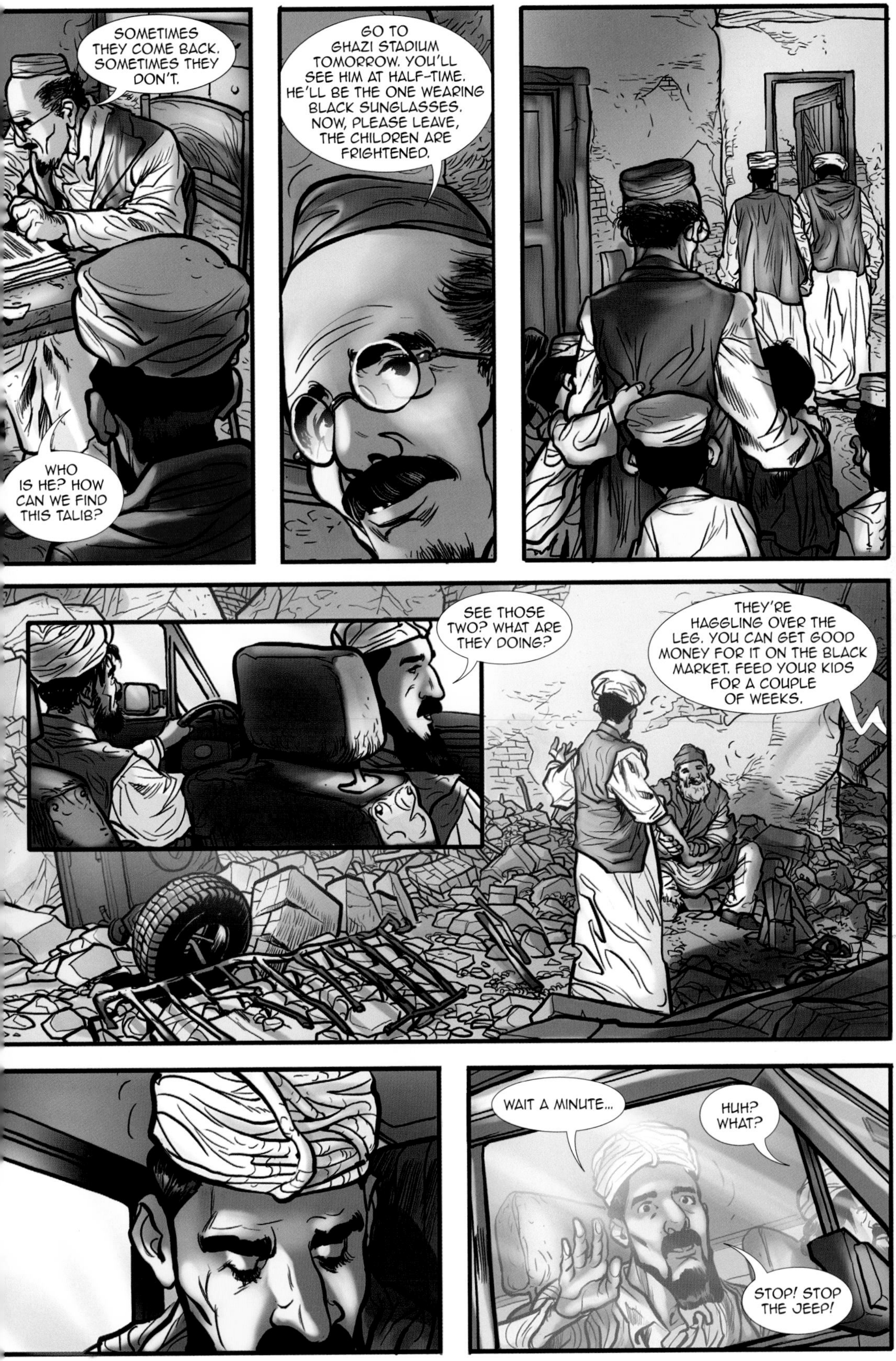
SOMETIMES THEY COME BACK. SOMETIMES THEY DON'T.
WHO IS HE? HOW CAN WE FIND THIS TALIB?
GO TO GHAZI STADIUM TOMORROW. YOU'LL SEE HIM AT HALF-TIME. HE'LL BE THE ONE WEARING BLACK SUNGLASSES. NOW, PLEASE LEAVE, THE CHILDREN ARE FRIGHTENED.
SEE THOSE TWO? WHAT ARE THEY DOING?
THEY'RE HAGGLING OVER THE LEG. YOU CAN GET GOOD MONEY FOR IT ON THE BLACK MARKET. FEED YOUR KIDS FOR A COUPLE OF WEEKS.
WAIT A MINUTE...
HUH? WHAT?
STOP! STOP THE JEEP!

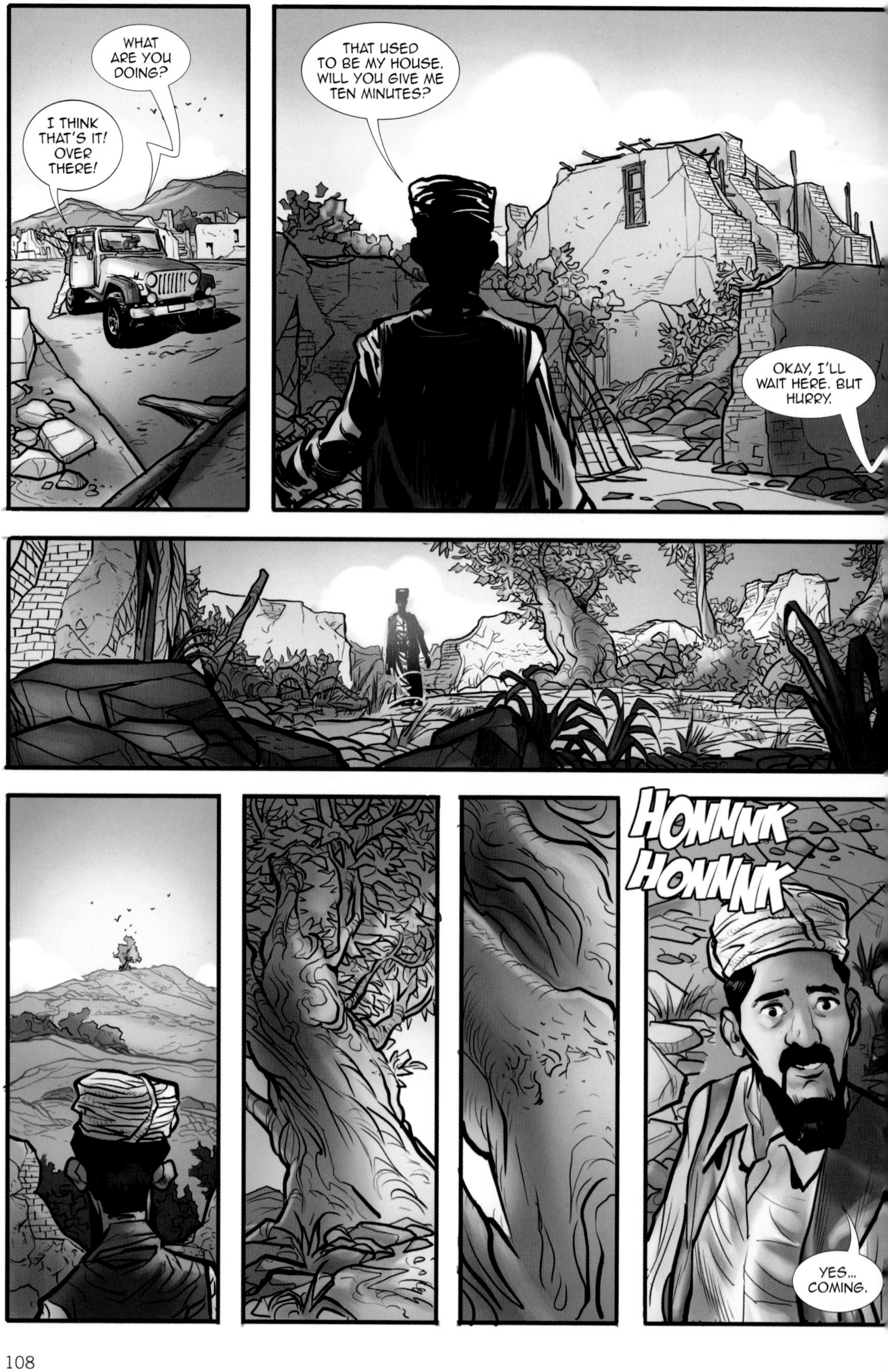
I THINK THAT'S IT! OVER THERE!
WHAT ARE YOU DOING?
THAT USED TO BE MY HOUSE. WILL YOU GIVE ME TEN MINUTES?
OKAY, I'LL WAIT HERE. BUT HURRY.
HONNNK HONNNK
YES... COMING.

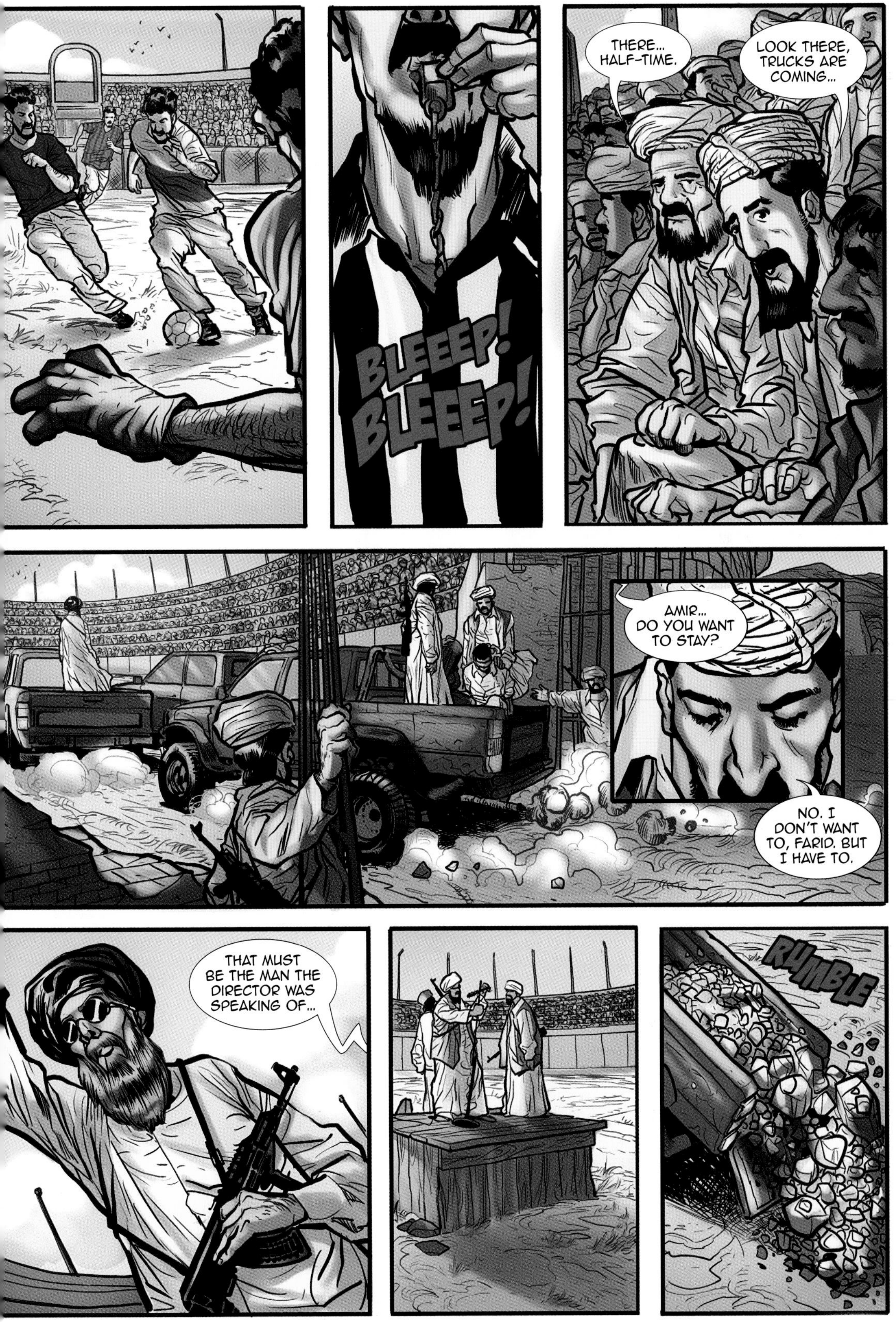
BLEEEP! BLEEEP!
THERE... HALF-TIME.
LOOK THERE, TRUCKS ARE COMING...
AMIR... DO YOU WANT TO STAY?
NO. I DON'T WANT TO, FARID. BUT I HAVE TO.
THAT MUST BE THE MAN THE DIRECTOR WAS SPEAKING OF...
RUMBLE

BROTHERS AND SISTERS! WE ARE HERE TODAY TO CARRY OUT *SHARI'A*. TO CARRY OUT JUSTICE. WE LISTEN TO WHAT GOD SAYS.

AND WHAT DOES GOD SAY? THAT EVERY SINNER MUST BE PUNISHED IN A MANNER BEFITTING HIS SIN. IT IS NOT I, NOR MY BROTHERS, WHO SAY THESE WORDS, BUT GOD HIMSELF!

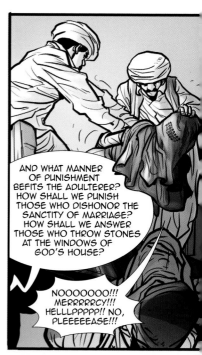

AND WHAT MANNER OF PUNISHMENT BEFITS THE ADULTERER? HOW SHALL WE PUNISH THOSE WHO DISHONOR THE SANCTITY OF MARRIAGE? HOW SHALL WE ANSWER THOSE WHO THROW STONES AT THE WINDOWS OF GOD'S HOUSE?

NOOOOOOO!!! MERRRRCY!!! HELLLPPPPP!! NO, PLEEEEEASE!!!

WE SHALL THROW THE STONES BACK!

CRACK

THUMP

CRACK

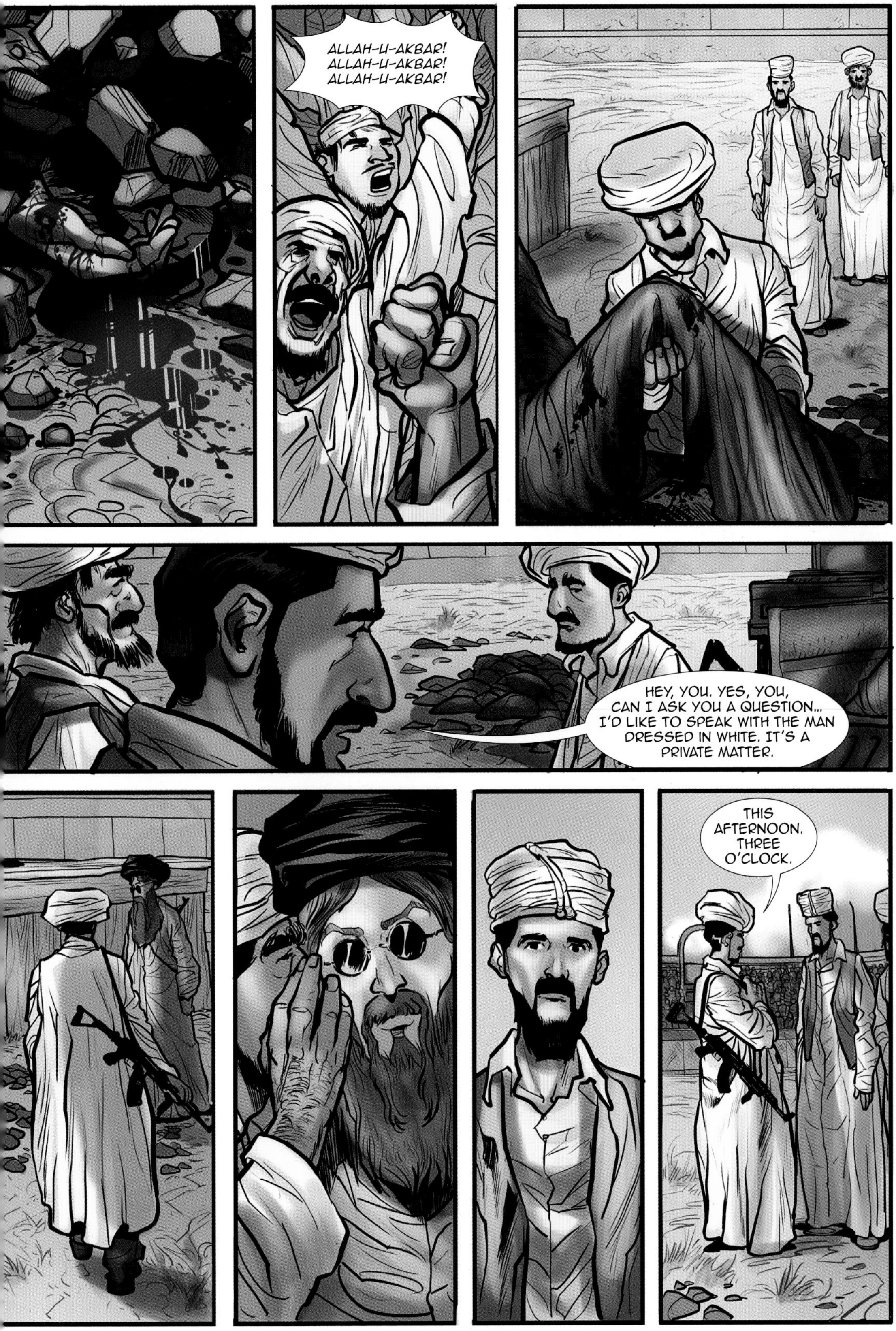
ALLAH-U-AKBAR! ALLAH-U-AKBAR! ALLAH-U-AKBAR!
HEY, YOU. YES, YOU, CAN I ASK YOU A QUESTION... I'D LIKE TO SPEAK WITH THE MAN DRESSED IN WHITE. IT'S A PRIVATE MATTER.
THIS AFTERNOON. THREE O'CLOCK.

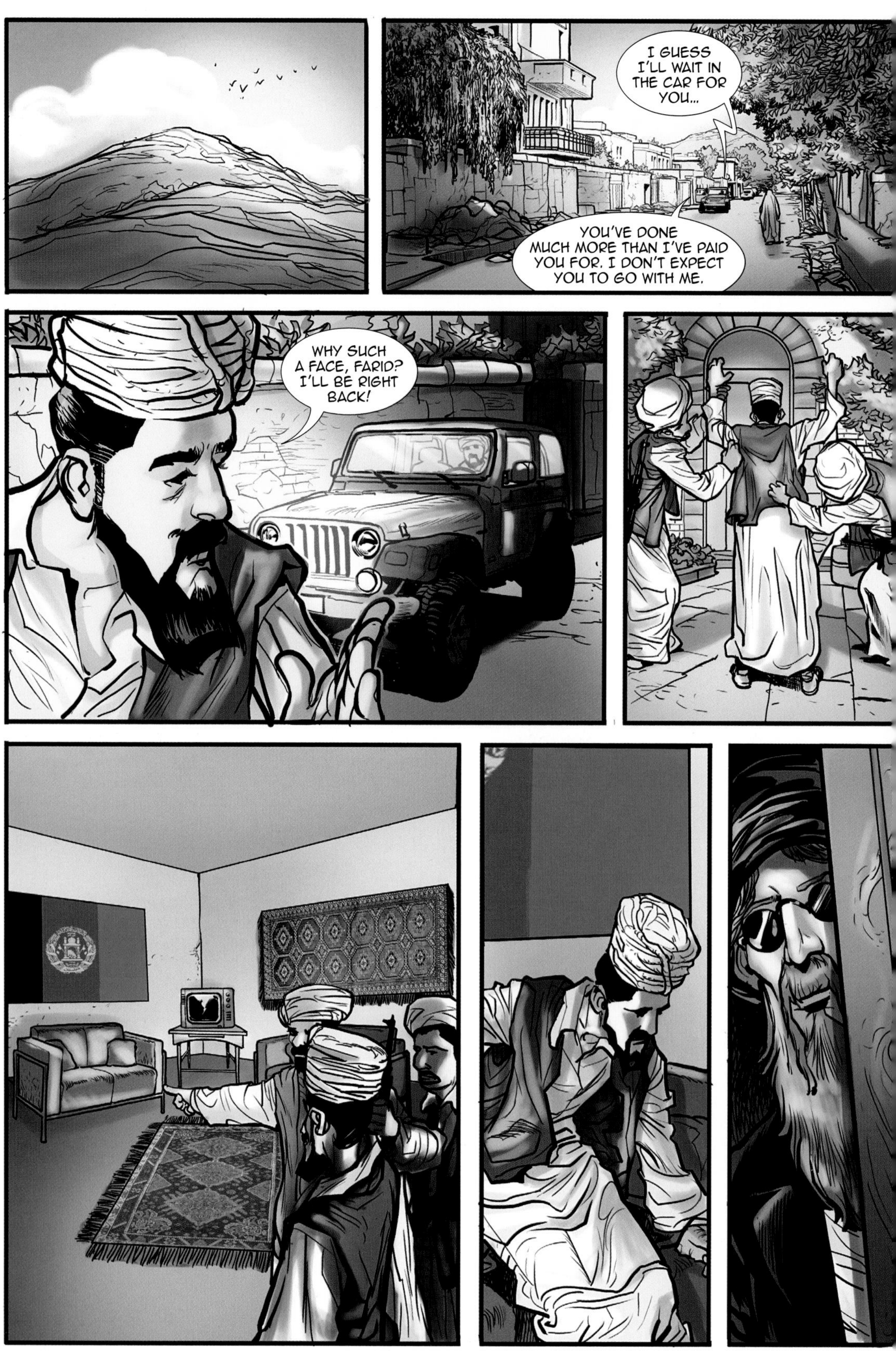
I GUESS I'LL WAIT IN THE CAR FOR YOU...
YOU'VE DONE MUCH MORE THAN I'VE PAID YOU FOR. I DON'T EXPECT YOU TO GO WITH ME.
WHY SUCH A FACE, FARID? I'LL BE RIGHT BACK!

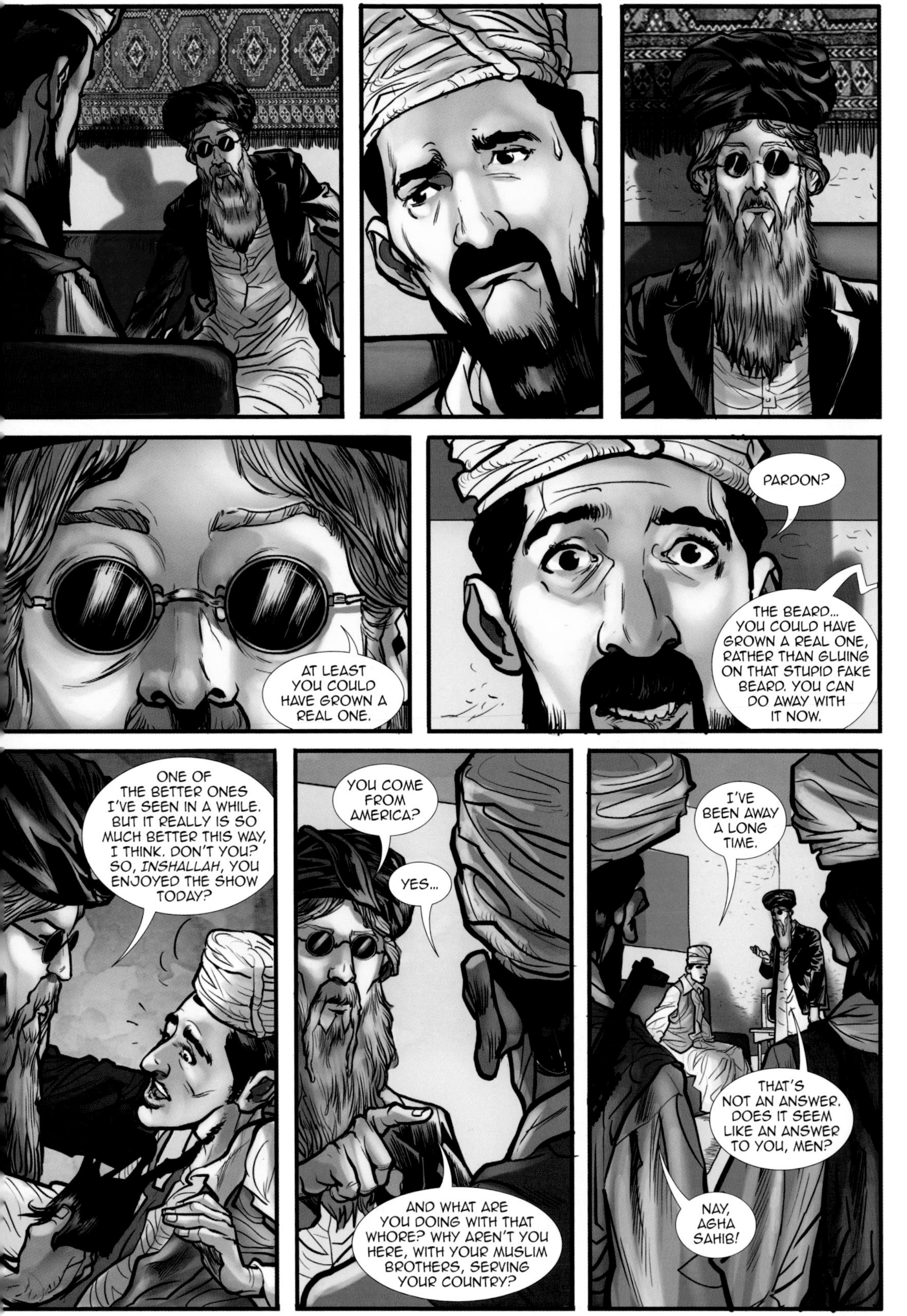
AT LEAST YOU COULD HAVE GROWN A REAL ONE.
PARDON?
THE BEARD... YOU COULD HAVE GROWN A REAL ONE, RATHER THAN GLUING ON THAT STUPID FAKE BEARD. YOU CAN DO AWAY WITH IT NOW.
ONE OF THE BETTER ONES I'VE SEEN IN A WHILE. BUT IT REALLY IS SO MUCH BETTER THIS WAY, I THINK. DON'T YOU? SO, *INSHALLAH*, YOU ENJOYED THE SHOW TODAY?
YOU COME FROM AMERICA?
YES...
AND WHAT ARE YOU DOING WITH THAT WHORE? WHY AREN'T YOU HERE, WITH YOUR MUSLIM BROTHERS, SERVING YOUR COUNTRY?
I'VE BEEN AWAY A LONG TIME.
THAT'S NOT AN ANSWER. DOES IT SEEM LIKE AN ANSWER TO YOU, MEN?
NAY, AGHA SAHIB!

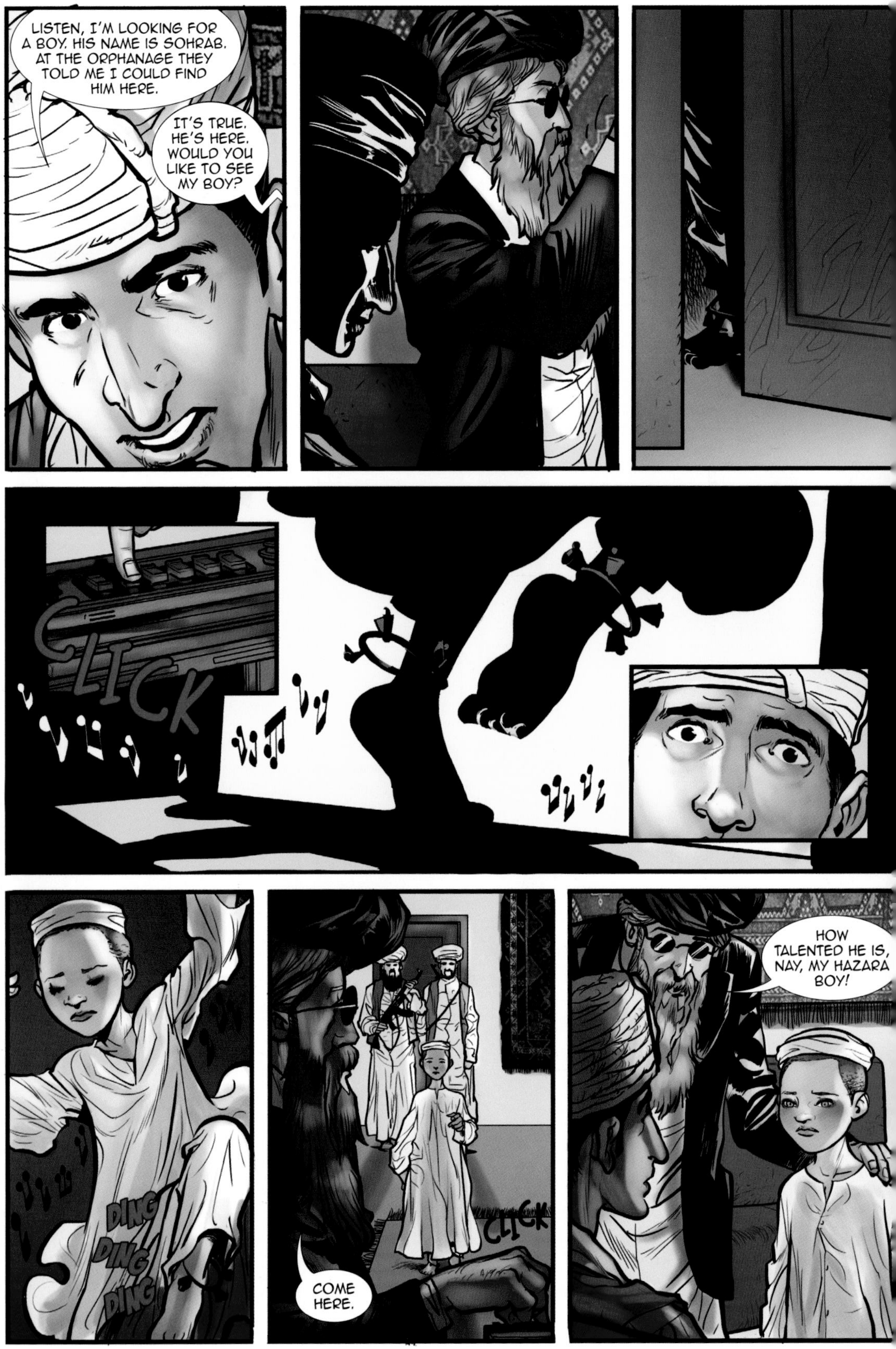
LISTEN, I'M LOOKING FOR A BOY. HIS NAME IS SOHRAB. AT THE ORPHANAGE THEY TOLD ME I COULD FIND HIM HERE.
IT'S TRUE. HE'S HERE. WOULD YOU LIKE TO SEE MY BOY?
CLICK
DING
DING
DING
CLICK
COME HERE.
HOW TALENTED HE IS, NAY, MY HAZARA BOY!

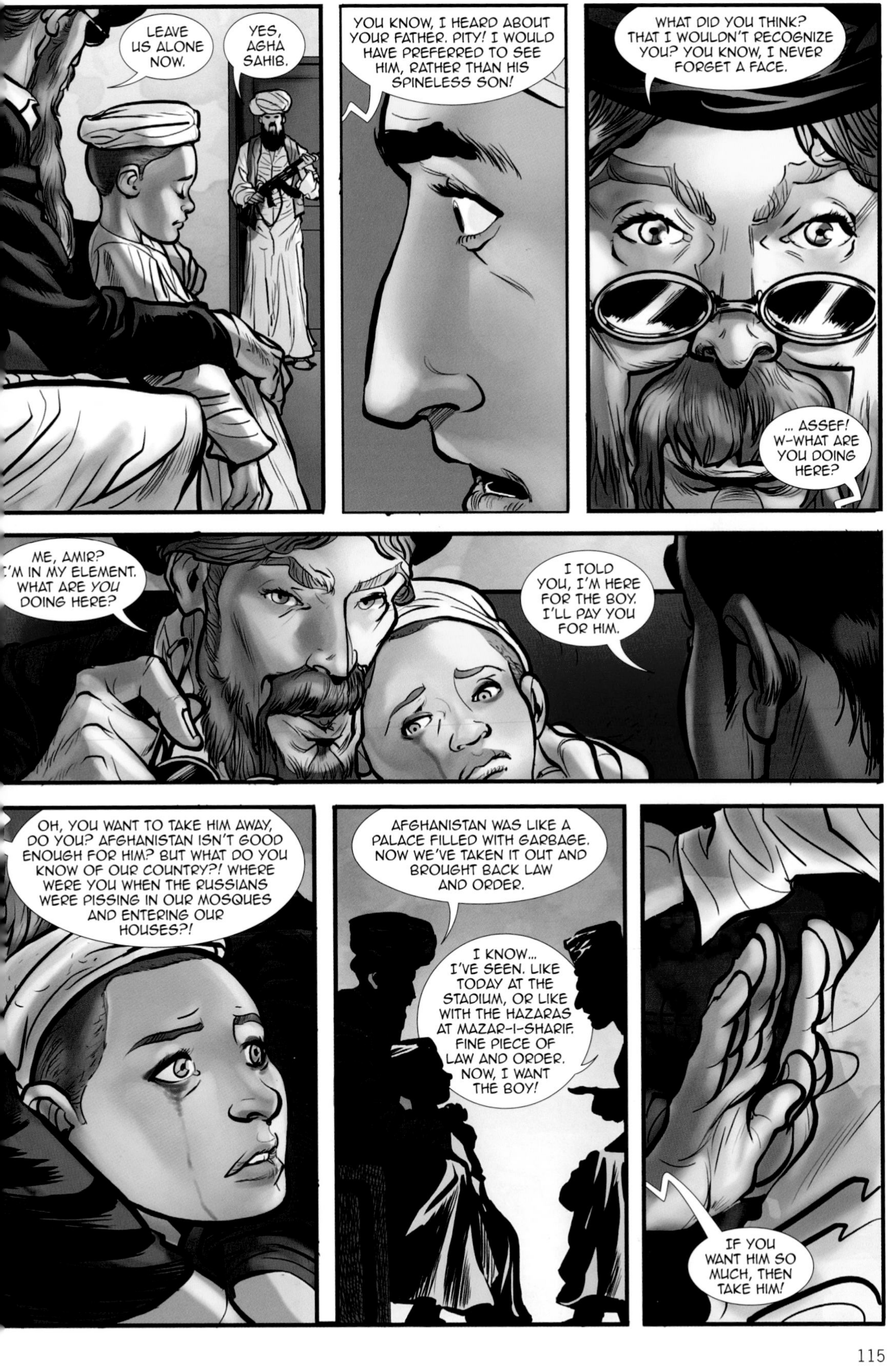
LEAVE US ALONE NOW.
YES, AGHA SAHIB.
YOU KNOW, I HEARD ABOUT YOUR FATHER. PITY! I WOULD HAVE PREFERRED TO SEE HIM, RATHER THAN HIS SPINELESS SON!
WHAT DID YOU THINK? THAT I WOULDN'T RECOGNIZE YOU? YOU KNOW, I NEVER FORGET A FACE.
... ASSEF! W-WHAT ARE YOU DOING HERE?
ME, AMIR? I'M IN MY ELEMENT. WHAT ARE *YOU* DOING HERE?
I TOLD YOU, I'M HERE FOR THE BOY. I'LL PAY YOU FOR HIM.
OH, YOU WANT TO TAKE HIM AWAY, DO YOU? AFGHANISTAN ISN'T GOOD ENOUGH FOR HIM? BUT WHAT DO YOU KNOW OF OUR COUNTRY?! WHERE WERE YOU WHEN THE RUSSIANS WERE PISSING IN OUR MOSQUES AND ENTERING OUR HOUSES?!
AFGHANISTAN WAS LIKE A PALACE FILLED WITH GARBAGE. NOW WE'VE TAKEN IT OUT AND BROUGHT BACK LAW AND ORDER.
I KNOW... I'VE SEEN. LIKE TODAY AT THE STADIUM, OR LIKE WITH THE HAZARAS AT MAZAR-I-SHARIF. FINE PIECE OF LAW AND ORDER. NOW, I WANT THE BOY!
IF YOU WANT HIM SO MUCH, THEN TAKE HIM!

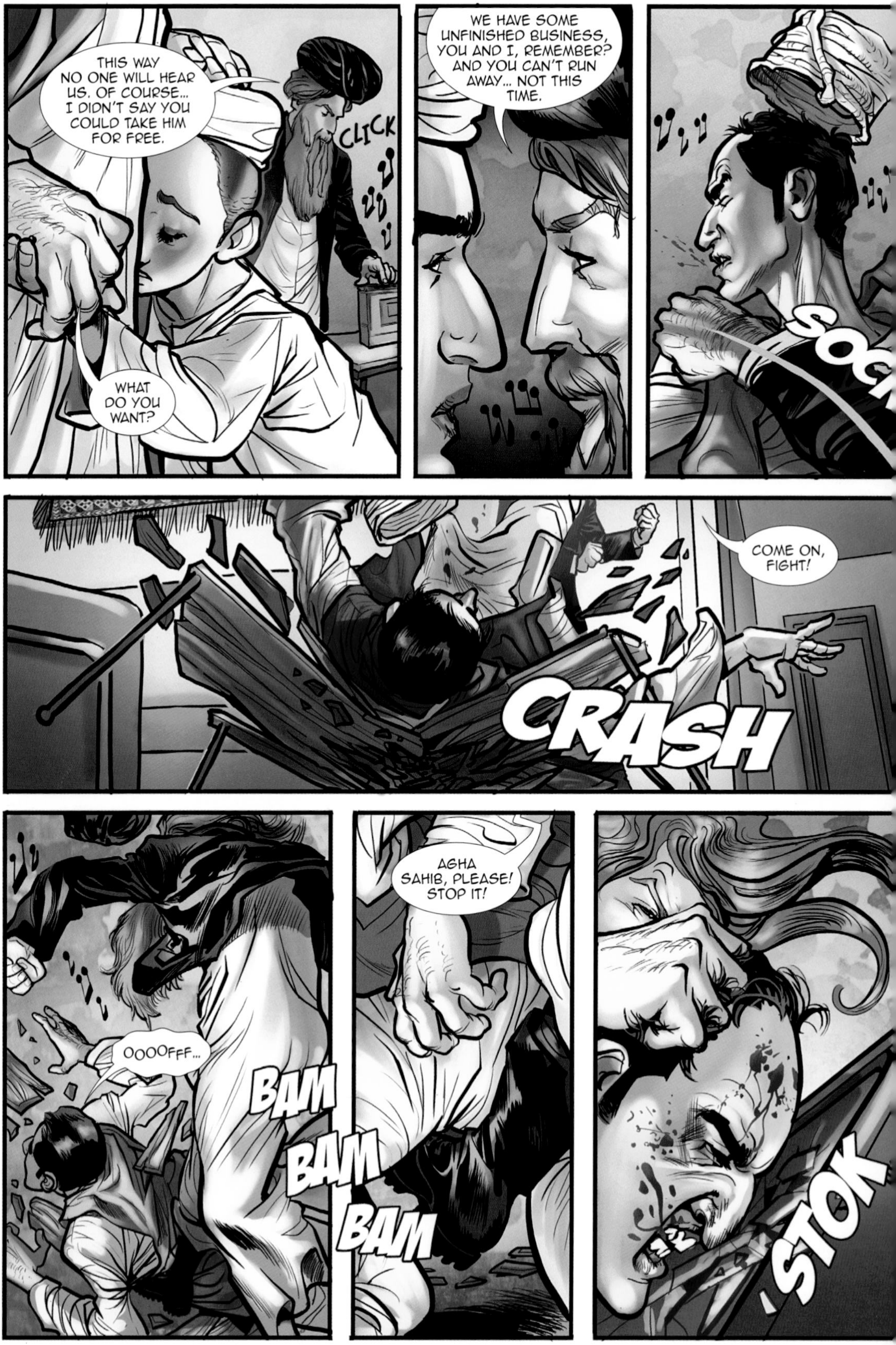

THIS WAY NO ONE WILL HEAR US. OF COURSE... I DIDN'T SAY YOU COULD TAKE HIM FOR FREE.
CLICK
WHAT DO YOU WANT?
WE HAVE SOME UNFINISHED BUSINESS, YOU AND I, REMEMBER? AND YOU CAN'T RUN AWAY... NOT THIS TIME.
SOCK
COME ON, FIGHT!
CRASH
OOOOFFF...
BAM
BAM
BAM
AGHA SAHIB, PLEASE! STOP IT!
STOK

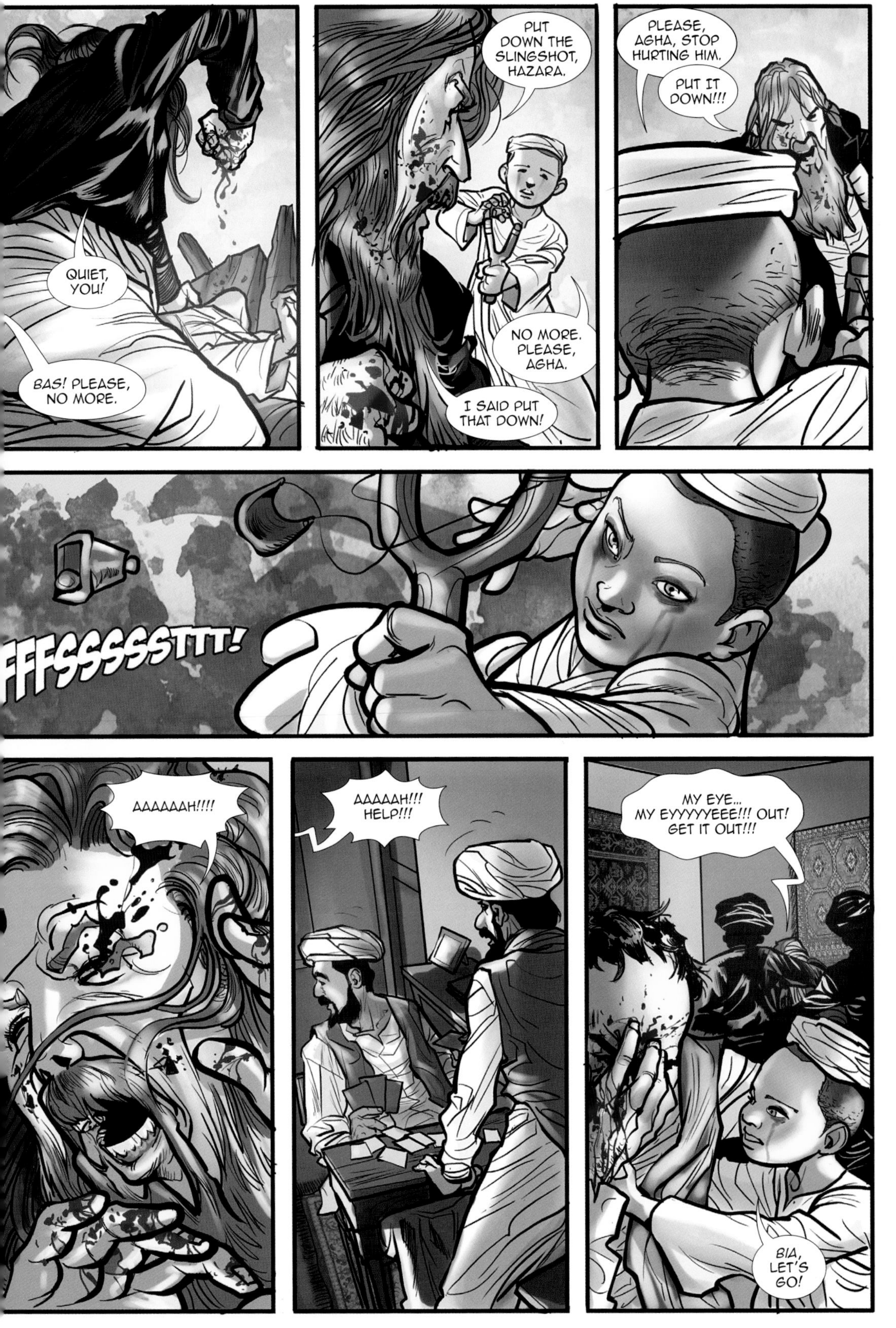
QUIET, YOU!
BAS! PLEASE, NO MORE.
PUT DOWN THE SLINGSHOT, HAZARA.
NO MORE. PLEASE, AGHA.
I SAID PUT THAT DOWN!
PLEASE, AGHA, STOP HURTING HIM.
PUT IT DOWN!!!
FFFSSSSSTTTT!
AAAAAAH!!!!
AAAAAH!!! HELP!!!
MY EYE... MY EYYYYYEEE!!! OUT! GET IT OUT!!!
BIA, LET'S GO!

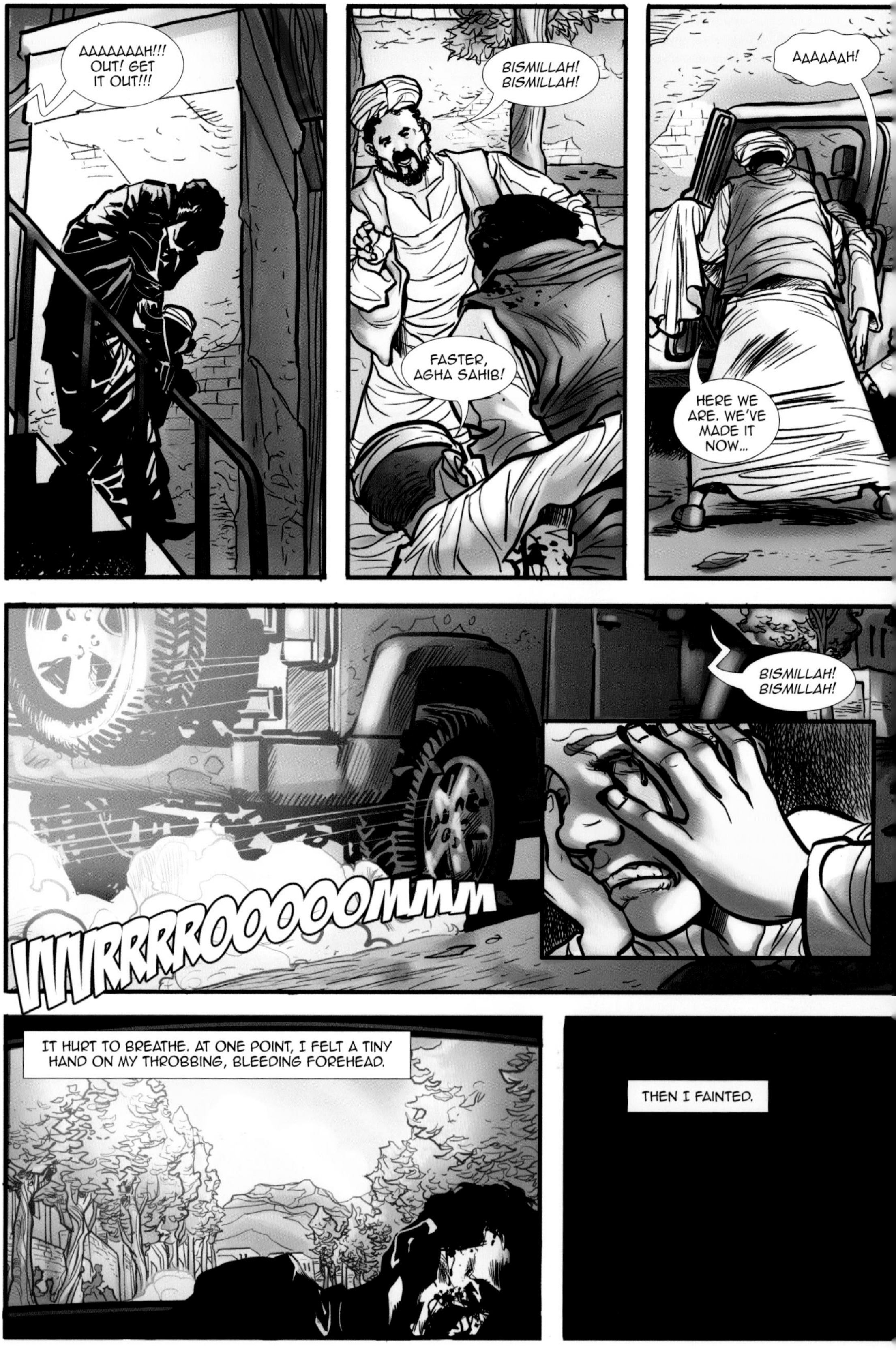
AAAAAAAH!!! OUT! GET IT OUT!!!
BISMILLAH! BISMILLAH!
FASTER, AGHA SAHIB!
AAAAAAH!
HERE WE ARE. WE'VE MADE IT NOW...
BISMILLAH! BISMILLAH!
VVVRRRROOOOOMMM
IT HURT TO BREATHE. AT ONE POINT, I FELT A TINY HAND ON MY THROBBING, BLEEDING FOREHEAD.
THEN I FAINTED.

TO THIS DAY, I DO NOT KNOW HOW MUCH TIME PASSED AFTER I ARRIVED AT THE HOSPITAL IN PESHAWAR. I REMEMBER THEY WERE ASKING ME IF I HURT AND IF I KNEW WHO I WAS. I KNEW WHO I WAS AND I HURT EVERYWHERE. BUT THE REST WAS CONFUSED. THE PAIN WAS SO GREAT I KEPT FAINTING.

HASSAN... ?

NOW I'LL SHOW YOU WHY THEY CALL ME TOOPHAN AGHA! HA, HA!

SOON WE'LL HAVE THOSE WIRES OUT, AMIR.

??

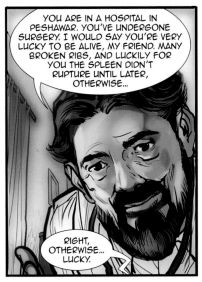

YOU ARE IN A HOSPITAL IN PESHAWAR. YOU'VE UNDERGONE SURGERY. I WOULD SAY YOU'RE VERY LUCKY TO BE ALIVE, MY FRIEND. MANY BROKEN RIBS, AND LUCKILY FOR YOU THE SPLEEN DIDN'T RUPTURE UNTIL LATER, OTHERWISE...

RIGHT, OTHERWISE... LUCKY.

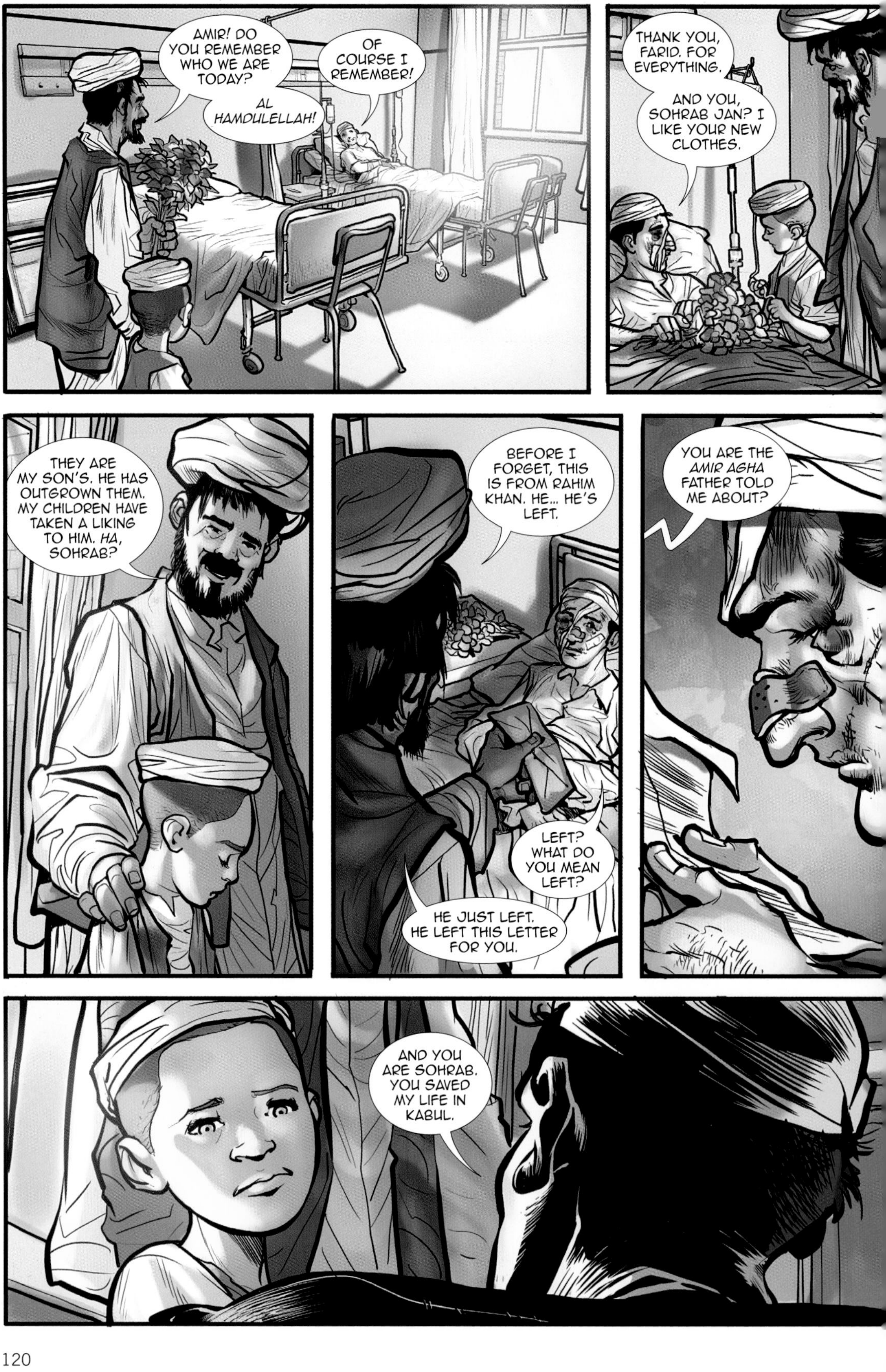
AMIR! DO YOU REMEMBER WHO WE ARE TODAY?
OF COURSE I REMEMBER!
AL HAMDULELLAH!
THANK YOU, FARID, FOR EVERYTHING.
AND YOU, SOHRAB JAN? I LIKE YOUR NEW CLOTHES.
THEY ARE MY SON'S. HE HAS OUTGROWN THEM. MY CHILDREN HAVE TAKEN A LIKING TO HIM. *HA*, SOHRAB?
BEFORE I FORGET, THIS IS FROM RAHIM KHAN. HE... HE'S LEFT.
LEFT? WHAT DO YOU MEAN LEFT?
HE JUST LEFT. HE LEFT THIS LETTER FOR YOU.
YOU ARE THE *AMIR AGHA* FATHER TOLD ME ABOUT?
AND YOU ARE SOHRAB. YOU SAVED MY LIFE IN KABUL.

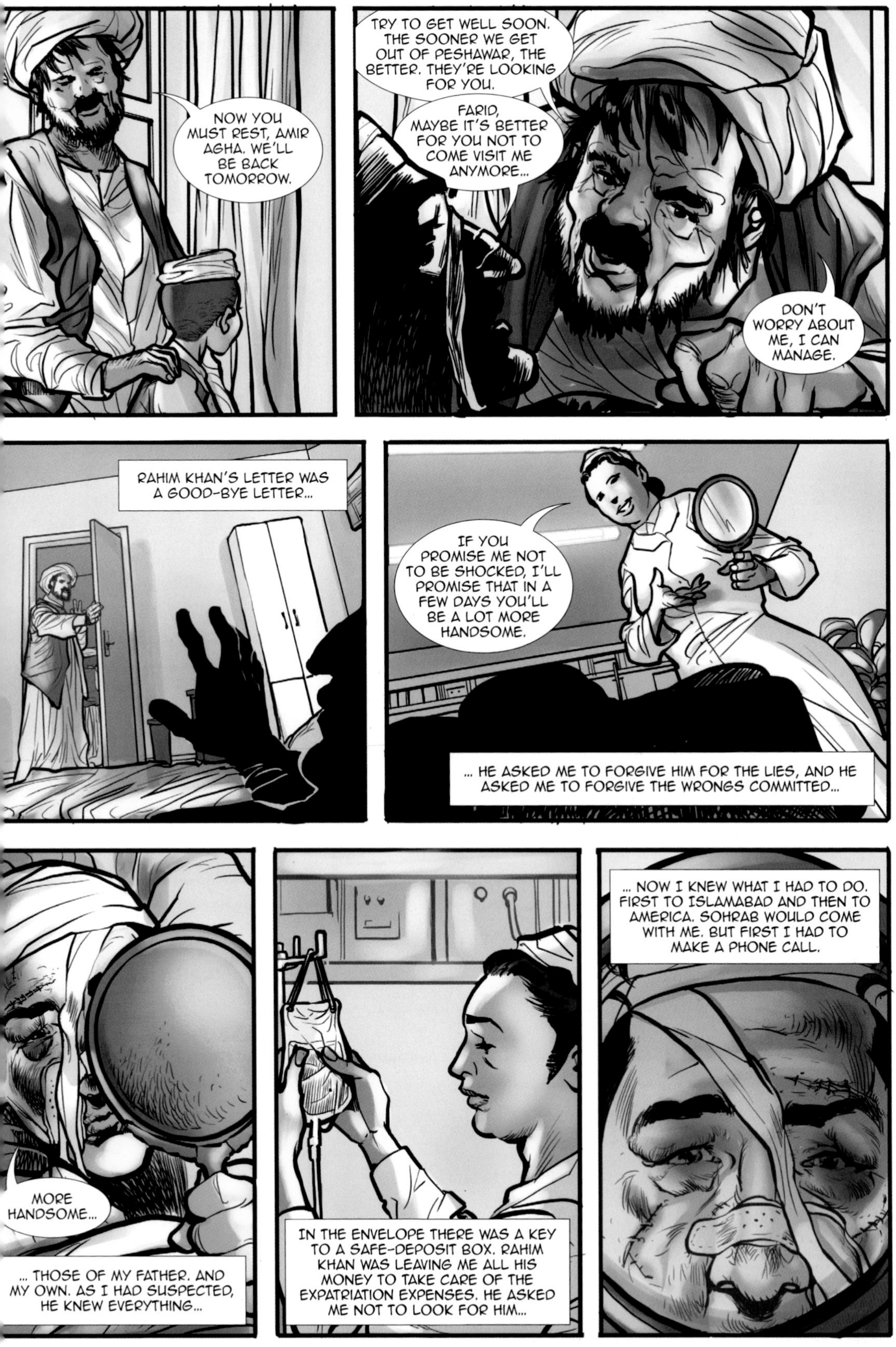
NOW YOU MUST REST, AMIR AGHA. WE'LL BE BACK TOMORROW.
TRY TO GET WELL SOON. THE SOONER WE GET OUT OF PESHAWAR, THE BETTER. THEY'RE LOOKING FOR YOU.
FARID, MAYBE IT'S BETTER FOR YOU NOT TO COME VISIT ME ANYMORE...
DON'T WORRY ABOUT ME, I CAN MANAGE.
RAHIM KHAN'S LETTER WAS A GOOD-BYE LETTER...
IF YOU PROMISE ME NOT TO BE SHOCKED, I'LL PROMISE THAT IN A FEW DAYS YOU'LL BE A LOT MORE HANDSOME.
... HE ASKED ME TO FORGIVE HIM FOR THE LIES, AND HE ASKED ME TO FORGIVE THE WRONGS COMMITTED...
MORE HANDSOME...
... THOSE OF MY FATHER. AND MY OWN. AS I HAD SUSPECTED, HE KNEW EVERYTHING...
IN THE ENVELOPE THERE WAS A KEY TO A SAFE-DEPOSIT BOX. RAHIM KHAN WAS LEAVING ME ALL HIS MONEY TO TAKE CARE OF THE EXPATRIATION EXPENSES. HE ASKED ME NOT TO LOOK FOR HIM...
... NOW I KNEW WHAT I HAD TO DO. FIRST TO ISLAMABAD AND THEN TO AMERICA. SOHRAB WOULD COME WITH ME. BUT FIRST I HAD TO MAKE A PHONE CALL.

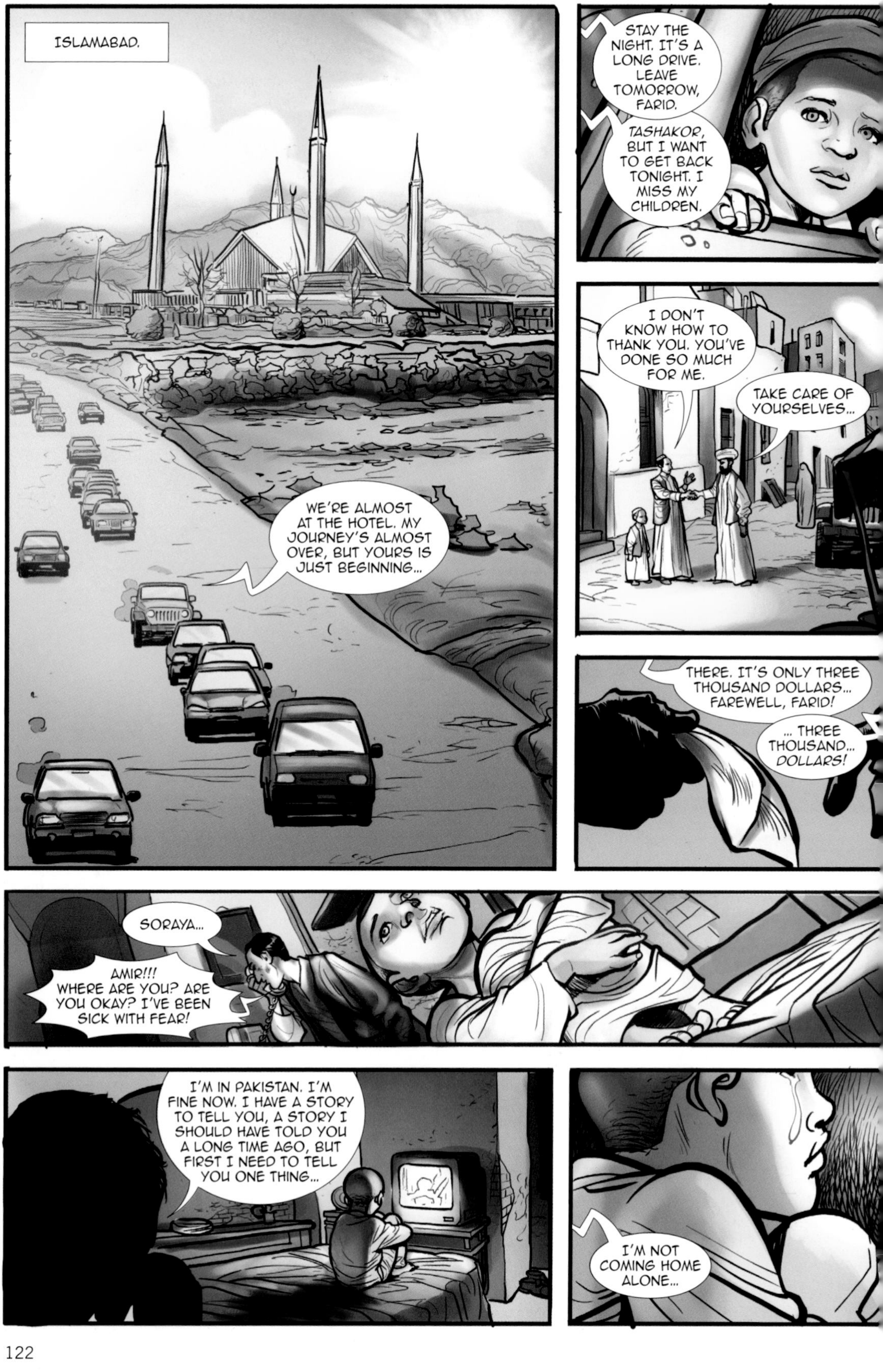

ISLAMABAD.
WE'RE ALMOST AT THE HOTEL. MY JOURNEY'S ALMOST OVER, BUT YOURS IS JUST BEGINNING...
STAY THE NIGHT. IT'S A LONG DRIVE. LEAVE TOMORROW, FARID.
TASHAKOR, BUT I WANT TO GET BACK TONIGHT. I MISS MY CHILDREN.
I DON'T KNOW HOW TO THANK YOU. YOU'VE DONE SO MUCH FOR ME.
TAKE CARE OF YOURSELVES...
THERE. IT'S ONLY THREE THOUSAND DOLLARS... FAREWELL, FARID!
... THREE THOUSAND... DOLLARS!
SORAYA...
AMIR!!! WHERE ARE YOU? ARE YOU OKAY? I'VE BEEN SICK WITH FEAR!
I'M IN PAKISTAN. I'M FINE NOW. I HAVE A STORY TO TELL YOU, A STORY I SHOULD HAVE TOLD YOU A LONG TIME AGO, BUT FIRST I NEED TO TELL YOU ONE THING...
I'M NOT COMING HOME ALONE...

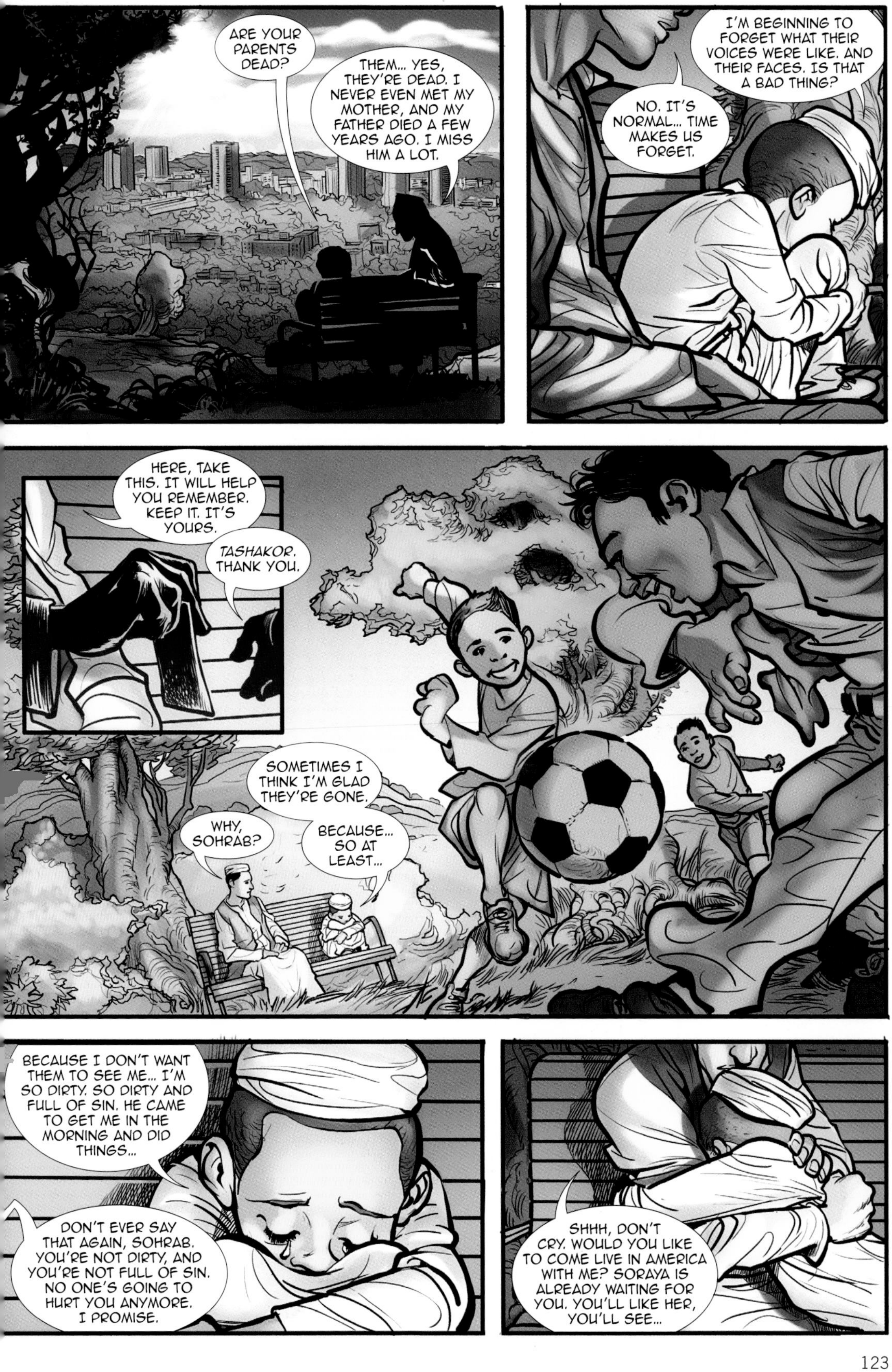
ARE YOUR PARENTS DEAD?
THEM... YES, THEY'RE DEAD. I NEVER EVEN MET MY MOTHER, AND MY FATHER DIED A FEW YEARS AGO. I MISS HIM A LOT.
I'M BEGINNING TO FORGET WHAT THEIR VOICES WERE LIKE. AND THEIR FACES. IS THAT A BAD THING?
NO. IT'S NORMAL... TIME MAKES US FORGET.
HERE, TAKE THIS. IT WILL HELP YOU REMEMBER. KEEP IT. IT'S YOURS.
TASHAKOR. THANK YOU.
SOMETIMES I THINK I'M GLAD THEY'RE GONE.
WHY, SOHRAB?
BECAUSE... SO AT LEAST...
BECAUSE I DON'T WANT THEM TO SEE ME... I'M SO DIRTY. SO DIRTY AND FULL OF SIN. HE CAME TO GET ME IN THE MORNING AND DID THINGS...
DON'T EVER SAY THAT AGAIN, SOHRAB. YOU'RE NOT DIRTY, AND YOU'RE NOT FULL OF SIN. NO ONE'S GOING TO HURT YOU ANYMORE. I PROMISE.
SHHH, DON'T CRY. WOULD YOU LIKE TO COME LIVE IN AMERICA WITH ME? SORAYA IS ALREADY WAITING FOR YOU. YOU'LL LIKE HER, YOU'LL SEE...

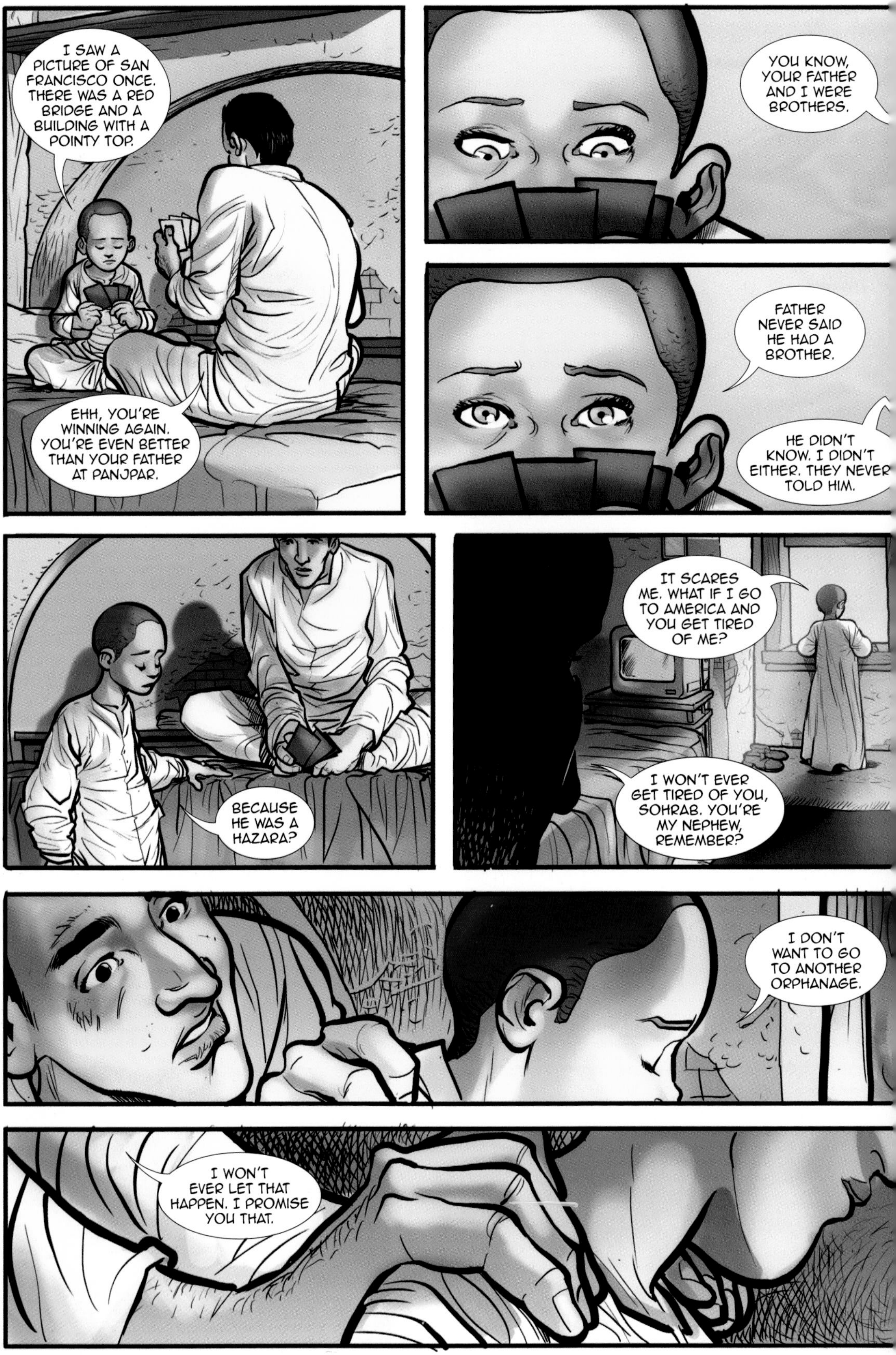
I SAW A PICTURE OF SAN FRANCISCO ONCE. THERE WAS A RED BRIDGE AND A BUILDING WITH A POINTY TOP.
EHH, YOU'RE WINNING AGAIN. YOU'RE EVEN BETTER THAN YOUR FATHER AT PANJPAR.
YOU KNOW, YOUR FATHER AND I WERE BROTHERS.
FATHER NEVER SAID HE HAD A BROTHER.
HE DIDN'T KNOW. I DIDN'T EITHER. THEY NEVER TOLD HIM.
BECAUSE HE WAS A HAZARA?
IT SCARES ME. WHAT IF I GO TO AMERICA AND YOU GET TIRED OF ME?
I WON'T EVER GET TIRED OF YOU, SOHRAB. YOU'RE MY NEPHEW, REMEMBER?
I DON'T WANT TO GO TO ANOTHER ORPHANAGE.
I WON'T EVER LET THAT HAPPEN. I PROMISE YOU THAT.

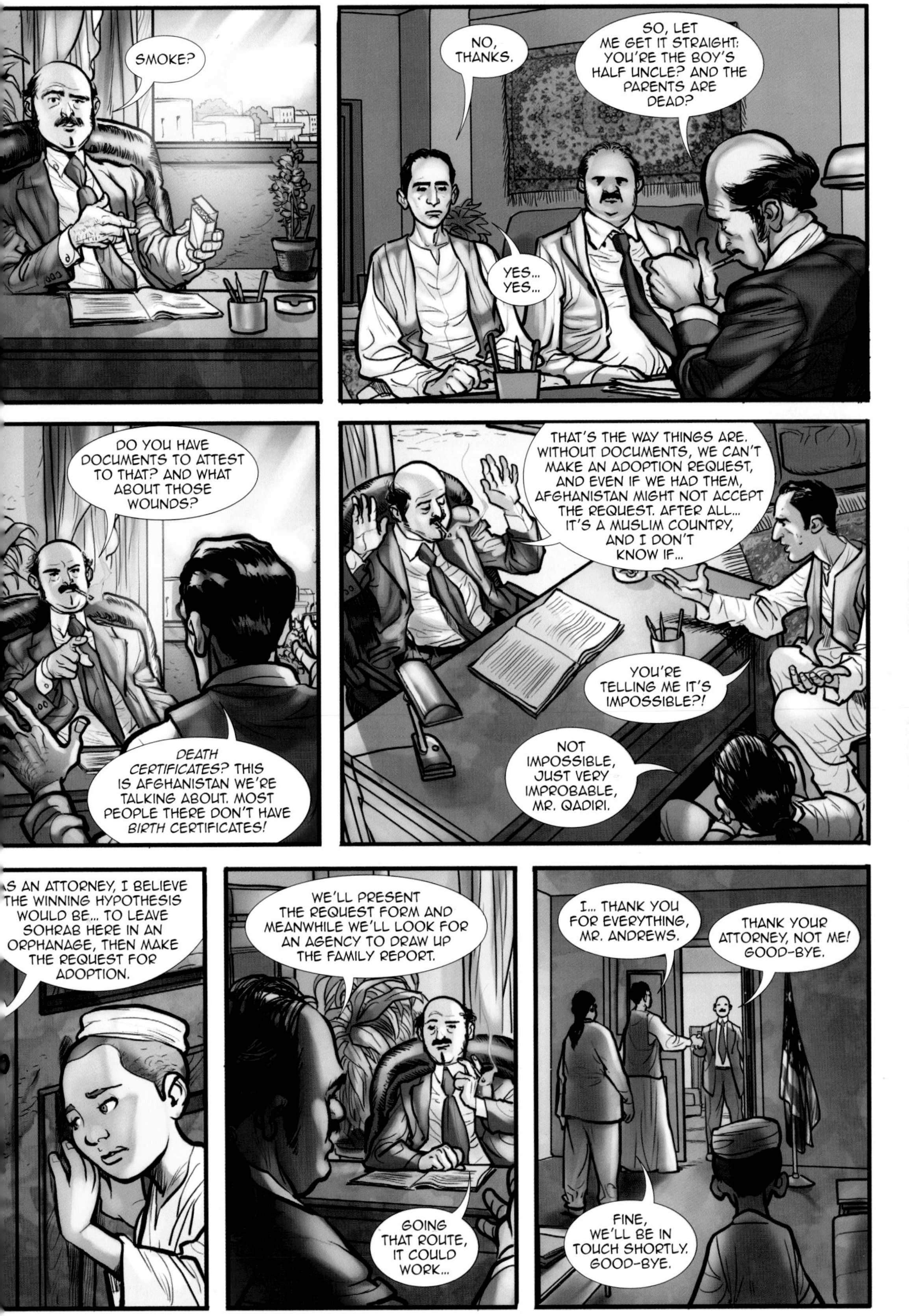
SMOKE?
NO, THANKS.
SO, LET ME GET IT STRAIGHT: YOU'RE THE BOY'S HALF UNCLE? AND THE PARENTS ARE DEAD?
YES... YES...
DO YOU HAVE DOCUMENTS TO ATTEST TO THAT? AND WHAT ABOUT THOSE WOUNDS?
DEATH CERTIFICATES? THIS IS AFGHANISTAN WE'RE TALKING ABOUT. MOST PEOPLE THERE DON'T HAVE BIRTH CERTIFICATES!
THAT'S THE WAY THINGS ARE. WITHOUT DOCUMENTS, WE CAN'T MAKE AN ADOPTION REQUEST, AND EVEN IF WE HAD THEM, AFGHANISTAN MIGHT NOT ACCEPT THE REQUEST. AFTER ALL... IT'S A MUSLIM COUNTRY, AND I DON'T KNOW IF...
YOU'RE TELLING ME IT'S IMPOSSIBLE?!
NOT IMPOSSIBLE, JUST VERY IMPROBABLE, MR. QADIRI.
AS AN ATTORNEY, I BELIEVE THE WINNING HYPOTHESIS WOULD BE... TO LEAVE SOHRAB HERE IN AN ORPHANAGE, THEN MAKE THE REQUEST FOR ADOPTION.
WE'LL PRESENT THE REQUEST FORM AND MEANWHILE WE'LL LOOK FOR AN AGENCY TO DRAW UP THE FAMILY REPORT.
GOING THAT ROUTE, IT COULD WORK...
I... THANK YOU FOR EVERYTHING, MR. ANDREWS.
THANK YOUR ATTORNEY, NOT ME! GOOD-BYE.
FINE, WE'LL BE IN TOUCH SHORTLY. GOOD-BYE.

AT THE EMBASSY THEY THINK THERE'S A WAY TO TAKE YOU BACK TO AMERICA...

SO WE'RE GOING?

WELL... IT'S A BIT MORE COMPLICATED THAN THAT. THEY SAID IT WOULD BE MUCH EASIER IF YOU REMAINED HERE FOR A TIME, IN A HOUSE FOR KIDS...

HOUSE FOR KIDS? YOU MEAN AN ORPHANAGE?

YOU PROMISED ME I'D NEVER GO BACK TO AN ORPHANAGE! THAT YOU'D TAKE ME WITH YOU TO SAN FRANCISCO! TO SEE THE RED BRIDGE!

I KNOW... I KNOW WHAT I PROMISED YOU, SOHRAB. BUT IT WOULD ONLY BE FOR A FEW MONTHS!

GOD, NO. IT'S NOT TRUE. PLEASE! NO... NO!

SOHRAB, CALM DOWN! EVERYTHING WILL WORK OUT!

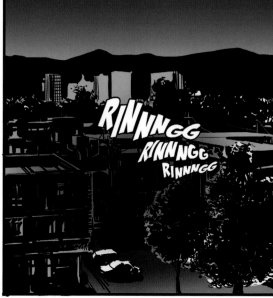

RINNNGG RINNNGG RINNNGG

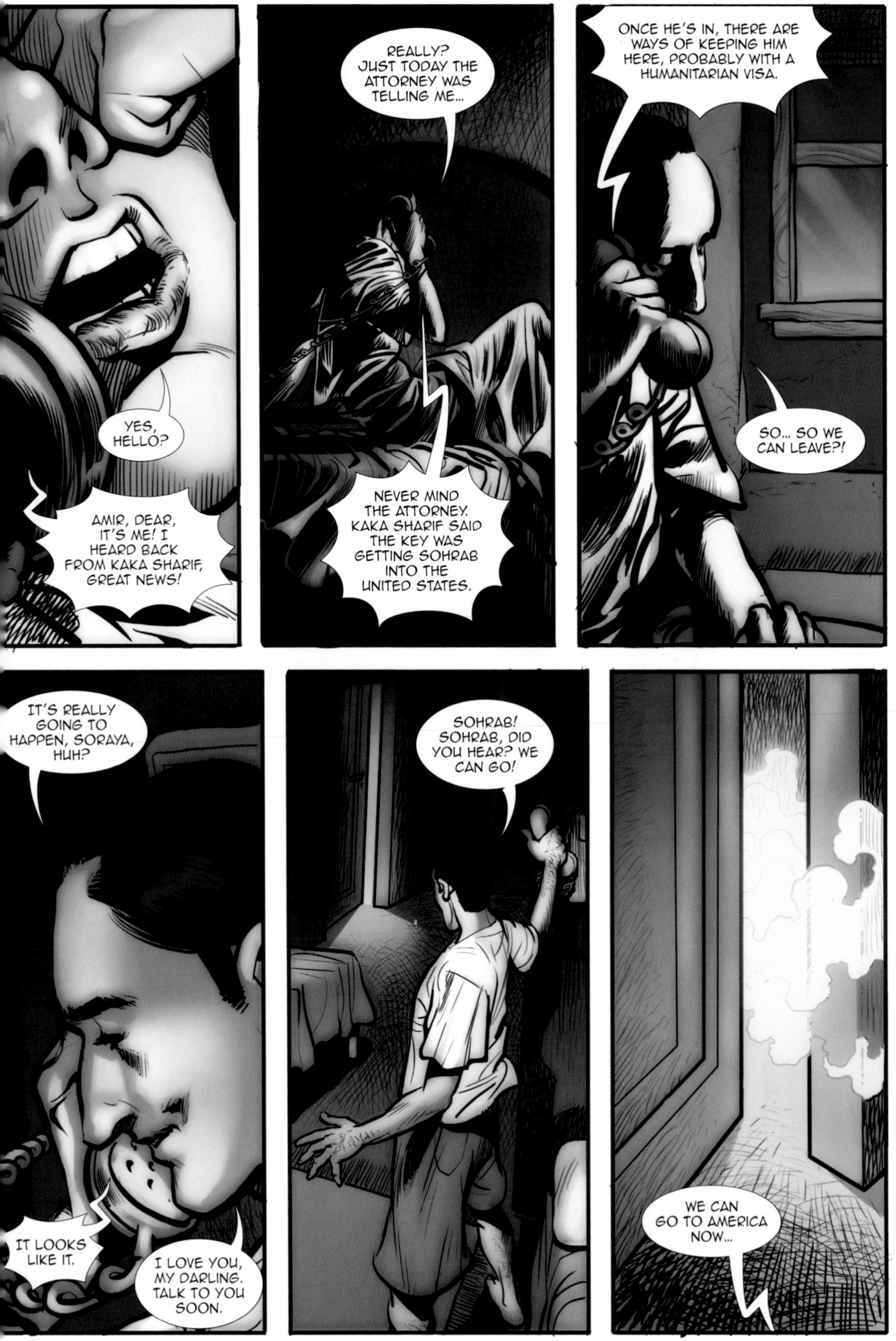
YES, HELLO?
AMIR, DEAR, IT'S ME! I HEARD BACK FROM KAKA SHARIF, GREAT NEWS!
REALLY? JUST TODAY THE ATTORNEY WAS TELLING ME...
NEVER MIND THE ATTORNEY. KAKA SHARIF SAID THE KEY WAS GETTING SOHRAB INTO THE UNITED STATES.
ONCE HE'S IN, THERE ARE WAYS OF KEEPING HIM HERE, PROBABLY WITH A HUMANITARIAN VISA.
SO... SO WE CAN LEAVE?!
IT'S REALLY GOING TO HAPPEN, SORAYA, HUH?
IT LOOKS LIKE IT.
I LOVE YOU, MY DARLING. TALK TO YOU SOON.
SOHRAB! SOHRAB, DID YOU HEAR? WE CAN GO!
WE CAN GO TO AMERICA NOW...

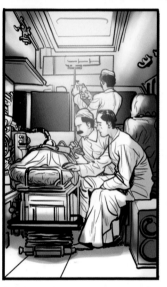

SOHRAB... PLEASE, EAT SOMETHING. LISTEN... I REALIZE I CAN'T GIVE YOU BACK YOUR PREVIOUS LIFE. I CAN'T BRING YOUR FAMILY BACK. BUT I CAN OFFER YOU A NEW LIFE, A FREE LIFE. I CAME INTO THE BATHROOM TO TELL YOU WE CAN GO.

ALL I ASK IS THAT YOU LET ME KEEP MY PROMISE TO YOU. I ASK YOU TO FORGIVE ME. TO TRUST ME AGAIN. SO... WILL YOU COME WITH ME TO AMERICA?

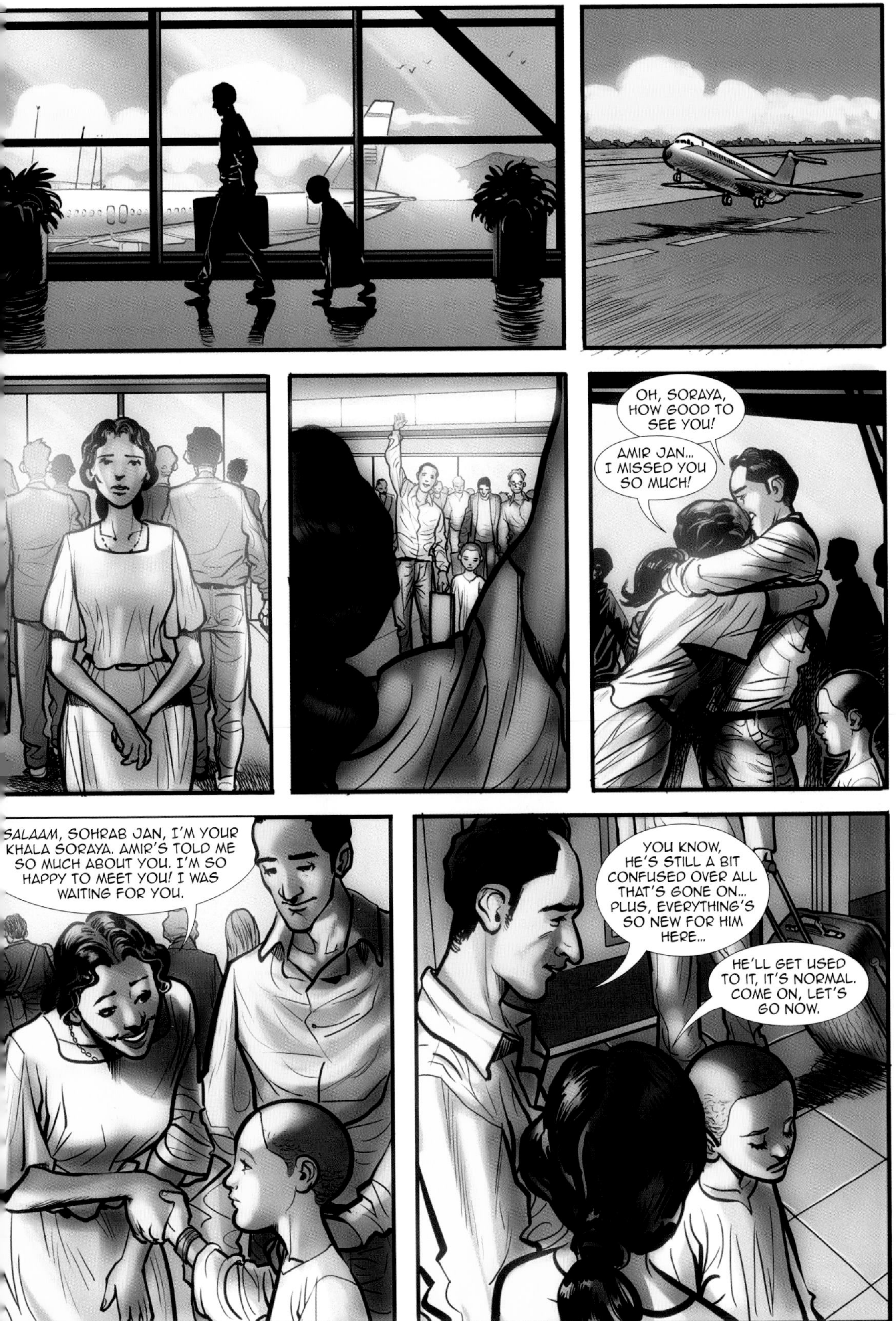
OH, SORAYA, HOW GOOD TO SEE YOU!
AMIR JAN... I MISSED YOU SO MUCH!
SALAAM, SOHRAB JAN, I'M YOUR KHALA SORAYA. AMIR'S TOLD ME SO MUCH ABOUT YOU. I'M SO HAPPY TO MEET YOU! I WAS WAITING FOR YOU.
YOU KNOW, HE'S STILL A BIT CONFUSED OVER ALL THAT'S GONE ON... PLUS, EVERYTHING'S SO NEW FOR HIM HERE...
HE'LL GET USED TO IT, IT'S NORMAL. COME ON, LET'S GO NOW.

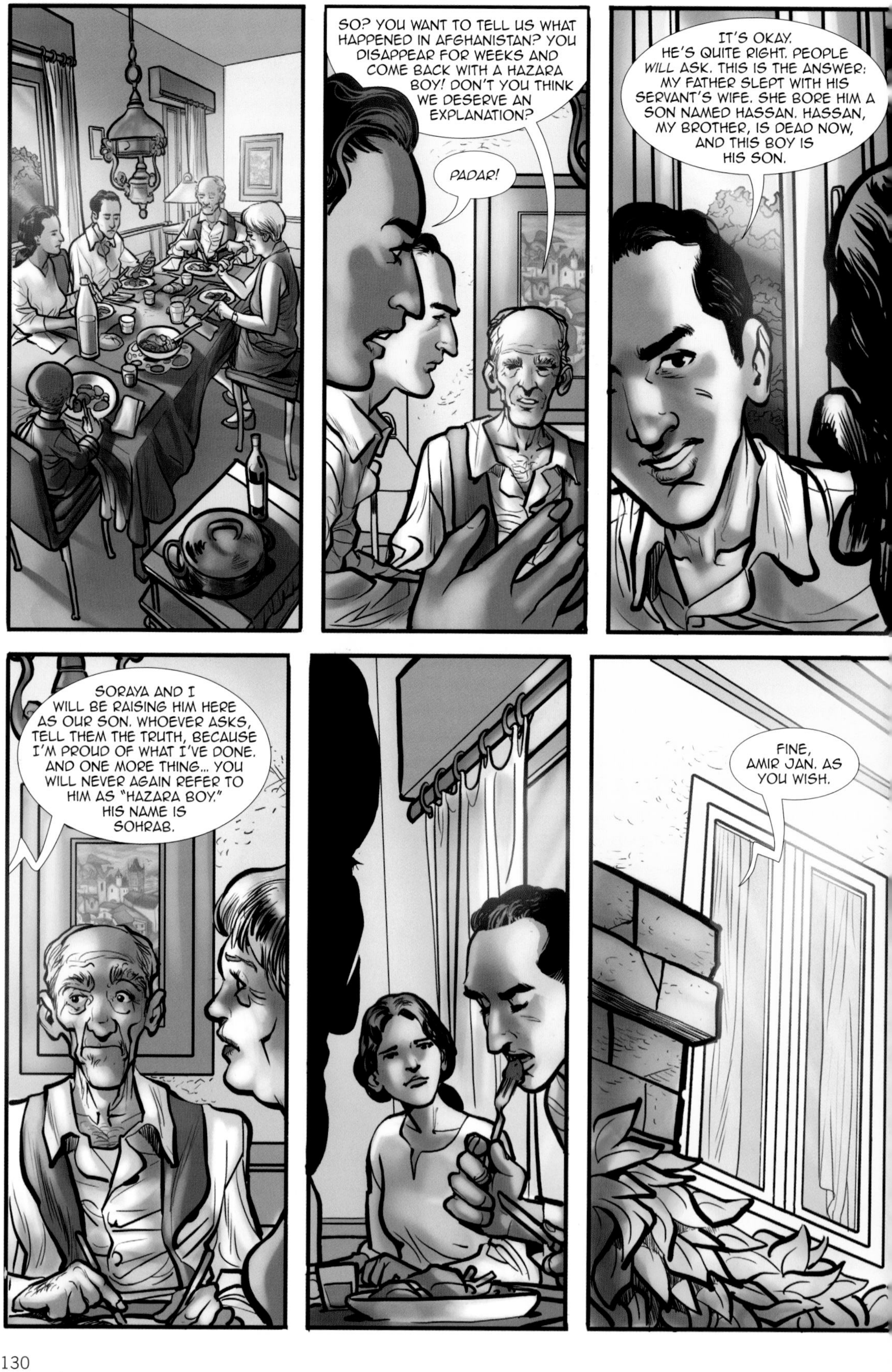
SO? YOU WANT TO TELL US WHAT HAPPENED IN AFGHANISTAN? YOU DISAPPEAR FOR WEEKS AND COME BACK WITH A HAZARA BOY! DON'T YOU THINK WE DESERVE AN EXPLANATION?
PADAR!
IT'S OKAY. HE'S QUITE RIGHT. PEOPLE WILL ASK. THIS IS THE ANSWER: MY FATHER SLEPT WITH HIS SERVANT'S WIFE. SHE BORE HIM A SON NAMED HASSAN. HASSAN, MY BROTHER, IS DEAD NOW, AND THIS BOY IS HIS SON.
SORAYA AND I WILL BE RAISING HIM HERE AS OUR SON. WHOEVER ASKS, TELL THEM THE TRUTH, BECAUSE I'M PROUD OF WHAT I'VE DONE. AND ONE MORE THING... YOU WILL NEVER AGAIN REFER TO HIM AS "HAZARA BOY." HIS NAME IS SOHRAB.
FINE, AMIR JAN. AS YOU WISH.

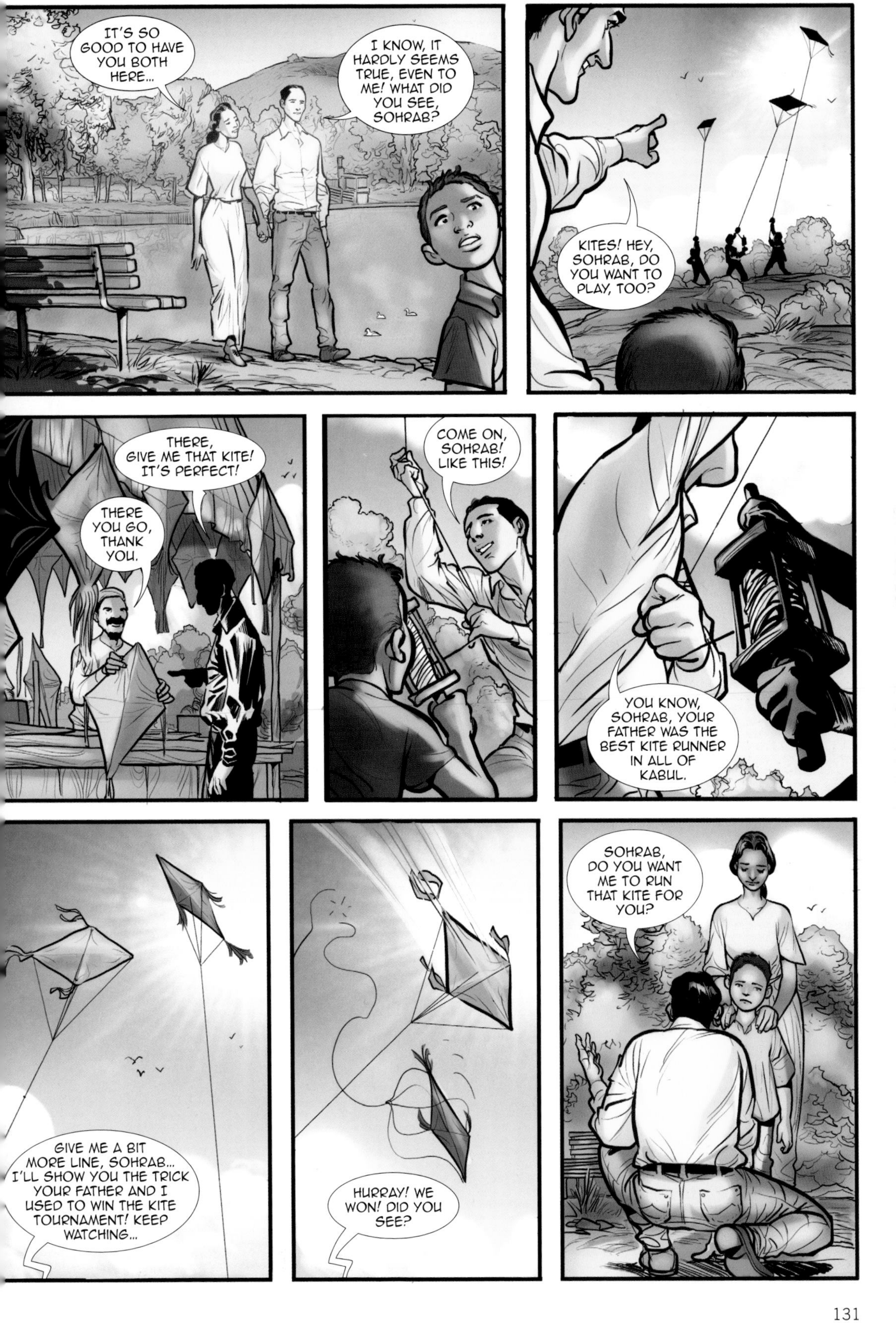
IT'S SO GOOD TO HAVE YOU BOTH HERE...
I KNOW, IT HARDLY SEEMS TRUE, EVEN TO ME! WHAT DID YOU SEE, SOHRAB?
KITES! HEY, SOHRAB, DO YOU WANT TO PLAY, TOO?
THERE, GIVE ME THAT KITE! IT'S PERFECT!
THERE YOU GO, THANK YOU.
COME ON, SOHRAB! LIKE THIS!
YOU KNOW, SOHRAB, YOUR FATHER WAS THE BEST KITE RUNNER IN ALL OF KABUL.
GIVE ME A BIT MORE LINE, SOHRAB... I'LL SHOW YOU THE TRICK YOUR FATHER AND I USED TO WIN THE KITE TOURNAMENT! KEEP WATCHING...
HURRAY! WE WON! DID YOU SEE?
SOHRAB, DO YOU WANT ME TO RUN THAT KITE FOR YOU?

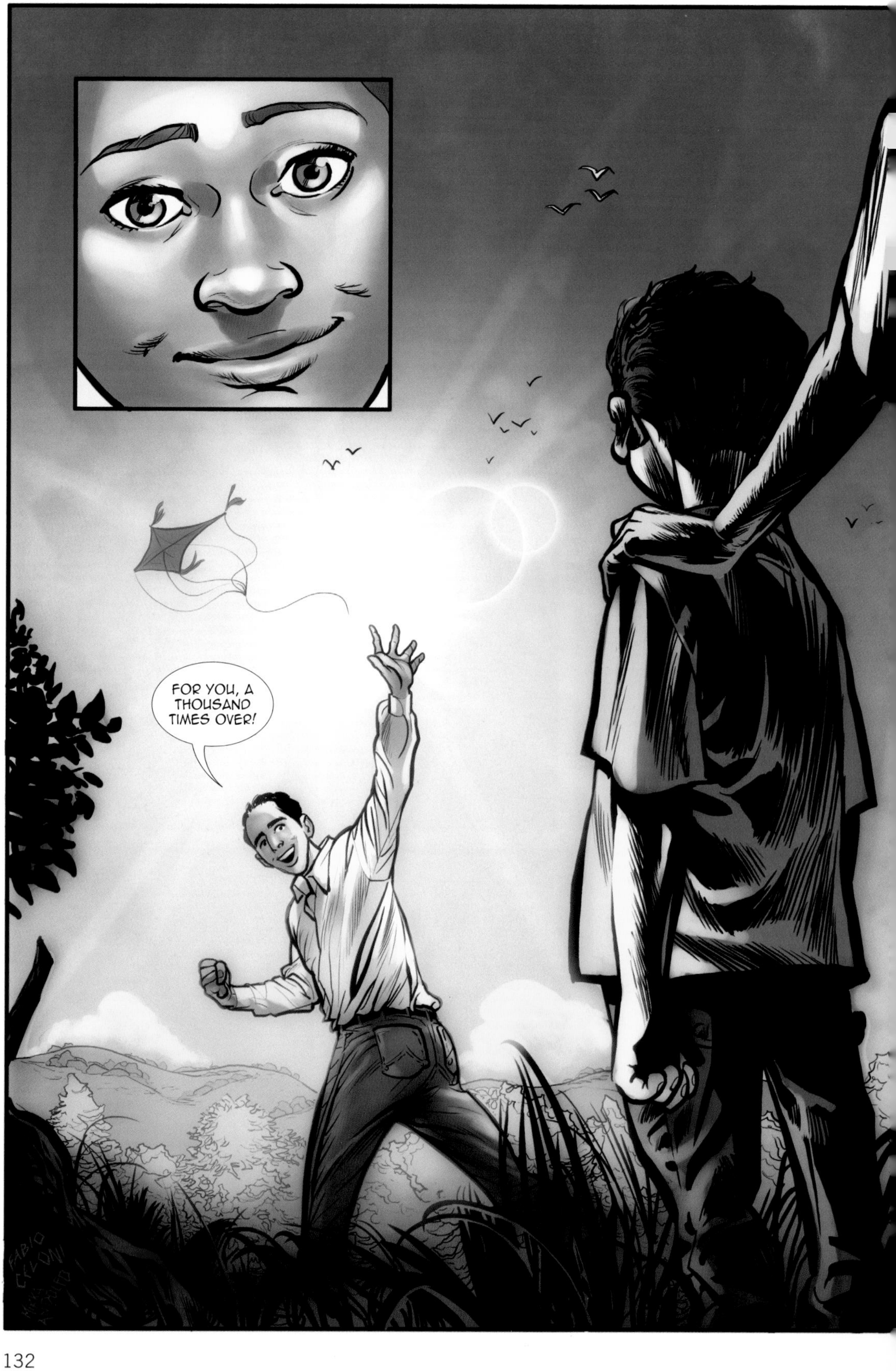
FOR YOU, A THOUSAND TIMES OVER!
FABIO CELONI